Independence!
A Tale Set in the Near Future

Independence!
A Tale Set in the Near Future

by
Tommy L. Attaway, Jr.

To My Parents,
Who Instilled In Me Appreciation For the Founders of the
United States of America and Their Sacrifices

Table of Contents

Preface

As with the preceding book in this series, this is the time at which the author makes his usual disclaimer that all events depicted are fictional, and any resemblance to any person living or dead is entirely coincidental. Again, such precautions have been made in the creation of this work, the creation of characters and the related events serve merely to further the narrative of the story.

This book is the continuation of my first novel, *We Defy!* While this story can stand on its own, a greater appreciation for the characters and story line depend on being familiar with that book. At the suggestion of readers, this book will have more character development, although as in the preceding work, the characters really do exist primarily to drive the tale forward.

The ideas presented via the story, is the central purpose of the book. While I hope that this work has some entertainment value, or at least enough excitement to make it readable to the end, I realize that I am not destined to write the Great American Novel. However, this book will have more measured chapter division and an easier flow for the reader to follow.

Finally, my literary efforts have been generally placed in the dystopian category of writing. However, that is not my primary intended audience. We live in a highly complex civilization, and many suggested solutions to the problems we face tend to be simple, straightforward, and unlikely to achieve the intended effect. If that diminishes the entertainment value to my writing, so be it. I hope to address themes here that will have to be dealt with, should the events of the world develop in the direction envisioned by this story.

I am also grateful to the readers of these books. I appreciate you not only for having bought and read these volumes, but for giving me more anecdotes of government misfeasance. Some of your experiences have been transformed into parts of this story.

In placing the characters in their proper roles and environment, they will use terms appropriate to them. This may impose a burden on the reader to determine some additional meaning to what is being said or done. This presented a dilemma in which the alternatives were to have the characters speak as they would to each other, thereby preserving the authenticity of their actions, or provide more explanatory context into what the characters were saying. I have chosen to keep the dialog as real as possible, in keeping with the idea that the story is one that could plausibly happen.

If there is one central theme to be stressed by this literary effort, it is that western civilization is in peril. Many useful solutions to the challenges we face, are to be found in the actions of the past. Similar situations were faced by our worthy ancestors, and their solutions merit our attention and consideration. The study of history gives us some predictive value to observed patterns. Our task is to correctly analyze the pattern in current events, in order to devise the correct course of action.

Lexicon

Battalion – a unit typically consisting of two to four companies and a headquarters company that provides support for the unit. Usually commanded by a Lieutenant Colonel

Black project – a secret activity undertaken in a manner that tries to prevent knowledge of the project from being known

Brigade – a unit typically consisting of two to four battalions and a support unit. Usually commanded by a Colonel

Commo – communications and refers to ability to communicate or the soldier responsible for communications in a unit

Company- a unit typically consisting of two to four platoons with a command and support troops. Usually commanded by a Captain

OPORD – Operations Order, the means by which a military unit is given a mission

Platoon – a unit consisting of three or four squads or a number of vehicles. Usually commanded by a Lieutenant

Squad – usually two teams and commanded by a Staff Sergeant

Team – usually four soldiers commanded by a Corporal or Sergeant

XO – the officer second in command of a unit.

Chapter 1

Elections Have Consequences

TO VOTE IS NOTHING, TO COUNT THE VOTES IS EVERYTHING. – JOSEPH STALIN

Many of the residents of Freedonia were gathered at the Green Dragon Tavern, watching the returns from the primary election held that day in Texas. Jim Roberts, Ed McMasters, and Ted Greenlow were the main characters at one of the large tables in the tavern. As three of the five Executive Directors of Free Texas, and some of the organizers of the Lone Star Party, they had more than just cursory interest in the election results. Dusk turned into night, and the televised returns were discussed by the group.

The Green Dragon was evidence of the growth of Freedonia. It was built across the town square from the first row of commercial buildings constructed in Freedonia. One of the businesses in that row across the square was the Freedonia Transaction Company, the scene of the attempted raid by the Internal Revenue Service, which had put Freedonia on the world stage. The subsequent actions resulting from that incident had created the dynamics reflected in this election. Those events had also lead to the growth of Freedonia, as more people had seen the attractiveness of less government intrusion into their lives, combined with the willingness to back that view of liberty with force. Some of those people felt the desire to live such a life themselves, and moved to Freedonia as a consequence.

The Green Dragon was named in honor of its namesake in Boston, which styles itself as the "birthplace of the Revolution". Being the meeting place of the Sons of Liberty and other related organizations the heritage of the name appealed to the owner. The Texas version more resembled a sports bar on the ground level. On the second story were the rooms for rent, in the manner of an inn or bed and breakfast. That arrangement also allowed the owner of the Green Dragon to have a good idea of who was in town, and why that visit was taking place. The basement, in addition to storage, offered a couple of private meeting rooms in case someone wished to host a small party or meeting, out of the view of anyone who just happened by.

On the north side of the town square a couple of churches had been built. The south side of the square had construction underway; including gasoline storage tanks being dug in for what would be a convenience store. The commercial growth was also attracting business from some people elsewhere in the county, who unlike the Freedonians, still transacted most of their business using United States currency. A few of those newer residents were also at the watch party at the Green Dragon.

Most of the watch party observers of the election results had two main items of interest. They were hopeful of the passage of the 10th Amendment Referendum that would express the will of the electorate that Texas should take action to enforce that part of the US Constitution against certain actions of the US Government. There was also some interest in how many incumbents of the state government would be defeated by more liberty minded challengers or face a run off election challenge. Both results would influence the future of the newest political party in Texas, the Lone Star Party.

The referendum was passing, although the margin of victory declined as the night wore on and the votes from urban areas was counted. It was left deliberately vague in specifying just what Texas was supposed to do to enforce the 10th Amendment, as that was the compromise needed to get the referendum on the ballot. Those actions to be taken as a result of the referendum passing would be the next political fight, and that led to the interest in the other election results.

The Lone Star Party had peeled off a few of the more populist oriented state representatives, and two state senators from the Republican Party. The first test of Lone Star would be the ability of these office holders to retain their seats in November from challengers. As Lone Star used the caucus method to select candidates, there was no primary voting for Lone Star Party members. There would be Republican challengers to those office holders in November as the Republican Party would try to reclaim those seats and put an end to the upstart Lone Star Party. There was also the potential that sympathizers in the Republican Party might eliminate a problem office holder or two in the Republican primary, and this was the other main item of interest at the Green Dragon.

Those hoping that recent events had caused a major shift in the political landscape of Texas, were being disappointed. At most only a handful of Republican office holders were poised for defeat, while Democrat incumbents had no serious primary challengers. The two largest political parties in Texas liked things the way they were. Democrats had become socialist, and appealed to that constituency. Republicans had mastered how to convince their voters that every one of their candidates for office was very conservative, and the reason why nothing conservative got done was because there were not enough Republicans were in office. It was almost a mirror image of national politics.

None of the statewide office holders were in danger of losing. They had successfully portrayed to the electorate that they were the guys standing up to Washington. That perception was annoying to the people who were the ones who had actually done so at considerable risk to themselves. As the results got close to 100% reporting in, McMasters said to Roberts "I guess this is not much of a surprise to you, Jim."

"Some of them had closer calls, than they were probably expecting. In November we will find out how many people are going to vote Lone Star rather than Republican. That will be the critical test. We probably live or die politically based on the results." Roberts answered.

"I'd hate for any of the office holders who jumped over to us to lose this Fall." Ted Greenlow commented.

"Six months is a long time in politics. Almost anything can happen. One thing we have to do is to get better at communications – we have to get the message out there as to who is really driving this train." said Roberts.

The waitress, who had been very attentive to them all evening, was back at their table. She must have been new in town, as none of those seated at the table remembered seeing her at the Green Dragon before. The population of Freedonia was growing, but there were few, if any, people who were not already known in town. Roberts was as curious as the others, and perhaps more so, as he detected that English was not her native language. Her attractiveness didn't discourage Roberts' interest either.

"Anything else you want?" the waitress asked.

Roberts decided to play his hunch. "Sind Sie Deutsche?"

"Östereicherin" she replied to the question.

"I was not aware that Freedonia had made the European tour guides." was Roberts' comment.

Roberts attempt at humor went past Lise Kirchner. "I am not here on holiday. I do not want to live in Europe the way things are now." she stated.

"Neither do I." Roberts agreed.

"But you have somewhere safe to go. I do not." Lise rejoined.

By this time, the conversation between the two had the attention of everyone at the table.

"Why here?" Ed McMasters was curious.

"Because everyone knows there is the most freedom in Texas. I want to be free and live the life I want. Europe is being overrun and it can not last. This is my last hope." Lise replied.

"Welcome to the free world. If we can make it last." Roberts added.

Lise gathered in the empty glasses and plates, glancing back at Roberts on her way to the kitchen. She had made her way to Texas, found Freedonia, and met some of the people responsible for making a great deal of news that had even become well known in Austria. The Texans were decidedly different from Europeans, but in a good way. They were friendly, but not willing to take any kind of abuse like too many Europeans were willing to do. One of the Texans spoke German, and had obviously lived in Europe. He would be of particular interest to Lise.

The evening was coming to a close at the Green Dragon for Roberts and the others at the large table. Their waitress was now a topic of discussion. Sarah McMasters turned to Roberts and asked "Jim, how did you know she was a foreigner? I didn't really hear an accent that seemed that odd."

"Speech pattern and the way a couple of consonants sounded were a clue. There are a few English sounds that are not natural for a native German speaker." Roberts told Sarah.

"But she spoke English very well. Not like I would expect from someone who hasn't lived here for a while at least." was Sarah's comment.

"The late to post Cold War western Europeans grow up hearing a good deal of English, mainly British English. Our popular songs play in English and the BBC broadcasts all over. English is just about everybody's second language now." Roberts told everyone.

Curiosity got to Sarah. "Jim, I wonder why she came here. I mean not some big city that most tourists go to or where there might be more of a social life."

"Sarah, I'm sure you'll find out. The US has always had a certain appeal to some Europeans with the perception of wide open spaces

6

and total freedom. Of course, they are aware that is really less true for the most part. In many ways we are much more freer than the free countries of the world. In some ways not so much. But after we hit the news by poking the Feds with a sharp stick, I can see that playing to the image of Texas being just slightly removed from the wild West. If you thought your own country was being inundated with savages, and you wanted out, what we have going might capture your imagination." Roberts replied to the question.

The election watchers headed home. The Lone Star Party would be in a fight for its future and the future of Texas. A fight against the federal government would be hard enough as it was. Being undercut by state Republicans along the way was going to be most unhelpful.

The next day, Roberts took a combination late lunch and early dinner at the Green Dragon. He wanted to time his visit so that there would be few, if any customers. As he suspected would happen, Lise came right over to the table to take his order. Roberts started with the small talk, "Schon weider da."

"English please. I know you can speak German, and that is nice of you. But this country speaks English, and so will I." said Lise.

When Lise brought the bacon cheeseburger and the rest of Roberts' order to him, he asked, "Why don't you get a meal for yourself and have a seat here? I'm paying."

"I'm working. I'm on my job." Lise refused the offer.

"Tell Bob I said that I want to talk to you. He won't mind." Roberts persisted. He was curious to hear more of her story.

Lise went back to the rear of the Green Dragon, found Bob Hooper, and repeated the substance of the conversation she had With Roberts.

"Not everybody gets a dinner invitation from Jim Roberts. You should take it." Bob told her.

Lise decided to eat just a sandwich and have some water, so it didn't take long before she was seated across from Roberts. "So, here I am with the Prominenz."

"I thought you wanted to speak English?" remarked Roberts.

"Some things don't translate well. Last night, I could tell you were important, but now I know how important. You are one of the leaders for freedom." concluded Lise.

"One day, the world will get along just fine without me. What about you?" Roberts asked.

"I am from a small village in Austria. It is terrible in Europe now, and I can't live there any more. I refuse to be treated like a slave in my own country." Lise replied.

"I learned to ski in Austria. Which town?" Roberts continued his mild interrogation.

Lise replied, "Pass Thurn, you have never heard of it."

"I've been there. It is at the southern end of the Kitzbühel Ski Safari. Beautiful view from the ski trail into town." Roberts remarked. It was also a nice graceful descent from the mountain into town, Roberts recalled. It was an easy way to finish a long ski run.

"It is hard to believe that you were there. When did you visit?" Lise was now even more curious about this Texan.

Now it was Roberts turn to feel a bit odd. "Possibly before you were born. It was a long time ago."

"We Europeans have a different view of time than you do. You may speak German, You may be familiar with Austria, but you are still a Texan." Lise told Roberts.

"Very true – while I have lived and worked in Europe, and I thought at the time that it would be an advantage to have children that would grow up in an international environment. I see that is not now what I would want for my children. And that was before we got a President that is culturally not an American because he grew up somewhere else. A child needs to know where he belongs and where his roots are. My children will need to be Texans. With much of Western Europe currently destroying itself, the decision is even easier to make." Roberts had concluded.

Lise was sympathetic to the argument. "I understand. We are now being thrown out of our own country because of the invaders. And no one fights for us."

Roberts pushed the idea a bit further. "What has made Americans what they are, and more especially true about Texans is that they fight for themselves, and then the neighbors will join in the fight. That was a part of our British heritage, which is also fast disappearing."

There was one more thing about Roberts that Lise had to know. "Why aren't you married?"

On Roberts' part the question was not unexpected. One of the things he liked about Europeans in general was that when they were curious about something, they just asked the question. "I've led a life that has been wildly unstable that would not be good for a family. And not meeting the right woman plays a role as well."

"Time grows short and you can't make everything perfect." rejoined Lise.

"Good point." admitted Roberts.

Thus ended lunch and Lise returned to work. Lise decided that she could end up in a much worse situation in life than a future with Jim Roberts. Or stated differently, life probably would not provide a much better opportunity.

Jim Roberts arrived at the same conclusion on his way out of the Green Dragon Tavern.

It didn't take long for the residents of Freedonia to conclude that the town was soon going to see its first wedding take place. Jim Roberts and Lise Kirchner had become what used to be referred to as an item of gossip. In a small town, any new development becomes a topic of conversation, and what could be an additional family in town was no exception. Lise and Jim as the objects of that curiosity, learned to accept it.

Jim and Lise were at the McMasters home for Ed's birthday party. Teresa Greenlow brought up the subject of when they were going to get married, and Lise had a reply, "I'm Catholic and don't believe in divorce."

Teresa also got a reaction from Jim. "I don't believe in divorce either, but I do believe in homicide."

10

Lise wasn't sure if Jim was joking or not. There are some questions that are never asked.

As Lise had decided on who was going to be in her future, the transition from Austrian to Texan had begun. One of Jim's tasks was to be Lise's firearms instructor. Lise had a slight hesitation about learning to shoot, because she was raised in a culture where firearms were for soldiers, the police, and hunters. Lise had noted that she was one of the few people in Freedonia not to carry a weapon. Although almost everyone was armed, she felt safer in Freedonia than she had in Europe the past few years. As it was destined to be part of her new life, she would learn to shoot as best she could.

Her first trip to the firing range was on a Sunday afternoon. Jim brought the weapons, shooting glasses and hearing protection. Lise found it interesting that the first lesson did not involve touching a gun at all. Jim had simply said to her "As you are right handed, point at that target with the first finger of your right hand."

Lise did as instructed, and then Jim told her to close her left eye. He then asked her "Is your finger still pointed at the target?"

"Yes" was her reply.

"Good, now open your left eye and close your right eye. Is your finger still on the target?" Jim inquired.

"No, it moved!" answered Lise.

"This means that you are right handed and right eye dominant. If you have to shoot using your left hand, you will need to close your right eye to improve your aim. But we are not going to worry about that now." Roberts told her.

Jim then showed Lise an AR rifle. In reality, a Jim Roberts AR was a semi automatic M16 or M4. Roberts liked having the weapons with the same function and feel as he used in the Army. Also for teaching purposes, it let the students use the military manuals to learn about the weapon, as they worked the same as the military version. He went through the safety rules, and how to load, unload, and fire the rifle. After mastering those steps, it was time to teach Lise to aim and fire the AR.

"You aim the top of the front sight post where you want the round to hit, and move the ring of the rear sight to where the top of the front sight is in the middle of the circle formed by the rear sight." Jim instructed.

"OK" replied Lise.

"Now slowly squeeze your hand around the grip and trigger until it fires." said Jim. A few seconds later there was the audible click of the hammer falling on an empty chamber.

"Good, that looked stable, but there will be more practice while balancing a washer on the barrel. This makes sure that the rifle is being held steady when the hammer falls. When everything is steady, you will fire live ammunition." Jim said and Lise was steady. Either she wasn't afraid of the rifle, or was saving her fear for live rounds. Either way, it was time to find out.

"Time to try live ammunition" Jim decided.

Lise showed her only concern when she asked "Will it hurt?"

"No" Jim reassured her, "This weapon was designed to be used by Asians and small stature people. In addition to soldiers, it is easy to use for women and older children." He then handed her a loaded magazine.

Lise loaded the rifle as she had been taught. "I'm ready" she announced.

"Fire when ready." Roberts was watching Lise to make sure that no danger was possible for either of them as Lise fired. He didn't have a spotting scope, but a pair of binoculars to look at the target. "Low and left in the 5 ring is very good for a rifle not having the sights adjusted to you. How did it feel?"

There was a hint of happiness in Lise's voice, "It did not hurt at all. It felt like I had great power but under control. Is that how it feels to shoot?"

"I think of it as being self confident of your capability to deal with whatever happens and who ever may have intentions to do you harm. That is how it feels to be a citizen of a republic. Go ahead and fire the rest of the rounds." suggested Jim.

Roberts judged the shot group as acceptable for a first time shooter. "That was good. Next time we are going to shoot pistols, then we will select the rifle and pistol you will use as your primary weapons for self defense."

"Shooting was fun, but it seems strange to say that." Lise remarked.

"You were raised in a culture where violence was to be managed by the professional police and military, and not the citizens themselves as a body. Our traditions are different. You may need to defend you own life, the lives of our children, and the life you save with that weapon may even be mine." Jim told her.

"Jim, that sounds scary." Lise replied.

"The world is a scary place. Evil is thriving." observed Jim.

The assessment of the town gossips was correct. Freedonia was indeed going to witness its first wedding. As practically everyone in town knew Roberts, considerable effort was dedicated to the appropriate preparations.

Lise's family arrived for the wedding, which proved to be the social highlight of Freedonia to date. While Freedonia may have been in the middle of nowhere in terms of the international jet set, the residents were not unaware of the world around them. And certainly, part of the world was aware of Freedonia. It turned out that a couple of the program hosts of Rampaging Elephants were capable of performing weddings. Thus it was obvious who should conduct the ceremony

As for the family of the now Lise Roberts, the oppressive heat of Texas seemed much more tolerable than what had become an oppressive society at home. They made plans to increase the number of Texas residents as soon as possible. The time had come to leave Europe while it was still possible to do so. Lise had been right. Europe was in danger of being over run by a horde of savages.

The Green Dragon Tavern now had an open position for wait staff person. Teresa Greenlow was still trying to get used to a Lise with an e instead of an a. Jim Roberts had told her it was a nickname for Liselotte. Lise then set about to redecorate their home.

Chapter 2

In the Supreme Court of the United States

THE LAW IS A ASS. – CHARLES DICKENS

In disputes between states and the federal government, the Supreme Court may exercise original jurisdiction. Thus, the case is heard in the Supreme Court without going through the federal court system. This saves the time of appeals which would end up in the Supreme Court anyway. In the case of the United States v Texas both sides in the dispute wanted the fastest possible final disposition to the case.

From the perspective of the Department of Justice, this was an easy case. Entities in Texas, if not the State of Texas itself, were negating federal supremacy by arresting and subjecting agents of the Federal Government to legal proceedings based on state laws. The case law was clear, once Congress legislated on a subject, the issue was removed from state jurisdiction. Some issues were complicated by the actors in the nullification of federal law being residents of the town of Freedonia, taking those actions possibly without sanction of the State of Texas. The State of Texas would be held accountable for the arrest of IRS agents and the attempted murder of DoJ agents by allowing the state legal system to prosecute those agents. The President insisted that Texas be brought under control and the Governor of Texas chastised.

The Attorney General of Texas had a clear mandate from the Governor and citizens of Texas via a referendum. The State of Texas would return the Federal Government to its Constitutional limits or else. The "or else" was indeterminate, but the political class of Texas was put on notice that the platform on which they had won election to limit federal power, was a demand by the electorate, and not a request. From the perspective of the State of Texas, repeated violations of the US Constitution by the Federal Government were clear and unmistakable.

Unlike the vast majority of the Supreme Court's workload, this would be a case actually tried before the court, rather than an appeal to the court. The case was a hot topic of conversation among the political class. A fairly clear line of demarcation had been set. Big government advocates supported the position of the Federal Government. Conservatives, Constitutionalists, and other annoyed at government over reach looked for a victory by Texas. The public discussion once again focused attention on Freedonia, and the events which led to the case before the Supreme Court.

This gave the visual media the opportunity to replay much of what had happened to create the present case. IRS agents intending to serve a search warrant on the Freedonia Transaction Company were detained by a local militia and arrested by the county sheriff. Those agents were then indicted by a Grand Jury, and bail was denied. The FBI and other agencies sent a 240 member task force to free the IRS agents and arrest the local militia that had detained the IRS agents. The task force ran into an ambush which led to their capture by the local militia and arrest by the county sheriff. Eventually, bail was granted and the agents released, but the charges remained. This massive disobedience, also labeled a rebellion by the leftist press occurred without the State of Texas acting to assist the Federal Government. Thus, legal action had been instituted to force Texas to comply with federal law.

A large number of Texans viewed events differently. At long last the massive federal overreach well beyond any conceivable limits set by the Constitution had finally been acted upon. Federal agents who executed laws and regulations unauthorized by the Constitution had been put on notice that such actions would have consequences for those agents personally. And if not the states themselves, there were citizens acting in concert willing to enforce the Constitution.

That attitude was also shared across the nation inside what was referred to as the liberty movement. Conservative talk radio and other media carried the discussion about the court case, and probable outcome as a hot topic of discussion. The right leaning think tanks started work to prepare their amicus briefs on what would be the defining case of the federal state relationship for generations. The last time there had been this much public discussion on the meaning of the Constitution was the federalist and anti-federalist papers prior to ratification of the document.

The states were extremely optimistic regarding a favorable outcome of the case. If the US Government won, the states would shortly be nothing more than administrative regions of the United States. If Texas won, the states would be well on their way to gaining the upper hand in the federal state relationship, and any not expressly stated federal power would be subject to curtailment by one or more states. The sudden death of one of the Supreme Court justices expected to vote in favor of Texas made the tension even greater. What would Texas do if the court was split or went 5 to 3 for the US Government? Would the court allow live video of the proceedings for the first time ever? Could there be a live audio feed instead of the usual recording? A court that had been trending toward the political considerations in the decision of cases, was now under more pressure than ever.

The case was scheduled to be the first case of the fall term. This was seen as a setback for the US Government, which was hoping to have the case heard at the end of the spring term, or the court convened especially to hear the case. This left matters pendant for at least six months without the federal agents being able to return to Texas without facing arrest. And the Texans would have at least six months of county sheriffs and local militias preventing the federal government from operating effectively in Texas. However, scheduling the case for the fall meant that it could still be on the docket when the President could nominate and the Senate could possibly confirm the Supreme Court Justice that would break a tie vote.

Finally, the can could be kicked down the road no further. There would have to be a clear statement from the Supreme Court as to what practical limits, if any, there was to the power of the federal government vis a vis the powers of the states. Did the ninth and tenth Amendments to the US Constitution have any meaning at all other than a statement of general principle when the US Government chose not to act, the matter was left to the states. The Democrats were optimistic that the last restraints on their ability to use the power of the federal government to accomplish their ends would be removed.

Conservatives were anxious about the outcome, but with the text of the Constitution itself, the whole dialog of the federalist papers, and contemporary legal opinion on their side, an unfavorable decision would look patently ridiculous. Simply put, there was no justification for the notion that a state was entirely subservient to the federal government and any law the Congress wished to pass, or an administrative agency could promulgate any regulation. The system was now in such a state that the federal judiciary was the arbiter of what the federal government could or could not do. A state, combination of states, and the people themselves were without any other recourse except rebellion.

One side or the other was going to be in for an ugly surprise when the Supreme Court rendered its opinion.

Assessing the implications of the decision going either way was the topic of discussion in Free Texas, the Lone Star Party, TEA Party groups, and others with an interest in the future of Texas and their own individual economic futures. Freedonia had become the de facto capital of Free Texas and the Lone Star Party. The pending oral arguments before the court were the main topic of discussion at the Green Dragon Tavern.

All five executive directors of Free Texas examined the issue at a working lunch, turning into dinner, on an otherwise dull Saturday. They took care of the board issues first with a review of finances and membership growth. The number of county organizations had grown to having over 150 of the 254 counties in Texas with at least one branch of Free Texas in operation. This mirrored the growth pattern and geographical areas of Texas where the Lone Star Party had made the difference in county and local elections as to who would be likely elected in November. There were also some 20 or more county directors in attendance, and the Green Dragon was packed with people to a greater degree that was usual for a Saturday.

When the topic turned to the impending case before the Supreme Court, the interest in the conversation among those gathered at the tavern and the county directors became more rapt. Ted Greenlow was the more optimistic of the Free Texas Executive Directors "Finally we are going to get our day in court. The contortions they are going to have to go through to claim the Constitution does not mean what it says will be pathetic."

Jim Roberts was on the other extreme. He had no confidence at all in the legal system "We are in the post modern world where the text of the Constitution and law is meaningless. These guys think that only a judge can figure out what all of that really means, and then will deliver the edit to us mere mortals. There is no rule of law in this country. We are living in a banana republic that can't even grow bananas."

More focused on the results of the decision and its implications was Ed McMasters. "What happens if it goes our way, and what happens if it doesn't?"

Roberts took on the question. "Best case is even with a miracle decision in favor of Texas, the immediate effect is to lock in the status quo. It potentially means the FBI stops hunting for us, but every act violating the Constitution will have to be litigated in order to annul it. The main advantage that I see would be that a state, and potentially us as individuals would have standing to sue, which almost no individual has now, unless the feds target you individually for some enforcement action. It will take a lifetime to get liberty back.

More likely is that we get more 'supremacy clause' shoved down our throats. This will be designed to make it clear to state governments that they are now no more than adjuncts to the federal government. As a practical matter, it puts Austin in the position of helping the feds to shut us down, or face the wrath of the federal government. The Governor and his friends in Austin will then have a decision to make. They can do the bidding of the federal government and hope the voters forget about this whole thing by November. Or, they may decide that staying in office requires them to take a serious look at Texas independence from the US. The current stance they advocate of taking the US Government to court will no longer be tenable. I predict the political class in Austin will find their self preservation somewhat difficult – either face angry voters, or angry party supporters. There is not going to be much happiness at the Capitol after this comes down."

Ed continued on "Jim what are we and you going to do to in response to the situation?"

Jim looked over at Lise Roberts with a grin. "Well Ed, my immediate plan is to order a bacon cheeseburger, fries, and a chocolate shake." Lise giggled. She couldn't help it. This was a deadly serious situation which could quickly make her a widow, but her husband was making light of the situation.

McMasters tried to get the conversation back on topic. "Dammit Jim, this is serious."

Roberts kept the gag going. "Ed, I take my dinner very seriously. You can't always be certain that there will be another one."

"OK, seriously, what is Free Texas going to do the position ourselves for the possible outcomes? What do we need to be prepared to do? Let's hear from the county directors, too." Roberts finally came back on topic.

Wise County's director spoke up "We want independence and we want it now. I'm tired of waiting for all of this to sort itself out."

Roberts addressed her "I know, but there is a path to be taken in order to get there. The decision will rest with a majority of Texans, and it happens when they decide they are ready for it. I think there are a considerable number of our fellow citizens that are hoping the federal government will be brought under control by the courts. They will not support independence until they are convinced the legal recourse method will not work."

The county director was still pressing the issue "How long will that take?"

Roberts replied "I suspect it won't be long. An arrogant class of judges and government officials will supply all of the help we will need. We only have to give them some time to do our work for us. I think the breaking point is near."

The county director went on "We have spent years on this. Why is it taking so long to wake up these people? It should be obvious by now. I see why there is so much contempt for the average person."

As an explanation, Roberts put forth the following reasoning. "My experience is that the human mind has a tendency to try to filter out things it finds too horrible to contemplate. Maybe that denial is some form of defense mechanism built in to keep us from worrying about things we can't mitigate or change. In any case, it seems to me the way forward is to send a message that we have the solution that makes life better for everyone. It is easier to sell a message of hope for the future than a disaster is on the way and you need to prepare for it in order to try and survive impending doom."

"But that doesn't mean that we still don't need to prepare for the future." Was the comment by Ed McMasters intended to ease the county director's concern.

Roberts agreed. "There are things we can do and should do as an organization to steer events in a favorable direction for us and deal with likely situations. We need to be even more vocal and get ourselves in the news, this keeps our message in the public discussion, gaining more support as more people realize that we have the winning argument. I suspect there are still a number of potential supporters that fear to be identified as part of Free Texas. Our success in various counties around Texas will convince more people to align with us publicly."

"We also need to have the public policy plans to back up our political stance of getting the US Government out of our business is good for all concerned. That means our alternatives to Social Security, Medicare, Defense, Veterans, and those programs we are going to eliminate. That also means realistic projections of revenues and expenses. Stating that we won't be paying income tax and other federal taxes, so there will be enough money and don't worry about it, just won't cut it. Reality is that we have to have a 'shadow cabinet' as they say in the United Kingdom and the Lone Star Party could do that. The goal is to demonstrate how Texas can take care of itself. That also means deciding what government is not going to do – and that is a real decision to make. A federal government that is running deficits of over $500 Billion a year is doing things it can't afford to do. Texas can't afford to do those things, and for many of them probably shouldn't be doing them either."

"And as an organization, Free Texas can be very helpful in another area. Running the militia support as an auxiliary organization is highly effective in making that limited military power more effective. It gives members who are not comfortable doing very public activities something very useful to do. Until Texas steps up and fully incorporates the militias into the Texas Military Forces, operational capability is going to be limited by funds and number of people who have blocks of time available for operations. Doing that as Free Texas, keeps it out of the realm of being tied to a specific political party, and thus capable of representing all of the people of Texas. It is also a very salient reminder that there is military capability in Texas that is not under the direct control of any politician. That is a powerful message regarding individual liberty and what we will or will not tolerate."

"That should be enough to keep us busy for the current quarter or at least until the next board meeting."

McMasters took over from there. "Seems like a plan Jim. We're open for discussion."

There was still a strong current of thought in Free Texas that they had the public policy part figured out good enough and the Lone Star Party should now pick up that ball and run with it. Others agreed with Roberts that if Free Texas was going to push for an independent Texas, how that was going to work financially and its impact on individual Texans would be a big part of selling the program. Greenlow felt it necessary to remind everyone that one of the member complaints making its way up to the Executive Directors was that Free Texas was not providing enough information on how an independent Texas was going to be able to sustain itself out to the membership. If the members didn't have that information, the potential supporters from the public at large also had to be uninformed. The talk continued into dinner.

Many of the county directors had left by the time the five Executive Directors were well into dinner. The organizational priorities had been set and members who wanted to get involved had no shortage of activities that could use their talents. And if not, Free Texas now had enough membership that it could steer resources into ensuring action on those activities. Such was always the challenge with leading a volunteer based organization.

One customer at the Green Dragon had arrived in the afternoon during the meeting of Free Texas and had said nothing throughout. He approached Roberts after dinner. "I thought you hated meetings."

"I do, however, they are a necessary evil. I'm glad you were able to make the ride out here Tom." Not everyone involved in the liberty movement was willing to accept motorcycle clubs as part of the movement. There was a wariness in the liberty movement that the clubs were bad news. In Roberts view, liberty included the freedom to ride motorcycles and to associate with other like minded individuals. Such clubs were the same as any other garden club as far as Roberts was concerned.

"What did the guys think, Tom?" Roberts asked.

"They like the idea of being a long range recon element. We share the same goals and have many of the same opponents. It is always nice to have more friends who can help each other out in times of trouble." was the response.

"Glad to hear it. We are building a militia Intel cell, and that should be the natural point of interface. Are you riding back tonight or staying over?" asked Roberts.

"Staying over. Some more of the Texas Patriots are riding in and we'd like to use the County Militia's range tomorrow if we may."

"No problem. The range is free this weekend I think. If it isn't I'll get you in." Roberts responded.

For the first time since the 2014 case of Kansas v Nebraska and Colorado, an original jurisdiction case was now before the Supreme Court, and the maneuvering had begun. The US Government used existing precedent from that case to have evidence and procedure to be used in this case to be the same as used in US District courts. The US Government seldom lost in District Court. The ruling by the Chief Justice was to accept that motion, as that was essentially how the court operated in all of the state v state cases the Supreme Court had decided in living memory. This was not entirely new territory, but original jurisdiction cases in the Supreme Court are rare, there being less than 250 examples to use as precedent.

Once before, Texas, had previously been a defendant in an original jurisdiction cases before the Supreme Court. In United States v Texas (1950) negating claims by Texas of the boundary of Texas extending 24 miles into the Gulf of Mexico based on a Republic of Texas claim. But the Texas lawyers still had one hope to tip the balance – as the defendant, Texas now demanded a jury trial. This had been done once before in another original jurisdiction Supreme Court case, Georgia v Brailsford (1794) in which Chief Justice John Jay instructed the jury: "It is presumed, that juries are the best judges of facts; it is, on the other hand, presumed that courts are the best judges of law. But still both objects are within your power of decision… you have a right to take it upon yourselves to judge both, and *to determine the law as well as the fact in controversy*".

Texas was going to invoke jury nullification to have the decision of constitutionality removed as a finding of fact from the Justices of the Supreme Court, and thus mitigate the loss of a key Justice. When the Chief Justice granted the motion for a jury trial, the outrage from the left side of the political spectrum was predictable, swift, and loud. The case would now depend on jury selection, and possibly not the makeup of the Justices sitting on the Supreme Court.

Chapter 3

To Repel Invasions

"... IF INSTEAD OF COLONIES YOU SEND TROOPS, THE COST IS VASTLY GREATER, AND THE WHOLE REVENUES OF THE COUNTRY ARE SPENT IN GUARDING IT SO THAT THE GAIN BECOMES A LOSS, AND MUCH DEEPER OFFENSE IS GIVEN SINCE IN SHIFTING THE QUARTERS OF YOUR SOLDIERS FROM PLACE TO PLACE THE WHOLE COUNTRY SUFFERS HARDSHIP, WHICH AS ALL FEEL, ALL ARE MADE ENEMIES AND ENEMIES WHO REMAINING, ALTHOUGH VANQUISHED, IN THEIR OWN HOMES, HAVE POWER TO HURT. IN EVERY WAY, THEREFORE, THIS MODE OF DEFENSE IS AS DISADVANTAGEOUS AS THAT BY COLONIZING IS USEFUL." - NICCOLO MACHIAVELLI

The average person thinks of an invasion as a military endeavor. As with the Geneva Conventions, this is a particularly western view of how conflicts may be fought. Other cultures have different views on how to conduct war. The United States was being colonized by waves of settlers from cultures with no concept of the western notion that individuals have rights which forbid intrusion upon by a government, groups of people as a society, or any other individual. The uniforms worn by the invaders were not that of an

28

army, and the weapons used were not always made of steel, but the effect on the people of the United States was the same.

If La Raza and the Islamic Caliphate adherents of resettlement of the Unites States had not read Machiavelli, they certainly were well versed in the means to be used for his preferred method of conquest. Massive settlement will subsume the native population over time. The battle will be won by the people able to produce the most children. It had been done before in North America, from 1607 to 1896. Millions of settlers had displaced the native population, and the regular military force required to perform the remainder of the task of subjugating the natives never numbered over 50,000 men. By the time the native population realized what was happening to them, it was too late to preserve their civilization.

Texas was being subjected to two invasions, and both were aided and abetted by the government of the United States. The loss of control of the southern border with Mexico allowed an almost unhindered flow of people and contraband into Texas and the rest of the United States run by various cartels. The Islamic migration was no less deadly. The resulting violence continued to escalate. While jihadi violence was mostly simmering beneath the surface, another threat had become more difficult to ignore.

There had been transit of goods across the border between Texas and Mexico dating back to the days before Texas became a state. Nobody really cared much about those movements until Prohibition was enacted in the United States, and then smuggling became a clandestine activity to bring alcohol in to the US, just as had also occurred on the northern border with Canada. Over time, the smuggling industry changed products, to meet demand for other intoxicants in the US, and some limited amount of recreational drug use.

The 1980s changed the dynamic with the start of the first Mexican drug cartel, focusing on the shipment of cocaine from Columbia and partnering with the Columbian Medillin cartel. The profitability of this enterprise created wealth for the cartel, corruption of government officials, and competitors for moving contraband into the United States. Cartel violence became the most efficient means of competition, and the murder rate rapidly surpassed anything seen in the "mob" days of the 1920s gangsters in the US. Ultimately, that competition led to territory controlled by each cartel, and fights along the borders of cartel control to expand influence or try to eliminate a neighboring cartel. Los Zetas and the Sinaloa cartel fight for control of central Mexico. The Gulf cartel, Los Zetas and the Juarez cartel control Mexican territory bordering Texas, attempts by Mexican police or Marines to capture cartel members created brief and intense battles in which numbers of uninvolved Mexicans were also killed.

The cartels themselves became de facto governments over parts of Mexico, extorting money from the citizenry, and engaging in various forms of terror in order to maintain their control. Murders in Mexico exceeded the number of murders in the US. Los Zetas took severe losses and new cartels formed. The Mexican government proved incapable, or in some cases unwilling, to get control of the country. The military was patrolling the streets, the Marines were used to try to capture cartel leaders, and the people themselves were left defenseless by Mexico's gun control laws.

Finally, some people in rural central Mexico had enough. The first Mexican militias (autodefensas) were formed. At first, they had little in the way of weaponry, disapproval from and possible arrest by the government, and no military training. But, they had the most important thing needed for success – the will to be free to live their lives as they saw fit. Drug cartel enforcers started to disappear and free elections for local political offices took place. The autodefensas started to be armed, first from captured cartel weapons, and then from lost police and military weapons. Gradually, some of the autodefensas established control over their towns and regions.

Their success was an embarrassment to the Mexican government. The Mexican federal government ordered the autodefensas to disarm and cede control back to the state and federal governments. The few who complied soon regretted that decision. The same problems returned, and the next time it was much harder to eliminate the cartel and their corrupt government puppets. The government then tried the next tactic – make the members of the autodefensas official police forces. In those areas controlled by the autodefensas, an uneasy truce held, occasionally having to repulse a cartel attack.

Each of the cartels had adjuncts operating inside the United States. They moved the goods and people north, while the resulting cash flowed south. Business was expanding, and not just geographically. Some entities did not want the presence of their people in the United States to be known to the US Government, or wanted to avoid the notice of customs authorities, and the cartels became the means by which illicit entry into the United States was effected. One of the consequences of the movement of populations from less developed regions of the world into the United States was that diseases not seen for decades were now not uncommon in what were labeled "immigrant" communities. County governments were incurring millions of dollars in expenses to provide medical care for non citizens.

As the cartels fought for control of regions of Mexico, their affiliates in the United States started to do the same to rival gangs and competitors in US cities and towns. So far, the impact to US citizens had been limited to those caught in the crossfire in Mexico and the competitors to the cartels that as a rule had a criminal history. The situation was now getting worse. The police labeled these activities "gang violence".

Some of the cartel revenue generating activities in Mexico involved kidnapping and extortion. This was a result of the highly competitive nature of the cartel business, the need to pay their "troops" and pure greed. Where there was corruption in the US, some of the cartel affiliates thought this activity would also be a source of revenue north of the border as well.

The first attempts were made on people who had either personal or cultural reasons not to involve the police. Thus, most of the public were not aware of the gradual escalation of violence. And to the extent more criminal conduct was noticed, much of it was attributed to other causes, such as political intimidation or ethnic agitation. The branches of the cartels operating in the United States grew stronger.

Texas property owners who were living on their property at or near the Texas border noticed the increase in illegal traffic across the border, and thus, their property. The transit routes trampled crops, and left a vast quantity of refuse behind. Human waste, water and food containers, luggage too heavy to carry an extended distance, clothing, and an occasional dead body became the price these land owners paid for owning property that bordered Mexico.

Border Patrol agents played a cat and mouse game with the smugglers. The agents also had to struggle against an agency management, under orders from Washington, which made sure that the agents had broken down vehicles, limited fuel to conduct patrols, and weaponry inferior to that of the cartels. Official policies discouraged the agents from using force to protect the border. Should an agent somehow overcome all of these obstacles, and manage to apprehend an illegal border crosser, the alien would not be deported, but after being caught, would be released into the United States, and told to later report for a court hearing. Few aliens bothered to appear in court, as the system was known to be a sham.

Many employers in the United States turned a blind eye to the issue, by hiring illegal aliens at below market and even minimum wage. This gave them a big cost advantage over their competitors, driving other companies that did not fire US citizens and replace them with foreigners from undeveloped countries out of business. Larger companies, rather than risk possible fines, and needing labor with some more advanced skills, spent money in Washington, for a visa program to avoid this risk. The H1B visa program allowed for the legal entry into the United States for people with marketable skills, who if allowed to enter the US on their own, could potentially change jobs to another employer that would pay them more, and thereby not depress the wages excessively compared to the US citizens. The H1B workers had their residence in the US tied to the employer who sponsored them. The indentured servant of the 18th and 18th Centuries had returned from the pages of history.

Eventually, over 25% of the work force in the United States consisted of non US citizens. Much of their health care paid by the public, and their "resettling" into housing and receipt of social services performed by US religious organizations and charities via grant money provided by the federal government. For the first time ever, living standards in the US began to fall. Formerly employed US citizens were reduced to using public assistance, and the percentage of the population on the federal food program reached 15%. The federal and state cabal of special interest groups funding political campaigns and using organized voting blocs to elect politicians who continued these programs were on the verge of destroying the middle class taxpayer.

These formerly middle class citizens who were now joining the ranks of either the working poor, or public aid recipients were angry. At first, that anger went into supporting the TEA Party organizations. The fight then went to the issue of control of the Republican Party. There was now a huge amount of stress inside the GOP. Could candidates chosen by the large financiers be replaced by those who would stop the invasion? That was the central question of the 2016 presidential campaign.

One quarter of inmates in federal prisons were not US citizens, in Texas the number was about one in ten. The pressure had caused the Texas legislature to increase the amount of spending on border security in 2015 to $400 million per year. This security effort took on the character of increasing the number of Department of Public Safety Troopers and augmenting the efforts of the Border Patrol. Washington could not control the Texas effort, and the state Republicans gave themselves credit for taking care of border security. Part of the GOP supporters bought that tale, and others, including the Lone Star Party and Free Texas didn't. The attitude of those organizations and the TEA Party Republicans had been summed up by Roberts in one of their meetings. "Great, illegally crossing the border into Texas is now about the same seriousness as a speeding ticket as far as the Governor is concerned."

Free Texas and the Lone Star Party were fielding the complaints from angry citizens who were demanding that something be done about the border. The Lone Star Party was campaigning on the basis of one of its primary issues as a party platform being to use Texas Military Forces on the border security mission, and take it away from the Department of Public Safety.

One of the Free Texas Executive Directors, Gene Smith had a close relationship with several people in the border counties, and they had been pressing hard on Gene to send out a militia call via Free Texas to put more aggressive border security into place. Gene couldn't take the pressure anymore and called Roberts. "Jim, I've got a lot of demand directed at me that we ask the militias to go to the border. I agree with them, and you know it is the right thing to do and we need to do it."

Roberts dreaded this conversation, and knew it was coming. "Gene, you know my feelings. This is a huge task that we can not perform successfully. We have neither the manpower nor the resources to perform serious border interdiction."

"Jim, what if you had to do it? Would you go and give it your best effort, even if it was only for show?" Gene asked.

"I'm sure there would be volunteers. Maybe even enough for the 52 one week rotations we would need as a real program. Otherwise, I'd think the guys would need to get paid in addition to the operational cost of the mission. If I was going to get involved in this, I'd rather do it in such a way that might lead to a change in the situation. Just plugging 10 out of 1000 holes in the dam will only be a temporary benefit to the owner of the property where we operate – that is until we pack up and leave. Something which has to happen one day with probable consequences to the property owner."

"Jim, if you're not going to do it yourself can you at least give me a plan that others can execute?" continued Gene.

"Here is what I suggest. We need an Executive Board meeting to discuss how Free Texas sponsors the border security initiative. The General and a couple of his retired Army officers need to be in on this. And we need some buy in from a few militia leaders. I'll help set that up. Is that OK, Gene?" answered Roberts.

"Let's do it." affirmed Gene.

The meeting took place just over a week later at the Green Dragon Tavern in Freedonia. This meeting did not take place in the main dining room like most of the Free Texas meetings. The twelve attendees were in the basement.

The General was the first to remark on the surroundings. "Is this like the White House Situation Room, but for Free Texas?"

Roberts answered the question. "Well sir, I think of it more like the wine cellar in the 21 Club in New York."

The General gave Roberts a quizzical look and Ed McMasters asked, "Care to explain that, Jim. Some of us don't travel to foreign countries like New York."

"The 21 Club was originally a Speakeasy on 52nd Street in New York City. As such, it had several security features to protect their patrons from undue attention. A lever would dump the booze from the bar into the city sewer if the place was raided. There was also a secret wine cellar behind a secret door. It eventually became a restaurant, and back in the day there were several traditions associated with the place. Women weren't allowed until the late 1990s, and even then only on the first floor bar and dining room, and not the second floor dining rooms. They now do private parties and such so that domino has fallen. In the wine cellar, there is a private dining room that seats 20, for small dinners hosted by ex Presidents and such. Having dinner in the wine cellar at the 21 Club is like the ultimate power symbol in New York, or at least it once was." Roberts explained.

Ted Greenlow asked "So when and with who did you eat in the wine cellar?"

Roberts replied "Never did. Nobodies like me ate in the dining room by the bar. But as far as Texas goes, we dozen have made it now. Hanging stuff from the ceiling as they do there at 21 would be a bit much in my view."

McMasters said "Maybe so. But I do find it fascinating to see how your mind works, Jim."

Roberts thought that after they heard the plan he was about to present, fascination might not be the word they were going to use to describe it. He had something in mind much bolder than sending a bunch of guys to the Rio Grande River and see if anybody tried to cross. He planned to have a real impact on the problem.

The first question was cost allocation. It was agreed that there would be one week rotations, the arriving unit travels to the site on Saturday, is deployed on Sunday, and departs the following Sunday. This only gave late Saturday afternoon and evening as transition time. It would be good to have longer rotations for a command group to smooth out the unit rotations, but that required qualified personnel who could spend more time on site. Roberts would be the POC (Point of Contact) to schedule units in and out.

As Roberts remarked, "That is the easiest part of this operation. Now it is going to get difficult. We're now talking logistics, and that means money. Food is $5 US per man per day. If we have a reinforced platoon, which is the smallest force we should send, that costs $250 US per day, and we have other needs such as tentage, water, generator fuel to recharge radio batteries, and so on. Even at this small scale, this is a $500 US per day operation. Can Free Texas support that? That is what this operation really comes down to, how much money we can raise and getting the manpower to volunteer. And at that we are going to have practically no impact on the situation. It is only a show for a PR stunt. Like with much of what we do – the real question is can the people who want something done, come up with the resources to make that something happen"

Smith quickly did the math. "I'm sure we can raise $100,000 US, but that won't last a year. Does it have to cost so much? I've gone with a few friends, and it seems like we didn't spend that much."

Roberts replied, "The four of you didn't spend $20 US per day? The issue is what would the four of you do if you had to engage an opponent? Does our intel tell us that we have enough people to handle an encounter? Where is the reaction force if you needed help? Being lucky so far is good for us. I don't like pushing that luck too far because one day it runs out."

"OK Jim, I see we are talking about a semi permanent presence. And that means some sort of camp, with sanitation required. So, maybe we only have six months for a run. It shows us doing something." Smith countered.

"Gene this covers less than one mile of a 1200 mile border. At a platoon a week, we will end up rotating a brigade's worth of troops through the operation. It will be good operational experience for each of the units that go, don't get me wrong on that, but this is more in the nature of training for us. Our people need the operational experience, and we need to see if we are any better at logistically supporting a long term operation than we have been so far. We were lucky that we didn't have to do it that long the last time.

The other issue is best location to do this. I'm assuming you have a spot in mind. If not, and we can believe the intel reports, most of the activity takes place between Laredo and Brownsville. I'd go for the Laredo area as where the Gulf cartel and Los Zetas may be fighting it out." said Roberts.

McMasters broke into the conversation, "This isn't going the way I had hoped. I thought we would be able to do more. Somehow we have to make an impact down on the border"

Roberts took this opportunity to make his pitch. "There are other options. For one thing, we can bring a larger force for a short period of time. After we get the coverage, reporters lose interest until somebody gets shot. It is just a matter of how you want to spend the money and man days, they are finite resources that we will ultimately exhaust. The other option is to make a show of our defensive efforts, while we put an offensive option into play."

Gene Smith thought he saw where Roberts was going. "You mean go after the cartels and smugglers? Maybe go after them in Mexico itself?"

"That is kind of the idea, but not us doing the chasing. If you look at Mexico, it is essentially a failed state. The government can't keep public order. Any organized armed group has a good chance of operating independently of any form of government control, especially if it can influence local government officials. According to historical record, the place is overdue for a revolution. The question is what comes next, the cartels or the autodefensas. It is in our interest that the autodefensas, the people themselves, end up in charge. We might be able to help that along."

Now it was Ted Greenlow's turn to break in, "Jim, there are times when I can't tell if you have come up with something brilliant, or have gone bat guano crazy. We can't overthrow the government of Mexico. I'm not saying it doesn't need it, just that we can't do it."

"I'm not suggesting that we do it ourselves. We might identify those in Mexico who would have an interest in doing it. Provide training and logistical support from our side of the border to help the natural course of history along is what I am suggesting. Our border operation would provide great cover for movement of the insurgents back and forth. They can run a government in exile and media from Freedonia on the quiet. Anyway, I've wanted to expand the ammunition plant into weapons production as well, the insurgents can do the field testing for me."

Phil Fuller, the fifth, and most recently appointed to the Free Texas board entered the conversation. "General, what do you think of this?"

Now it was the General's turn to speak. "As you must know in Free Texas, the first Republic of Texas essentially went bankrupt trying to meet its security needs on the southern and western borders. It would be a pity for the same thing to happen to the second Republic of Texas, and even more so before it was successfully established. Giving the people of Mexico a government that was responsive to their needs is probably the best form of security assistance we could have from our southern neighbor. Anything done of a military nature done from this side had better never see the light of day. That would better be accomplished by an intelligence agency covert operation. In any case, providing a safe haven on this side of the border for those who wish to reform Mexico is a necessary first step for the operation." The other retired officers nodded in agreement.

Roberts rejoined the dialog. "Ted, the difference between brilliance and bat guano crazy may be a very thin line. It depends on whether or not the subject has lost touch with reality."

"I wasn't expecting an answer to the question. Now you're going to make bank by selling us weapons, too." Greenlow remarked.

"Benjamin Franklin referred to it as doing well by doing good. He made sure that he got the business of printing official government documents and proceedings. Gene, you have the best contacts in south Texas. Let's find out who has an interest in making Mexico a better place for the people of Mexico to live and work. Some Mexican journalists might even want to tour Freedonia. That may give some people in Mexico very dangerous ideas indeed." Roberts summarized.

The Free Texas fundraising drive for border security started the next week.

Chapter 4

The Central Bank That Wasn't

THE AMERICAN REPUBLIC WILL ENDURE UNTIL THE DAY CONGRESS DISCOVERS THAT IT CAN BRIBE THE PUBLIC WITH THE PUBLIC'S MONEY. - ALEXIS DE TOCQUEVILLE

The Freedonia Transaction Company was doing well. Income from mortgages, loans, rents, and credit card usage now more than covered manager Beth Dunwoody's 150 TXD monthly salary. There were an extremely large number of deposits and new accounts being opened almost every day. The FTC had plenty of capital to invest, and it was being invested first in Freedonia, and then elsewhere to assist what was now being called the "Liberty Movement".

Beth had a 1000 TXD mortgage on a quarter acre lot with a shell of a very small house, taking a 1.25% note at 15 years from the FTC. She paid 7.50 TXD per month on the mortgage and planned to retire the note early. Beth, as did most Freedonians, lived modestly preferring to "pay as you go" rather than take on debt. Internet service from the Freedonia Technology Company, and a mail box at the Freedonia General Store cost 1 TXD each per month. Splurging for food and drink at the Green Dragon Tavern every day would seldom cost over 30 TXD per month. Water and electric service from the Freedonia City Utilities accounted for another 5 TXD per month. Living below the income tax threshold meant a monthly disposable income of some 100 TXD per month that could be used on finishing out the house and a trip to Lubbock for major purchases after exchanging some TXD for US currency. In the liberty Movement, US paper money was referred to as FRNs, or Federal Reserve Notes, in order to distinguish them from real money, meaning silver or gold coins and FTC TXD promissory notes which could be exchanged for real money.

The same idea was taking hold in other parts of Texas, with local equivalents to the Freedonia Transaction Company being established on the same model of using US silver coinage as the benchmark of value. Most of the organizers of the effort asked the FTC for the benefit of experience before starting, and the FTC was eager to help. Printing the FTC promissory notes was expensive because like any currency, it took some effort to put anti counterfeiting measures into place. This was especially critical, as a one TXD promissory note had a value in excess of $10 FRN, so the FTC had watermarks and other security measures in all of the notes, even the fractional one cent note. People had to have absolute confidence in anything used as money. After coming away unscathed from the encounter with the IRS, there was absolute confidence in the value of the FTC promissory note, and at any time, they could be redeemed for US silver coinage. No one had ever been turned away from redeeming a FTC promissory note for silver coinage.

So far, all of the other companies had agreed with the reasoning suggested by the FTC to use FTC promissory notes. They were already established, it would make it easier for people to use the same form of payment in all Liberty Movement areas of Texas, and it formed a basis for the companies to do business and transfer funds among themselves without having to take the risk of transporting large quantities of silver coinage to make payments. The mechanism was simple. Each company opened an account with the FTC, and traded some silver coinage for FTC promissory notes, which were then put in circulation as a customer opened an account or traded currency or coin for the FTC notes. The company account numbers at the FTC were structured like American Banker's Association routing numbers, and then the follow on individual account number gave the FTC the capability as acting as the clearing house for the Texas Financial Network.

The creation of the Texas Financial Network had other benefits. The Discover Card network found itself perfectly willing to issue cards to members of the Texas Financial Network, even if member institutions were not members of the American Banker's Association. Rather than risk pumping new life blood into Discover, Visa and MasterCard also suddenly dropped the ABA membership requirement. It was now much easier for the transaction companies to issue credit cards.

The size of the operation was now creating challenges for the Freedonia Transaction Company. The vault could no longer hold all of the coinage which backed the FTC Promissory Notes, more FTC Promissory Notes needed to be printed and stored to meet demand. Additionally the Internal Revenue Service decided to take another run at the Freedonia Transaction Company and the people using FTC Promissory Notes as currency.

Land was getting scarce in Freedonia and the Freedonia Transaction Company needed a depository for storage of reserve coinage and currency. It was time to make a deal. Freedonia needed to expand and as is the case in rural Texas, inherited property comes on the market when the children of the deceased owners prefer city life to the slower pace of life in the countryside. The Freedonia Transaction Company invested in those properties in the county although they did not border the town of Freedonia itself. This set the stage for a land swap with one of the owners of property bordering Freedonia. As part of the deal, all expenses were covered by the Freedonia Transaction Company, including moving the owner's house whole to the traded property. Freedonia could now expand, and that expansion included a depository for the Freedonia Transaction Company, guarded by the Borden County Militia.

Freedonia Transaction Company Promissory Notes were an interesting item. The fractional notes were less than half the size of US currency, with a look something of a cross between Republic of Texas currency and military payment certificates. In addition to the wording "The Fredonia Transaction Company promises to pay the Bearer on demand" the amount in silver lawful money, there was a portrait and a watermark. The Texas Dollar notes were almost the same size as US currency and also had other security features. Each denomination used a different color scheme. The notes were printed by a European company that also printed bank notes for various countries. The Texas series featured the following:

One Cent – Patrick Henry
Five Cents – Thomas Jefferson
Ten Cents – James Madison
25 Cents – George Washington
Fifty Cents – Benjamin Franklin
One Dollar- Sam Houston
Five Dollars – William Travis
Ten Dollars – Benjamin Milam
Twenty Dollars – David Crockett
Fifty Dollars – James Bowie

100 Dollars – Juan Sequin
500 Dollars – Jose Navarro
1000 Dollars – Mirabeau Lamar

It was rare to see anything larger than the 20 TXD note in circulation. Every day, the exchange rate between FRNs and the TXD was posted. The rate depended on the price of "junk silver" US coinage. For most of the residents of Freedonia, that exchange rate was of concern only when buying items in the larger cities in Texas, where the FRN still was the currency of choice.

The Internal Revenue Service considers gold and silver coin transactions at face value as frivolous claims for the purpose of income tax declarations. Accordingly, a cause of action was opened against the Freedonia Transaction Company in US District court in Dallas, Texas. Service was performed on the corporate attorney in Austin, who then notified Roberts, a member of the Board of Directors of the FTC, of the action.

"Is this the usual administrative regulation tax evasion claim?" Roberts asked.

"Yeah, that's about it. I assume you want to reply." said the attorney.

"Yes we do. First move venue to out as close to here as you can. I want at least one juror to be holding FTC Promissory Notes in his pocket during this case. Second, how about a motion to dismiss as the IRS claim is frivolous as conflicting with the SCOTUS decisions we discussed on starting this thing. And the backup plan is for discovery on the Dallas Fed to see if they maintain adequate amounts of gold and US securities as required by law to back the FRNs they have issued. Relevance is that we can't establish a market value of the coins without placing an artificial value on FRNs.

And we are going to send out a killer press release Friday after the markets close that might cause a stir. I'll get a copy worked up and sent to you today. This should be a wild ride." Roberts said to the attorney.

"OK, talk to you later after I get the release." replied the lawyer.

Roberts' next move was to contact Beth Dunwoody and let her know that the next battle with the IRS was on, and she would play a key role in this scuffle as the public face of the Freedonia Transaction Company. She then started to contact the members of the Texas Financial Network to advise them of the IRS action and to set up a conference call on the FTC response. Strategy on how the companies would be protecting their depositors would also be part of the call.

Next task was for Jim and Beth to work up the Press Release.

FOR IMMEDIATE RELEASE

Freedonia Transaction Company, Freedonia, TX Friday 4:30 PM

The Freedonia Transaction Company (FTC) has been notified that it is the subject of legal action instigated by the US Department of the Treasury, Internal Revenue Service. The IRS claims as to the valuation methods used by the FTC relating to US Currency, coinage minted by the US Treasury prior to 1965, and FTC Promissory notes are without merit and refuted by prior statements made by the Department of the Treasury, and case law established by the US Supreme Court.

As the Department of the Treasury states on its website: "Federal Reserve notes are not redeemable in gold, silver or any other commodity, and receive no backing by anything.........Congress has specified that a Federal Reserve Bank must hold collateral equal in value to the Federal Reserve notes that the Bank receives. This collateral is chiefly gold certificates and United States securities. This provides backing for the note issue."

The Freedonia Transaction Company will ask the court to allow us to audit the Dallas Federal Reserve to ensure that there is adequate backing as required by law for all of the currency it has issued.

The question as to whether stated value or market value of US coinage applies to debts such as the wages an employer owes employees or debts incurred as a result of a contract has been settled by the Supreme Court and invalidates any regulation or administrative decision by the IRS.

U.S. SUPREME COURT

THOMPSON V. BUTLER, 95 U.S. 694 (1877)

"One owing a debt may pay it in good coin or legal tender notes of the United States, as he chooses, unless there is something to the contrary in the obligation out of which the debt arises. A coin dollar is worth no more for the purposes of tender in payment of an ordinary debt than a note dollar. The law has not made the note a standard of value any more than coin. It is true that in the market, as an article of merchandise, one is of greater value than the other, but as money -- that is to say, as a medium of exchange -- the law knows no difference between them.

This judgment is for coined money, which at the time it was rendered and now is worth more in the market as merchandise than

48

paper money; but our jurisdiction is to be determined by the amount of money to be paid and not the kind. If, instead of paper dollars and gold dollars legalized as money, the law had provided for silver dollars and gold dollars, and this judgment had been for payment in gold, we think it would hardly be contended that this Court could take jurisdiction because when the judgment was rendered, gold happened to be worth more in the market as merchandise than silver; but in principle that case would not be different from this."

Effective immediately, the Freedonia Transaction Company and certain other members of the Texas Financial Network will no longer accept US Currency as a medium of exchange.

END OF RELEASE

Dunwoody asked Roberts "This seems so straightforward. How did all of those other guys get tripped up and convicted for tax evasion?"

"Easy, some of them minted their own coins – not classified as legal tender, and got caught up as bartering. Or, they used post 1985 minted silver or gold, which the US Code specifies are numismatic items sold by the US Mint at market value. One guy declared the silver coin face value on the W-2 forms, but actually paid employees in FRNs. We have consistently used pre 1965 coinage which is legal tender that can be exchanged one for one for FRNs at any Federal Reserve Bank." Roberts explained.

The conference call took place a 4 PM. Dunwoody took the lead. "By now you should have a copy of the press release we will issue on Friday. We are going to respond to the legal action and fight it in court as we have ample legal precedent on our side. This may scare some of your customers and we think that is what the real purpose of the action is. If the IRS suspects a taxpayer is reporting what it thinks is low income based on real money, they will audit and assess penalties that may include the $5000 penalty for a frivolous argument claim. We think the more publicity this gets, the worse it will be for the IRS. That might be why they have not held a press conference on this. They are doing some selective intimidation, and any of you may be in the same situation if you do not cave in."

"Beth, this is Keith Miller in Quanah. CNN is reporting the IRS filing on you guys now. There is plenty of snark on tax cheats, right wing extremists, anti government groups, and so on. You might get a reporter or two wanting to talk to you."

"Thanks Keith, I'll prepare for that." In the past, Beth had her home and all other assets seized by the IRS in a tax dispute. Any competent reporter would be aware of that before interviewing her.

"Beth, what I was going to ask before getting off track with CNN, is are we going to stop trading FRNs for TXD? Do our customers have to make the trade themselves and bring us the silver coins?"

"It is up to each of you how to proceed. Either no change from what you do now, or join what is essentially a FTC boycott of US currency. Of course, our customers can still make FRN purchases with their credit cards. But we are going to get out of the cash trade of FRNs for TXDs until this blows over. It is up to you to manage your risk, just like any prudent banker should.

We are prepared to loan to you from our silver reserves what you may need to cover a run, either in coin or Promissory Notes. That is one reason we are suspending the FRN trade, we can't get caught short with a pile of FRNs and run out of silver. This may go the other way, and people start lose even more confidence in the US Dollar. That is the angle we are going to play. If the US Dollar was a sound currency, the IRS wouldn't be doing this." Beth told the listeners on the call.

The rest of the call concerned which companies wanted to increase their silver or FTC note holdings. This led to the creation of the Texas Financial Network TIBOR (Texas Inter Bank Overnight Rate), which is how the participants would meet short term cash flow needs among themselves.

News of the IRS action did get some minor news coverage as it seemed to relate to the conflict between some Texas groups and the federal government, and the Freedonia Transaction Company was asked to comment. Reporters were told there would be a press release and conference Friday afternoon at 4 in the afternoon.

Rumors started to go around on social media that some banks in Texas were no longer going to accept US Dollars. When Texas Financial Network customers went to their institutions to check out the rumor, they were told that as of Friday, some members would no longer trade FRNs for TXDs, so customers were encouraged to complete such transactions by Friday. Thus, the social media rumors were confirmed as true. This increased the business of the companies. Very few customers bailed out. By their vary nature, customers of entities such as the Freedonia Transaction Company had more faith in silver and private enterprise than they did the US Government. Those customers felt that their faith was more than justified when it was backed up with men carrying rifles who had previously arrested IRS agents trying to shut down the Freedonia Transaction Company.

Most of the financial action went the other way. FRNs were being dumped into the Texas Financial Network for various reasons. Some did it as a show of support for those standing up to the federal government. Some did it as a hedging strategy, mindful that during the depression, the government had confiscated private gold holdings, but having FTC Promissory Notes could be as good as having the silver itself. The notes would either not be subject to confiscation (the government deeming them worthless) or be easier to hide. Others decided that now was the time to make a break with the US Dollar, before disaster struck.

Businesses in Freedonia had readily adopted the idea. Prices in US Dollars disappeared, and only the Texas Dollar, being a coin of 90% silver weighing 26.73 grams, or .77345 oz., or containing 371.25 grains of pure silver, or its equivalent, was acceptable as payment for any debt. The few reporters who traveled to Freedonia to attend the Freedonia Transaction Company press conference were the first to be bemused by this happening. The only way they could pay for anything in Freedonia was by using a credit card. Their personal experience would only reinforce the point to be made at the press conference.

Only six reporters attended the press conference. Dunwoody went over the points from the press release and asked for questions. Most of the questions pertained to how the Freefonia Transaction Company thought it could operate without using US Dollars. She pointed out that all the reporters needed to know about that point was seen in town. Nobody needed US currency, and life went on as normal. Based on that experience, she guessed most of the stories were going to be about the town in a dispute with the IRS that thinks it can do without the US Dollar. That would be a good message for Freedonia. It would take some of the air out of the tax scammer argument in the public conversation.

To the extent that the dispute and the reaction by the Freedonia Transaction Company was covered, it hit the press wires by 5 (a good press release writes at least half of the story for the reporter), and got local TV coverage from the Fox station in Lubbock, which had always had an interest in Freedonia since the IRS raid. CNN took it as a blurb in order to have a laugh at the Texas banks who thought they could no longer accept US Dollars. The news about the Texans not accepting US Dollars also became a crawl item on CCN International, as most of the news of the week had been reported, and it was now after close of business on the east coast.

Saturday is a normal work day in Asia, and the CNN crawl about the Texas banks no longer accepting US Dollars intrigued a Japanese reporter, who thought the story interesting. He decided to check into it, found the press release online from the Freedonia Transaction Company, and social media posts confirming that there were people being told that they could no longer take US Dollars in to the bank for trade. He wrote up the development and put it on the Japanese press wire with the headline "Texas Banks No Longer Accept US Dollars" shortly before 9:30 AM Japanese time.

The article written by the Japanese reporter caught the attention of a currency trader at one of Japan's largest banks. This information was immediately brought to the attention of his boss. More calls around the bank took place. It was determined that Freedonia was the center of a movement challenging the US Government and the rebels had a string of success behind them. As a precautionary measure, the bank would reduce its holdings in US Treasury bonds and sell US Dollars, and these actions would take place now because Japanese markets had an hour head start on the Chinese markets and a 90 minute head start on the Singapore market.

A trader in Shanghai, China noticed a 15 basis point rise in interest rates on the US treasury 30 year bond on the Tokyo Exchange. The US Dollar has also fallen slightly in value. He decided to sell some of his firm's US Dollar assets before their value decreased any more. He notified his supervisor of his actions in case developments warranted his supervisor's attention. Singapore traders noted the decline in the price of US Treasury securities and the Dollar as well. It was thought prudent to adjust their positions on holdings denominated in US Dollars. Traders all around Asia were now taking an interest in the value of the US Dollars and yields on US Government securities.

While Washington slept, the US Dollar had lost 2% of its value and interest rates on US Government securities had risen .15% by early afternoon in Asia. There was plenty of US Government debt being held in Asia. The PRC held about $1.25 Trillion, and various Japanese entities held another $1.15 Trillion in debt, so even a fraction of a percentage of a change in holdings moved the market. On any given day, about $600 Billion of US Government debt instruments change hands. That amount of trading in Asia had already been surpassed by noon in Peking. PRC banking officials scheduled a meeting for 1 PM Peking time to discuss the situation.

At the meeting, it was decide to execute a test of a plan designed to send a message to the United States in upcoming negotiations with the PRC. That afternoon, the total amount of US Government debt to be liquidated would be $100 Billion, with preparations made to liquidate another $100 Billion before the US markets opened on Monday.

Most of the buyers of US Dollars and Treasury bonds had been the after hours traders in Europe and the US. They had seen the initial drop in price of US Dollar assets as a buying opportunity. Toward midnight, they realized that the market had decided on a lower price for the US Dollar and US Government debt. The fall in value was noted by the financial press that published on Saturday in Europe and the US. An alarmist bear or two in the US wondered if this was the start of a crash.

By Sunday, more of the press was aware of the actions of the Asian markets, and speculation was rampant on what would happen when the markets reopened on Monday. There was also speculation as to what triggered the markets in Asia to sell. Was it concern about the election in November? Was it concern about the debt load soon to exceed $20 Trillion? Was it concern about the refinance in a few days, where over $100 Billion of debt was to be auctioned?

Monday started the cycle again in Asia. The $100 Billion in US Government securities dumped on the market by the PRC indicated there would be no recovery for the US Dollar. The Asian markets closed Monday with the US Dollar off 5% from its Friday close, and interest rates on US Government debt yielding almost .5% higher than on Friday. There had been a 45 basis point change in the yield on US Treasury 30 year bonds over two days trading in a 54 hour period.

The European markets opened with an intervention by the European Central Bank to buy the US Dollar and take on some US Treasury Bonds. European banks started to worry about their derivative positions and started to hedge. The fall seemed to have been arrested, but at the lower level is where that new stability occurred.

The US market opened before Europe closed. The Federal Reserve intervened by buying $500 Billion in US Government debt on the open market. That sent a message and the markets stabilized at the new found interest rates and exchange rate for the US Dollar. The Secretary of the Treasury thought it necessary to have a meeting Monday afternoon with the Federal Reserve, Comptroller of the Currency, and a few agency heads within the Treasury Department.

The Secretary of the Treasury started the meeting off with a question. "Can anybody tell me what happened over the weekend?"

The representative from the Office of Terrorism and Financial Intelligence replied, "We have no information of deliberate targeting, other that we do think for some reason the Chinese Communist party instructed the People's Bank of China to sell some $200 Billion of US securities over the weekend. We are not sure if that was to start the events or take advantage of them."

Office of International Affairs asked "Why would they do that? They need to hold our debt to keep their cost of exporting down relative to the Dollar."

"Possibly to send a message to a Presidential candidate about trade policy." was the reply from the Intelligence representative.

"There was one odd thing we saw, but it makes no sense. There was a news blurb in the Japanese media that said banks in Texas were no longer going to accept deposits in US Dollars. Like I said, the translation into English makes no sense." said the representative from International Affairs.

The Commissioner of the IRS gave the Intelligence analyst a startled look. That caught the attention of the Secretary of the Treasury. "Out with it."

The IRS Commissioner wasn't sure how to express it. "Well sir, we are involved in an enforcement action on some tax evaders in Texas. They have a fake bank that they are operating and we started legal action on them last week .... Well it seems they issued a press release late Friday that said they were no longer going to use US currency. A couple of media outlets covered it."

At this point the Secretary was livid. "We have an over $100 Billion refinance this Thursday, 30 Year Bonds, 10 Year Notes, you name it, and if this interest rate rise holds it will cost the US Treasury over $500 Million that we won't get at auction. Why does it seem that every time I have to explain something to the President it involves the IRS and Texas? You idiots have three days to fix this.

I find it incredible that some nobody in Texas can issue a press release that some Asian can't translate and it almost crashes the US securities market as a result." remarked the Secretary of the Treasury.

Chapter 5

A Businessman in Texas

THE MORE PEOPLE WHO OWN LITTLE BUSINESSES OF THEIR OWN, THE SAFER OUR COUNTRY WILL BE, AND THE BETTER OFF ITS CITIES AND TOWNS; FOR THE PEOPLE WHO HAVE A STAKE IN THEIR COUNTRY AND THEIR COMMUNITY ARE ITS BEST CITIZENS. – JOHN HANCOCK

Removing a substantial part of the federal tax burden on a small business via having accounts at the Freedonia Transaction Company or a local version of the FTC was a boon to those businesses, and in many cases was the difference between continuing to struggle and starting to grow. It also made some businesses viable that otherwise would fail. One of the consequences of a growing business environment, is the creation of more jobs and a potential for higher wages as the supply of workers starts to become limited by skill, citizenship, or geography. This effect was enhanced by successfully being able to ignore the federal and much of the state regulatory burden, too.

The Freedonia Transaction Company and Free Texas, supported these efforts to bring the financial system in use in Freedonia to the rest of Texas via the Texas Financial Network of member institutions. Whenever possible, the Freedonia Transaction Company would assist in the creation of another member of the Texas Financial Network. As there was no capital requirement or bank charter requirement in order to join the network, a number of entrepreneurs ran with the idea. Expanding the reach of the network, and more people opting to use FTC Promissory Notes was in the best interest of the Freedonia Transaction Company.

Part of the expansion of the Texas Financial Network was the FTC being a clearing house for what were in essence interbank transactions among member institutions. This volume of work was expanding as more small business opened accounts and participated in making payments to each other. Instead of the conventional check, the Texas Financial institution used a variation of the system used in Europe, so that numbers for amount and account to be credited were written in boxes in a form that went through optical character recognition software and then entered in to an electronic payment stream, just like online payment instructions. Not being tied to the existing American Banking Association clearing system allowed for a different, more efficient, and thus less costly way of processing payments.

By design, the fee schedule for processing transactions for member institutions was modest. As Beth Dunwoody explained it, "If we try to really make money off of this, somebody else will come in, undercut us, and put the network at risk of breaking up. We can't afford that." Of greater importance to the Freedonia Transaction Company, was that it meant a job was created in Freedonia.

Keith Fuller, who owned the transaction company in Quanah called Beth Dunwoody about an item of interest to him. "Beth, I own the transaction company in Quanah, and I'm also on the board of the State Bank in Quanah, and I'm wondering why The Texas Financial Network doesn't allow existing financial institutions chartered by the state of Comptroller of the Currency to join?"

"Who said we don't allow that? Nothing stops them from joining. All of the internal accounting around that is your issue to deal with, not ours. All it takes is opening an account at the FTC, compatible file formats for data exchange, and using compliant forms for individual transactions if you want to support them." Beth answered.

"Good to know." was the reply. In smaller communities, community credit unions, credit unions, and state banks found a way to participate in the Texas Financial Network.

The entire health care system in the United States and Texas had become a complete disaster. Doctors were frustrated with getting multiple layers of approvals to treat patients, hospitals had to bill according to approved codes and in formats that insurance companies and the government via Medicare or Medicaid demanded, and the people who were sick got less care at greater expense to either themselves or their employers. This meant an opportunity for an entrepreneur.

Texas had more than one such entrepreneur. The idea for the business opportunity was sparked by asking a few questions to doctors and hospital administrators. How much of your revenue is eaten by complying with insurance and government requirements? If an alternative was presented to you where all you had to do was present a bill that got paid, how much would your price decrease? Would you participate in such a program? The questions for the patients were also designed to test the market. If you could get basic health care for up to half of Obamacare costs, would you be interested? Additional coverage that still costs less than Obamacare, but instead of the right to sue a doctor or hospital, you would settle directly with the insurance provider, would you use it?

One model used the concept of the Health Savings Account. Instead of paying almost $2000 per month for an Obamacare plan, $1000 per month was paid into the Savings Account. The doctor or hospital sent the bill to the patient, who could then gage the cost and amount remaining in the account. This provided the incentive for the patient to control costs by ensuring value for the service. If your needs exceeded account balance, there were two options: pay yourself, or shop for a plan that might cover your need. As you got older, the balance in the account should be increasing until the point was reached that very expensive treatments might be needed.

The other model was a variation of group insurance without the bureaucracy. In any case, a way had to be found around the Texas Department of Insurance, which regulated insurance companies. Here the savings account model had the advantage, because it could be claimed that it was not an insurance plan. Would the State of Texas want to press the issue was the open question.

Free Texas and the Lone Star Party made a conscious effort to reach small businessmen and make known their efforts to eliminate undue government interference in the free market. By showing the development of Freedonia was the model they had for Texas, Free Texas thought it had a powerful message. Targeted for the light manufacturing industry and into middle class suburbs was where the liberty movement could really pick up support and become the dominant force in Texas politics. The media role was being performed by Rampaging Elephants Radio.

Inquiries were met with the explanation that freedom for business and people was an integrated systematic approach. It took political action locally, the force of a militia to back up that political will, and a system of financial independence that matched political independence. One of the concepts worked only in conjunction with the others. One of the more interesting examples was situated near Houston.

Seeing a need for incandescent light bulbs to be made in Texas, after the EPA had put every manufacturer in the US out of business, and claiming protection under a law specifically targeted to provide for such manufacturing, a Texas businessman found the equipment from one of the shut down light bulb plants. He had the equipment moved to Texas and placed out from a Houston suburb. He asked for advice from Free Texas as they had experience setting up production "in the middle of nowhere", attracting a work force, and keeping the feds away from interfering. How could it work here?

The suggestion was the best way to find a work force for the plant was to reach out to some contacts which Free Texas had with pastors in the black community, hire and train some black Christians because religious people don't steal, and have an ethic for honest work. Good jobs would mean the people would become more prosperous, and then support the Lone Star Party as part of making that possible. There were also bound to be some vets among the group, which could help form the local militia. The various Free Texas communities tended to buy products from other Free Texas communities.

As Roberts had remarked, one of the things about tight knit communities is that they support each other. That needed to be true of Free Texas, and Texans in general. When people see their wealth increase by so doing, the principle becomes self reinforcing. This was the key to growing Freedonia, and the concept should be universal.

One of the goals of Free Texas and the Lone Star Party was to grow from its current rural base to attracting the more suburban and possibly urban population as well. As Roberts explained to the other directors, the target was Republican financial supporters, soccer moms, and people who vote for Democrats out of habit, but would rather have jobs. The message is that liberty makes your life better, and then we show them how we make that true. If Lone Star could pick up Tejanos, black conservatives, and more TEA Party Republicans, the Republican Party would collapse like a balloon. If they could persuade Christian blacks that the Democrats were culturally hostile to them, and give us a try, they might shave off enough Democrat support for Lone Star to win some races across the state, and maybe sink some incumbents in the state Senate and House.

The economic boom in Freedonia was the message of the Lone Star Party and Free Texas as an organization. Texas liked to claim its vibrant economy as the "Texas miracle" to the rest of the United States. If that was the case, then Freedonia had become the "Texas miracle" of Texas. Most of the land acquired for city expansion had already been sold, and population was poised to increase to some 5000 people.

The Freedonia Army Ammunition Plant was an example of the economic growth of the town. The Plant is privately owned, so there is no group of investors influencing management to sacrifice the long term health of the business in order to maximize next quarter's profit. The owner reinvested most of the profit into expanding the manufacturing capability of the facility. The plant started with one production line making 5.56mm M193 ball ammunition. The single line could produce almost 25,000 rounds in a single shift. Triple shifts could increase production to 70,000 per day. This yielded a profit of between 75 TXD per day to 150

TXD during all out production. In three months, another production line had been opened for 5.56 mm ammunition.

The most expensive part of the round is the brass case. These were part of the production line at the FAAP. The last machine in the line, took the brass case, added sealant and the primer, poured in the powder, put the sealant around the case neck, and inserted the bullet. The ammunition was then placed into 10 round stripper clips, which were assembled into a bandoleer of 120 rounds. The last step in production packed 7 bandoleers into a M2A1 ammunition can, labeled the can 840 Cartridges, M193 Ball 10 Rd Clips, Bandoleers, and then TX, year and month of manufacture with the lot number. The FAAP sold cans and two can cases of ammunition to any who visited, or to dealers in Texas. At least 20% of production was reserved for Free Texas and its sponsored militias.

The plant now ran four production lines. One line was for pistol ammunition, alternating between .45 cal. M1911 ball and 9mm M882 ball. Two production lines produced 5.56mm ammunition, a combination of M193 ball, M855 ball, and M856 tracer. The fourth line produced 7.62mm NATO ammunition, either M80 ball or M62 tracer. The machines on the 5.56 and 7.62 lines could be converted to make the other calibers with two hours down time for changeover.

The next most expensive part of the round is the bullet. One of the issues in ammunition panics in the US that occur during fears of gun bans, is the limited number of manufacturers of the key components of bullet, powder, and the case primer. Production at the FAAP was subject to those same constraints, so the next round of investment was designed to solve that problem. Machinery needed to make bullets was purchased, so that constraint on production was removed. Case primers were the next easiest component to attack and produce internally.

Gunpowder of the modern "smokeless" variety is not so easy to produce. Modern gunpowder is nitrocellulose based. Production requires careful quality control and the correct mix of chemical components, including some that are highly explosive and unstable. Experiments in making small quantities of powder were undertaken in a remote underground location. As Roberts remarked to the chemist working on the project, "Blowing up the ammunition plant would be really bad for business."

Getting gunpowder production right for the 5.56mm rounds was the hardest challenge the project would face. The powders for the other calibers didn't have the same structure that had to be maintained to get the proper burn rate for the 5/56mm ammunition, and thus velocity of the bullet which made semi automatic and automatic weapons function properly. Ironically, the easiest propellant and explosive to produce would be for one of the "black" projects – mortar rounds.

A byproduct of this project would be used in another "black" project. The manufacture of the explosive C-4 was next on the list. This would give the supported forces a demolitions capability and the ability to produce the M18A1 anti personnel mine, commonly known to generations of GIs as the "Claymore". Except for the M4 blasting cap, the other components of the mine could be easily made or obtained. The Claymore mine is ideal for a fixed defensive position and would cause terrible carnage to uninvited visitors.

Small arms production was still just a dream, but a self sufficient Texas would have a need for such things. The Freedonia Army

Ammunition Plant was preparing to meet that need. The US Government took a different view, as the activities of the Freedonia Army Ammunition Plant, actual or planned required the appropriate licenses, facility inspections for safety and regulatory compliance, and the payment of certain fees and taxes once approvals were granted. It was much easier to get something done when one could act without bothering with all of that procedure.

Most of the labor force at the plant were also members of the Borden County Militia. This presented a challenge during deployments, as this also tended to be times at which the plant needed to operate at peak production. Initially, the crunch was alleviated by family members of the plant workers working part time. It also happened that at these times there was also featured a large transient population in Freedonia, so there was at least some labor which could be trained and used. Over the longer term, the growth in population allowed for part time work at the plant, which became full time or overtime during periods of high production. New employees started with the packing of ammunition, and once familiar with the process could be trained to load the machines with materials, and then finally learn to operate the machines.

Growth also meant the expansion of city services, meaning water and electricity. The water system had been planned for this to occur and the tower capacity planned accordingly, so it was just a matter of laying the additional pipes. Electrical generation was an issue requiring more investment. Freedonia had been conceived on the idea of community preparedness, rather than individuals generating their own electricity and water. It was much more cost effective for the community to do that and ensure its electrical system was hardened. Various concepts for power generation had been considered.

The Freedonia Utilities used more than one method of electricity generation. One of the issues in operating independently of the rest of the Texas electrical grid, was the ability to meet peak demand. The three main sources were solar, steam, and water or wind turbine. The steam generator was linked to the incinerator for trash disposal. If the Environmental Protection Agency had been able to inspect the whole setup, it would have disapproved the engineering effort as not friendly to the environment. To date, no one in Freedonia has died of air pollution.

Growth meant construction. That construction took the form of more housing, even a small apartment complex, more industry, and more businesses forcing another street of commercial activity to exist. Madison Street was built as an addition to the opposing streets on the town square of Washington and Jefferson. Cross streets of Travis, Bowie, Crockett, and Burnet were added to the previously existing streets of Austin, Houston, and Rusk.

All of this activity and growth led to a sedan displaying US Government license plates arriving in Fredonia. The driver asked to find city hall or the city manager. After being informed that there was no such thing in Freedonia, the driver asked if there was any property to be had in the community. The driver was told to go to the Freedonia Transaction Company, as they handled the real estate in the town.

A short walk across the square brought the stranger to the office of Beth Dunwoody. "Can I help you?" she asked.

"I hope so." the stranger answered. "I'm with the US Postal Service, and Freedonia is going to get its own Post Office and I'm here to obtain the land for it."

"There is no land in Freedonia for sale to the US Government." Beth told her visitor.

"But the Postal Service is its own entity." he protested.

"Is it still a federal felony to posses a firearm on Postal Service property?" Beth asked.

"Of course, we care deeply about the safety of our employees and customers." was the answer to her question by the Postal Service employee.

"There is nothing for you in Freedonia that you can buy. If you are thinking of eminent domain, you can ask the IRS or FBI how well that works here. Go away and good day to you." Beth dismissed the visitor.

Madison Street soon featured the Freedonia Postal Center where citizens of Freedonia had their mailboxes, and daily stops by the USPS, UPS and FedEx. Mail internal to Freedonia addresses was free.

Although Freedonia had grown to over twice its size in less than a year, there were three things Freedonia failed to provide for its citizens that other communities in Texas did. The town of Freedonia had no property taxes, traffic control lights / signs, or police force.

Chapter 6

Evinces a Design to Reduce Them Under Absolute Despotism

IF PARLIAMENT MAY TAKE FROM ME ONE SHILLING IN THE POUND, WHAT SECURITY HAVE I FOR THE OTHER NINETEEN? – RICHARD HENRY LEE

Keisha Jones of the Texas Department of Health and Human Services (Family and Child Protective Services) was driving toward the town of Freedonia. There had been an anonymous tip that told CPS that there were children in the community not attending school, not properly cared for by parents, and left to roam about without proper supervision. Had anyone in the state agency bothered to investigate the tip, it would have been traced to a phone number in Washington, DC and in use by the government of the United States. That was of no concern to anyone at the Department, all that mattered was a tip had been received they thought to be credible.

This was the first time that Keisha had an occasion to drive to Freedonia. Normally, she would have no interest in the happenings of a tribe of ignorant rednecks with an anti-government reputation. However, if the tip proved to have some truth to it, she would be retuning to this location many more times in order to save the children from their bad parents.

Thirteen year old Cash Miller belonged to one of the families in Freedonia that believed in home schooling. This was not unusual in Freedonia, although the public schools in the county had been under the careful supervision of a school board that had thrown out the state recommended books and associated curriculum and returned to teaching methods and resources in use prior to 1970. These methods and materials had produced the scientists and engineers that made the most rapid economic progress in human history. Some families felt their children were better served by home schooling, even if the public schools in Borden County were not political indoctrination centers for the American version of the Young Pioneers youth organization of a communist party.

Cash had finished his school work for the day, and just after 3 PM was on his way to the horse pen to saddle his horse and ride out to check on the crops his family had planted. His backpack contained the usual precautions taken for outdoor activity in west Texas. He had checked his pack before leaving home to ensure he had two half liter bottles of water, some candy bars, matches, a solar blanket, basic first aid kit, and the family AR-7 survival rifle which was broken down and packed in the stock. Rabbits and other varmints had a habit of feeding on the seedlings and crops as they matured. Or, a rabbit or squirrel stew could be in the family's future.

As Keisha turned off the Farm to Market road and onto Washington Street toward the town square of Freedonia, she saw something most unusual and frightening. Every person she saw was carrying a gun. Some of the men looked like they were carrying assault rifles. The oddest thing about the entire scene to her was that nobody acted like there was something unusual going on. It was as if all of these people thought it was normal to walk about carrying guns. She had been told by her agency co-workers to be prepared to encounter redneck central, but seeing this display of firepower in person was still startling. She glanced down at her badge and ID suspended from her neck. It was a subconscious gesture to remind herself of her superior authority given to her by the State of Texas.

As Keisha approached Rusk Street, she glanced left and saw some distance away, toward the end of the street, what appeared to be a young person wearing a cowboy hat and a with a backpack on his back. At just after 3 in the afternoon, he could not have made it home this soon from the school complex over in Gail. The reports of neglected children must be true. She turned onto Rusk, and prepared to pick up the neglected child.

Cash heard the car approaching from behind him. At first he didn't think anything of it as there was occasional traffic down the street. As the car got closer, he became curious about it, and finally it passed him and stopped in front of him. He saw a woman get out of the car. She had a card holder suspended from her neck. It was like he had heard about what big city schools did to the kids – make them wear badges in school so they knew where the kids belonged. The Freedonia kids who had moved there from the larger cities referred to the school badges as cattle tags. No student or staff of the Borden County Schools wore a cattle tag. Cash noted that the woman also had a badge on her cattle tag.

Keisha approached Cash and asked "What is your name young man?"

The reply was curt, "None of your business, Ma'am." The last word came out a bit surly as Cash wasn't sure if word of this encounter was going to get back to his parents. If it did, he wanted to be able to say that he was polite to an adult.

"Well, Mr. none of your business, I'm Ms. Jones of the Texas Department of Family and Protective Services and why aren't you in school?"

Cash hesitated to tell the woman he was home schooled. Stories about what they did to families who home schooled were legend among the home schooling community. Cash decided the best answer was "I'm done with school for the day."

"Let's go talk to your mother about that." decided Ms. Jones

That statement played right into Cash's fears about this encounter. "Leave my momma alone!"

In training protective services workers it is often noted by psychologists that abused children often keep very deep emotional attachment to highly abusive parents. Ms. Jones reverted to her training. "Its OK, we're going to see your momma."

By now, Cash had decided there was no way this encounter was going to end well. He had nothing else to lose. "Leave us alone and go away, or I'll shoot you in your butt!"

"Now you really need to be careful about making threats, and especially about threats to state agents. If you were an adult, you could go to jail for that." Ms. Jones did not like her authority being challenged.

By the time that statement had been uttered, Cash had the backpack on the ground. The stock of the AR-7 was in his hands.

Keisha had not previously pondered a possibly perforated posterior to be a possible permutation of the progression of events. When the stock of the AR-7 opened, and the receiver attached to what was no doubt about it a gun barrel appeared, she realized the teen Texan's statement of intentions was about to be matched with capability. Keisha beat feet as fast as her heels would allow, dialing 911 on her way back to the car. Cash had the rifle assembled and loaded by the time Ms. Jones of Family and Protective Services had locked the car doors.

"911 What is your emergency?" the operator asked.

"Thank God something in the hillbilly heaven is normal and works. There's a kid with a gun and he's going to shoot me!" the caller almost was screaming.

"Where are you and have any shots been fired yet?" the operator was trying to obtain useful information from the call.

"This hickville called Freedonia and he just loaded the gun. Send the police now!" Ms. Jones was panicking.

"I'll contact the Sheriff and let him know. He will be on his way as soon as he can." reassured the operator

"But I need him here now!" Ms. Jones was now concerned that this youth might have among his friends and relatives, some of the armed people she had seen earlier in Freedonia.

"I'll stay on the line with you until he arrives." The operator was trying to calm the caller.

Cash saw the woman in the car talking with someone on the phone. At this point, he was unsure as to what course of action he should take. As she was locked in her car, it didn't seem necessary to shoot her, but who knew who she was talking to on the phone and what she was saying. He decided to wait and let the situation develop. Maybe she would just drive away.

The 911 operator put the call on hold and buzzed Sheriff Connors. "There is trouble in Freedonia. Call from a woman says a kid with a gun is going to shoot her."

"Recognize the caller?" asked Connors.

"No, it's a mobile number with a 512 area code." the operator told him.

"If I didn't know any better, I'd suspect someone from Austin just got herself in trouble with someone in Fredonia. I'm on the way." Connors told the operator.

It took just a few minutes for Sheriff Connor's truck to make it to Freedonia. He figured the Green Dragon would be the best source for information. "Anybody know anything about a woman possibly from the Austin area and a kid with a gun?" he inquired.

He got the answer he was looking for, "A car with state exempt plates and a some seal on the door turned left on Rusk sometime ago. That's where I'd start looking if I were you." one of the customers said.

"Thanks a bunch." replied the Sheriff.

Sheriff Connors saw what he was looking for as soon as he turned on to Rusk. At the end of the street was a car, and in the middle of the street between the car and himself was a teen holding a rifle. Connors decided to take the slow and easy approach to keep the teen calm. As he approached, he noticed that it was indeed a state agency car with government plates.

After bringing the truck to a stop, and making sure he had been noticed by the teen, Connors got out. He slowly approached Cash, and asked in a casual tone "Say youngster, what happened?"

The response from Cash was immediate "She was going to take me away!"

Connors replied, "I see. Well its OK now son, you're not going anywhere, so you can put up the rifle now."

Cash unloaded the rifle and started to take it apart. "Can I go now?"

"Sure, I'll get your statement later." Connors told Cash.

As soon as it was clear that the Sheriff was in control and the rifle was unloaded, Keisha was out of the car. "It took you long enough! What are you doing! You're letting him get away!"

"Just hold on ..." Sheriff Connors was trying to sort out who was visiting Freedonia and why.

"I'm from Family and Protective Services and we are taking that child ..." stated Ms. Jones.

"No you're not." Sheriff Connors told her.

"I work for the State of Texas, you can't tell me what I can and can't do." insisted Ms. Jones

"I can certainly inform you of your rights." Sheriff Connors had enough.

"My rights? What for?" MS. Jones seemed confused.

"You are under arrest for attempted kidnapping." said Sheriff Connors while reaching for a pair of handcuffs.

Ms. Jones' supervisor was expecting her to call with a report on what she had found in Freedonia. The news that Ms. Jones was now a resident of the Borden County Jail was unexpected. His subsequent call to talk with Sheriff Connors was unproductive, so he escalated the matter to the District Attorney to have the charges dropped and his employee released.

The District Attorney told him "Some kid minding his own business is not evidence of neglect or abuse. The charges stand. I'm sure the judge will grant bail. Good day."

Ms. Jones supervisor then called the regional office responsible for Borden County. He asked how many cases they had in the county. He was told that there were no cases because CPS personnel did not go to Borden County. When he asked why no investigations were conducted there, he was told the CPS workers did not want to get shot or arrested over nothing.

This would not be the last time a car belonging to the State of Texas was seen in Freedonia.

Jim and Lise Roberts were having dinner at the Green Dragon. Ed and Sarah McMasters came in and Jim immediately waived for them to sit at their table. Ed was agitated.

Roberts noticed his demeanor. "You look annoyed Ed."

76

"I am. I really thought we were making it. We were restoring freedom. And now it all falls apart." Ed was annoyed.

"What's happened?" Jim asked.

Ed continued "I had a visit today from some twenty-something working for the Texas Commission on Environmental Quality. Told me I was operating an unlicensed land fill, and I had 10 days to dispose of everything properly and show receipts from a licensed facility and that I had paid for them to take it."

Lise was perplexed "Landfill?"

McMasters continued with the story. "You know that I and my partners have built many of the houses in town. From those jobs we have some scrap left over. We just dump it on my property until we use some if it in another house, or use it for firewood, or whatever."

Roberts could see where this was headed. "I gather that this offends the proper authorities? What's unacceptable about burning it?"

McMasters was starting to see some humor in the situation, as expensive as it was going to be for him. "I asked that very question and was told the material might have some paint among it, and some of the possible paint might have lead in the possible paint, which if burned, would be released into the atmosphere and lead to the end of civilization as we know it."

Roberts was curious about one other point. "Ed, how did they find out about this renegade landfill of yours? Have any idea who ratted you out?"

"You won't believe it." Ed told him.

"Try me." Jim insisted.

"They compared Google Earth images from two years ago to last month, and my dump appeared where it had not been there before." Ed said.

Roberts had not expected that answer. "That is really disturbing because (1) big brother is watching and (2) somebody in Austin has too much time on his hands. I'm getting tired of visits from vehicles belonging to the State of Texas and their occupants. Do you know when this person is returning?"

"Ten days" Ed replied.

"How about if we just spread the stuff around and burn or bury it. I'll set up the reception committee for the next visit." Jim suggested.

"I won't be able to show a receipt for proper disposal." Ed responded.

"Let the reception committee address that minor detail." Jim concluded.

True to the promise, ten days later a car with the seal of the Texas Commission on Environmental Quality rolled up to Ed McMasters house. Ed was on the front porch. The young perky recent graduate of the University of Texas at Austin noticed that there were more men on the porch. One wore a checked shirt, blue jeans and a Sheriff's Star. The other six men were carrying assault rifles and some kind of military gear.

Ed's voice seemed friendly enough, "I see you're back."

"Yes, I'm checking on compliance." the driver of the car said.

Now it was Sheriff Connors turn, "Miss, do you have a search warrant?"

"No, we don't need one. It is a compliance matter." the Sheriff was told.

Roberts broke into the conversation. "May I suggest that the Sheriff was hinting at you may be trespassing on private property."

"That doesn't apply to us. And who are you anyway?" she said as she indicated her ID and badge."

"We are Mr. McMasters personal security detail. We wouldn't want anything untoward to happen to him." Roberts replied.

"If you just show me that everything has been properly disposed of, that will end the matter." The TCEQ employee was trying to avoid additional unpleasantness at this point.

"I am in the employ of the owner of this property and have control of this property. Unless you show me a valid search warrant, you are ordered to leave immediately, subject to arrest for criminal trespass should you fail to do so." Roberts now made it legal.

"Look I said that does not apply to me." she stated.

"Sheriff?" Roberts asked.

"Miss, your next destination is either Austin or the Borden County Jail. Which will it be?" Sheriff Connors asked.

The Texas Commission on Environmental Quality never got a receipt for the proper disposal of waste materials from Ed McMasters.

Roberts later remarked to McMasters, "You know Ed, it's getting to be that the State of Texas is as bad as the feds."

"Sad, isn't it?" was all that McMasters could reply.

On the farm to Market road leading to and from Freedonia, a sign had been posted to the rear of the city limit sign, with the dimensions of four feet by eight feet. Anyone leaving town could not miss it. The sign stated:

Attention! You are leaving the American sector

Achtung! Sie verlassen sich den Amerikanishen Sektor

Attention! Vous Sortez Du Secteur Americain

Atención usted está abandonando el sector americano

Chapter 7

God is Great!

THE MOST EXTRAVAGANT IDEA THAT CAN BE BORN IN THE HEAD OF A POLITICAL THINKER IS TO BELIEVE THAT IT SUFFICES FOR PEOPLE TO ENTER, WEAPONS IN HAND, AMONG A FOREIGN PEOPLE AND EXPECT TO HAVE ITS LAWS AND CONSTITUTION EMBRACED. NO ONE LOVES ARMED MISSIONARIES; THE FIRST LESSON OF NATURE AND PRUDENCE IS TO REPULSE THEM AS ENEMIES. – MAXIMILLIAN ROBESPIERRE

Being a devout Muslim in a land of infidels was very irritating to Abu al Zaidi. Every day and in every hour of the day his senses were assaulted by the infidels. Their language, the way the infidel women acted like whores, and worst of all, their impiety toward Allah the merciful and his Prophet, may peace be upon his head. The infidels had no sense of shame, they allowed homosexuals to conduct their perversions without rebuke. Every kind of immorality and vice was celebrated among them

Thanks to the wisdom of Allah the merciful, great amounts of wealth had been provided to the faithful, and even the western infidels gladly paid their due, even if not in the amounts required by the Holy Koran. From time to time, as a vision of paradise to come, Allah the merciful had provided him with the pleasures of an infidel whore. It was obvious that these infidels were stupid and easily manipulated. Unfortunately, these infidels had clearly been manipulated for decades by the Jews. It was impossible to bring any number of them into the one true faith, to receive the wisdom of the Prophet, may peace be upon his head, and the knowledge contained within the Holy Koran.

The one place of peace in his life was at the Mosque. There he could observe the tranquility and happiness of being among the faithful. The women covered themselves and were obedient to their men, as Allah the merciful had willed it. The men discussed important matters of faith and community without the petty concerns of women being heard. If only the infidels would submit to the will of Allah the merciful, all would be well with the world. The infidels were a constant source of trouble. Just their impiety alone should condemn them, but their constant interference and their presence in the land of the Prophet, may peace be upon his head was intolerable.

But what to do about the infidels? Was this a test of faith by Allah the merciful? Was it the will of Allah the merciful that the true faithful were to be separated from the others by seeing who was willing to conduct jihad. Or was it that Allah the merciful willed the presence of the infidels to see if the faithful did not stray from the one true faith. These questions were puzzling, and only by prayer and study of the Holy Koran with learned Imams could the will of Allah the merciful be discovered.

After the call to prayer one Friday, he was approached by one of the faithful. "My brother, I see that the faith is strong in you and that you are a true follower of the Prophet, may peace be upon his head. Will you join me and a select number of other true brothers with our Imam?"

"Brother you are very kind to make such an offer, and I can only hope to learn more of the correct path as Allah the merciful wills me to go." Abu replied to the gracious invitation.

The Imam spoke about the duty that every true believer has to do the will of Allah the merciful, and imitate the life of the Prophet, may peace be upon his head, to bring the infidels to the one true faith. It was the will of Allah that brought the faithful to the land of the infidels now here before him today. The faithful had long been tolerant and taken every care to show the infidels how to act, how to come to the path of true enlightenment. The infidels have refused to submit to the will of Allah the merciful. If the infidels continued to resist the will of Allah the merciful, the day would surely come when Allah the merciful would call the faithful to jihad. The faithful must be prepared to do as Allah the merciful commands.

"Did the words of the Imam reach your heart, my brother?"

"They did. I realize that I am not properly prepared and may not be able to follow the path on which I may be commanded to go. This must be why my mind has been so troubled of late." Abu said.

"Come with me my brother. I know of one who can teach us what we must be able to do."

One more recruit to help build one more cell in the organization had been acquired. The infidels were so stupid and lazy. Allah the merciful had made them so in order that they could be the more easily conquered. The infidels thought of war as a short term activity performed by a small group on men using their infidel tools. The infidel tools could not stop the unlimited number of faithful waging jihad who had already infiltrated among the infidels. The infidels would soon be shown the power of the faithful carrying out the will of Allah the merciful. Their inherent weakness would turn them into slaves, or come to the one true faith. Success to date had shown the wisdom and strength of those who followed the will of Allah the merciful.

The plan had been underway for years, the wealth acquired from oil had been used to expand the reach of Islam world wide. Western culture was particularly easy to target. The west was already a target of subversion by adherents of communism, and their socialist front. The subversives willingly assisted the Muslim migration into western countries. In their arrogance, the communists were certain that history was on their side, and the Muslims could be controlled by them just as they planned to control the generations to be subjected to their control via indoctrination of the children of successive generations. The Muslims took a different view of who would end up in control. The allies would fight among themselves later.

Most westerners view terrorists as a few dozen radical truly committed political or religious kooks who think they can impose their will on others by force. Any serious student of insurgency warfare knows this is not true. The armed component is only a small percentage of the effort. There is a huge auxiliary support network which provides supplies, recruits, operational cover, a political action arm, and most importantly a mass of people and networks which allow the armed element to have a cover which makes the guerrillas more difficult to detect. There is also an underground, which operated in the target environment, which works to cripple effective response from the target of the insurgency. Vital to the success of the plan was placing Muslims in key positions of the US Government.

The upcoming election in the United States and recent elections in Europe were of concern. There were efforts underway to stop or reverse Muslim movement to western countries. A change in government policy or personnel hostile to Islam would risk the plan to possible exposure or perhaps the loss of valuable resources. The risk would be taken of proceeding with the plan now, although the collapse of western civilization could not be assured. Even if it was weakened, the west would then collapse after the next large effort. Messengers with the relevant orders were dispatched.

The curriers headed for Texas were not going to risk direct entry into the United States. Transit via Mexico into Texas with a well paid cartel was much more secure. While the cartels had a reputation for abandoning their human cargo on the slightest pretense, it was not so with entities that the cartel used for sourcing heroin and other opiates. Both sides had an interest in maintaining the relationship. The curriers made it through to their contacts in various cities in Texas. There are thousands of Muslims in the Houston and Dallas areas. Islam academies had been established as part of the school systems in larger school districts so that the infidels could help pay for Islamic indoctrination of the youth. The influx had become so great thanks to various church organizations accepting government money to resettle refugees that even Amarillo had a vibrant Muslim community. Such was the power of Allah the merciful over the infidels.

Abu was approached at the Mosque at prayer. "Brother the day we have been waiting for is approaching. Meet us here tomorrow prepared for a journey of many days."

"Allah the merciful be praised. I will be ready to follow the path of righteousness." Abu said to his benefactor.

They met at the Mosque the next day. There were the four other faithful from the class with the Imam that he recognized. They took a van which drove them out of town to a rural location. There they met another group of the same size. They all were addressed by the brother that had recruited them. Several large boxes were in the room. One box contained AKs, another chest rigs for spare magazines, and a box contained masks and dark clothing to wear over their own clothes. They fitted the clothing and chest rigs to themselves. Late in the day, they tested the AKs. They were told that they would be staying there for the night. The ritual shaving and clothing before going into battle preparations consumed the rest of the evening. They would be ready in the morning. Allahu Akbar!

The next morning, the rifles and gear were packed into the two vans, and both groups of jihadis returned to the Mosque. There were other such groups arriving. Abu's leader and some other groups were directed to a room. There were some 30 jihadis assembled in the room. The Imam spoke to them. The time for jihad had arrived and the judgment of Allah the merciful on the infidels had been pronounced. The brothers assembled would be the sword of Islam.

The group leader was introduced to the faithful who did not yet know him. He told them that they would be waging jihad on a collection of infidels gathered in a building. They could expect well over a thousand infidels to be there. They would take the infidels hostage and then the infidels would accept Islam and the rule of Islam over the land. There would be other faithful who had been trained in explosives and would bring the explosives and wire the building with explosives, so that if they were attacked by the infidels, all of the infidels would die. The infidels would soon see the power of Allah the merciful. They were told to wait there for further orders. Allahu Akbar!

Larger police departments have an intelligence section that tries to monitor known criminal elements for clues regarding future gang or drug dealer activity. Terrorism also falls within their purview. One officer noticed a number of vans bringing in men to a Mosque, and there were also some boxes being moved in. He reported that activity as suspicious. He was called back about an hour later and told not to worry, they had checked with their liaison and that observed activity he reported was preparation for a Muslim holiday.

Those Texans who for some reason happened to be watching news channels at sometime after 1 in the morning heard that there were rumors of terrorist attacks in Europe at various locations. The number and type of attacks were as yet unknown. By the time most of Texas was awake, it was clear that there had been a number of bombings on public transportation during the morning commute in countries all across Europe. It was clear that many major European cities had been hit. The number of lives lost had wildly divergent estimates. There were now reports of schools being attacked in those same countries.

Then the breaking news hit – the New York subway system had been bombed. While Texans were trying to take in all of this information, the first reports of more local concern hit the airwaves and cable. There had been explosions at several highway intersections around Texas. Bridges at the intersections of the Interstates and Loop 610 were down. Some of the bridges had collapsed on Beltway 8 traffic, and now there were reports from Dallas was well. Similar things had happened around Loop 635. There was now a report that part of the elevated section of I-35 through Austin had collapsed. Thousands, perhaps hundreds of thousands, maybe even a million commuters in Texas were now stranded in traffic.

The response stretched the police and fire departments to the breaking point. Both the Houston and Dallas areas, possibly Austin, too had a thousand people each killed or wounded. The usual terrorism talking heads were now on television, the more prescient of them told the audience that some 250 or so bombings could be expected throughout the United States based on what was observed in Europe and the pattern of attacks seen so far in the United States.

It wasn't just the scale of the damage, which was bad enough, but the fact that the metropolitan police an fire departments had multiple locations with extensive damage. Civilian emergency management is based on the Incident Command System which is how police, fire departments, Red Cross, FEMA, and Homeland Security manage incidents. The system is not designed for one organization to manage multiple simultaneous incidents occurring. City leaders had to decide which location got resources first. States and now even the federal government had the same dilemma. What was the extent of the damage and who got resources first?

One thing quickly became clear to the Governor of Texas. Any resources Texas was going to be able to use were already in Texas. The federal government's first priority was the New York, Baltimore, Washington area corridor where the important people live. Commercial communications were starting to fail, either due to damage or traffic load. Already, one question was forming in the Governor's mind. Were the feds going to let the states use their National Guards, or were the feds going to federalize them under national control. Of course, thousands of Guardsmen were probably stranded in the mess as well as the rest of the population.

Abu's group awoke in the morning to the glorious news that infidel Europe was ablaze. The group leader told them that other faithful were already conducting jihad and the time had now come to join them. They ate, got geared up with their rifles and got into the vans. Their target was only a few blocks away.

On the news of the bombings, almost every school district in Texas went on lockdown. Students and staff were to stay in their current classrooms or locations and await further instructions. School Resource Officers, being a polite name for school district policemen, roamed the halls to ensure everyone was in place. No one knew how long the wait would last.

Because the target was so close, it did not take the vans much time to arrive at the high school. The group leader took part of the group to the main entrance, while Abu's team following his team leader from the Mosque, went to another entrance by the gymnasium. In keeping with the school lockdown policy, both doors were locked. The glass portions of the doors were shot out. Then, group members reached in and opened the doors. As the group entered the high school, they set off the metal detectors. All of the noise had attracted the attention of the Resource Officer, who hustled toward the sound. As he rounded the corner from a hallway to view the main entrance, 8 AKs were fired at him. Before his hand could touch his pistol, he went down in a pool of blood.

The main part of the group went into the main office, where an infidel whore was talking on a phone. She was shot in the chest, and the rest of the infidels were herded out of the office. Those infidels were handed over to the explosive team jihadis who started to move the infidels toward the gymnasium. The rest of the main group of jihadis started down the halls toward the classrooms.

Abu's team went for the gymnasium. There was already a collection of infidels there. At lockdown, all of the PE classes got dressed and sat in the basketball stands awaiting further instructions. The jihadis herded the infidels to one side of the gym, brought out two trash cans and told everyone to put their phones and all of their electronic devices in the trash cans. They were then moved to the far side of the gym, to make room for more of the infidels who would be herded in soon.

The explosives team went to work setting up the bombs and wiring to trigger them in the gym. Explosives were placed around the walls, and suspended along mid court in the air. The message was clear, if the bombs went off, no one in the gym would survive. The wiring of the explosives was still under way as more infidels started to arrive in the gym. So far the plan had worked perfectly. There was really no resistance to speak of, Allah the merciful be praised, and with all of the other destruction taking place, the only people who knew that the school had been taken were the jihadis who took it and the hostages in the gym. As the main group of jihadis searched the school, the gym filled with infidels. With the search complete, guards and watches were posted. The watch was looking for any attempt by the infidels to come and rescue the infidels being held in the gym. The guards watched the infidels in the gym, and manned the triggers for the explosives. This left about half of the jihadis free to amuse themselves and rest.

As the lockdown continued, the school district office started to all around to the schools to give them instructions to go ahead and have the cafeteria staff, if present to prepare to serve lunch. Not every school answered. There should have been staff present at all times. Not even school administrators' phones were being answered, and this was a disturbing development to those at the administration building. School Resource Officers at the main admin building were sent to check on the schools not answering their calls. The Resource Officers at the schools were not answering their radios either. Something was very wrong.

As the School Resource Office patrol car approached the high school it was taken under fire by the watch. That told the officer sent to check out what was happening at the high school all that he needed to know. He backed the car out of the line of fire as best he could, taking a couple of slight wounds in the process. He radioed in that the school had armed intruders who had just shot him. Urgent backup from the city police was needed to handle the situation. It would take some time for that help to arrive.

As soon as it had become obvious that a major incident was underway, the police forces of most towns in Texas and across the nation sent the message for all officers to report in for duty. Because of the resulting traffic congestion, it took hours for the majority of officers to arrive in the cities where bombs had exploded. Vehicles and equipment had to be allocated to the various locations where emergency services were needed. Now that it was known there were schools occupied by armed intruders, this stretched the local police forces past the breaking point. Two patrol cars, with six police officers total, was all that could be allocated to the high school. They tried to set up a security perimeter around the school. There was no barricade material to be had, just the two patrol cars, some flares, signs, and the six officers.

The senior officer present had a bullhorn, and tried to start a dialog with the intruders. The only thing the jihadis had to say was Allahu Akbar! No one knew if or when a SWAT team was going to arrive.

Two armed men wearing masks and dressed in black had entered Julie's classroom. The students and teacher were told to move to the gym. Everyone complied because the men were carrying rifles. The men told them to remain silent and not say anything. As the class of students approached the gym, they saw the body of the Resource Officer lying on the floor. One of the girls who was about 10 feet ahead of Julie couldn't help letting out a scream when she saw the body. The girl was shot in the back and crumpled to the floor.

As they turned the corner from the hall to enter the gym, they were told to put their phones and any other electronic devices in the trash cans by the door. Julie thought about keeping her iPhone in her purse, but the men might search her looking for phones from those who did not put something in the trash cans. She didn't want any of those men to touch her, so she dropped her phone in the trash can. She wanted to call her father. Daddy had a gun. Julie wished her father would come to rescue her.

All of the students and teachers were going to the gym. They were ordered to sit on the floor and not to say anything. Julie noticed there were wires running round the walls and elevated above them and that the wires had packages attached to them. Once everyone was in the gym, they were told that there were bombs all over the school and in the gym. If anyone tried to escape, they would all be killed. A boy's phone rang. He had not put the phone in the trash can as directed. One of the masked men unholstered a pistol and shot the boy in the head. As bad as the thought was, Julie was glad she wasn't near the boy when he was killed.

Abu and his team were among those not immediately needed to guard the hostages or on watch. His leader led them out to the gym, and said to the rest of the team in Arabic, "Look at how Allah the merciful has rewarded us. We shall have our choice of the infidel whores." He then grabbed one of the girls, made her stand and started to tear at her clothes. Abu and the others joined him and soon the girl was naked. She was then dragged to a room off to the side of the gym. When the door opened for some of the masked men to enter or leave the room, Julie and the others heard screams.

Julie prayed that would not happen to her. She looked down at her bracelet, the one with the Alamo charm on it. Her father had bought it years ago when they visited the Alamo. It reminded her of the story how men had died rather than submit to tyranny. Julie would not let them do that to her. She would fight and die before she went into that room.

Before Abu went into the room with the infidel whore, he noticed the blonde infidel girl, she had a look of defiance about her. Before long, Abu would teach that blonde infidel girl her place and submission to the faithful. He would enjoy it very much. He doubted it, but if she was a virgin it would be even sweeter. It would be a view of the heaven to come for the faithful jihadis such as himself.

The hostages had missed lunch, and the day had gone on almost to the time that they would have left school and gone home. Abu and his team were now back in the gym. Abu walked over to the blonde infidel girl, the one with the defiant look. Julie's heart stopped when the masked man walked over to her. He then grabbed her, and she tried to hit him, but he hit her on the side of her head. She felt faint, and was losing her strength. Now two other men were grabbing her. She tried to fight, but hey were too strong. She could tell that her shirt was gone and they were pulling on her blue jeans. Julie tried to fight harder, but it was no use. All of the others in the gym were afraid to help her, just as she had been too afraid to help the other girl. Her bra was gone, and they were taking her to the room off of the gym. She had to grab a gun .....

Then there was a sudden violent explosion, and Julie felt like her body was being crushed. Julie's last thought was "Daddy it hurts really bad."

Chapter 8

Mobilization

THE OFFICERS OF A PANZER DIVISION MUST LEARN TO THINK AND ACT INDEPENDENTLY WITHIN THE FRAMEWORK OF THE GENERAL PLAN AND NOT WAIT UNTIL THEY RECEIVE ORDERS. – FIELD MARSHAL ERWIN ROMMEL

Roberts' personal assistant at the ammunition plant gave him a call. "The State Adjutant General's Office has been trying to reach you. They want you to call in for orders. Do you have the number?"

"I was in a meeting with some of our guys about the situation. I'll call in." It took Roberts several attempts to complete the call to Austin. He assumed with the day's events so disruptive, the phone lines were over capacity. The series of bombs were going to hamper traffic in major cities and disrupt the Interstate Highway System for some time. He estimated it would take over a week just to clear rubble and wreckage. Now there were reports that schools were being targeted for attack.

"Major Roberts, the Governor has ordered a general mobilization of the National Guard, State Guard, and other Texas Military Forces, to include able militias. Will your militia in Border County comply with the order?" he was asked by the Adjutant General's office.

"We will. What are we to do?' It had taken a catastrophe of this magnitude to get the state serious about having a reserve military. More critically, now that a reserve military force was needed, it was too late to build it.

"Mobilize the available units in the county and await orders. You are to report to Camp Mabry for a briefing at 1800 today if you can make it." Ordered the Adjutant General's Office.

"I think I can. It will depend on how bad traffic is messed up." Roberts said.

Roberts make a few calls to the militia leaders in the county, informing them of the Governor's order, and they would probably be ordered to go somewhere when he returned from Austin.

Not everyone in Texas had a formal or informal relationship with the Texas Military Forces, and thus mobilized themselves. The urge to do so was especially strong among parents with children who had not returned home from school. Calls to the schools had gone unanswered, and the school district would only say an incident had occurred and schools were on lock down. Parents started to fight the traffic to make the trip to the schools where their children attended.

Jeff Rogers was one such parent. Like many people that day, he was one of those who left work early. Besides the bombs, there were more and credible reports of schools being attacked and children being held hostage. Initial reports were that right wing extremists were suspected of trying to overthrow the government. Jeff and other Texans had decided that line was getting old, because it never turned out to be true. As Jeff neared the school his daughter attended, his path was blocked by a police car in the intersection and two police officers.

"You can't go any further. So, go left, right, or turn around." one of the officers told Jeff.

"I'm going to pick up my daughter at school. I need to get through." was Jeff's response.

"Sorry, there has been an incident at the school, and this is the security perimeter. You can't get any closer." The officer told him.

"What happened and when can I get my daughter?" Jeff's fears were now realized.

"All we know is that there has been a shooting and the building is not safe. It would be best to go home and wait." The officer said.

Jeff decided to park on a side street and to have a look at the situation for himself. As he approached the school, he noticed a small crowd, possibly parents of some of the students, had gathered. He asked what had happened and was told there were armed gunmen holding the school and the students inside hostage. Two police officers kept the small crowd back. Jeff asked the officers "What are you going to do?"

"We're waiting on SWAT to arrive." the officer said.

"How long will that take?" Jeff wanted to know.

"We're not sure, just be patient. There are a number of them in there. Too many for us to take down." the officer told Jeff.

One of the parents thought the answer unsatisfactory. "Who knows what is going on in there. I'm going home to get a rifle." Other parents thought the idea had merit. So did Jeff, so he decided to drive home, arm himself and then return. The day had been another disaster in the history of the United States and who knew what would happen next. It took only a few minutes to arrive home. Jeff went straight to where he kept the firearms. He didn't tell the officers he was carrying a pistol, so he already had that weapon with him. He got his AR, three magazines, and then bad news. He only had three 20 round boxes of ammunition for the AR. It was now instantly clear to him why at the gunshows every veteran he saw bought ammunition by the case.

His wife had also come home early from work, and their son was also at home. Thank God his wife and son were safe. "I'm going back to the high school. I think Julie is being held hostage by gunmen." Both wanted to go with him, but Jeff told them that if Julie was released, she would head home, and someone needed to be at home if Julie arrived. If no one was home when she got there, Julie would be even more worried.

When Jeff returned to the high school, more parents were there waiting and more than a few of the parents were armed. One of the men asked "Any other veterans here?" and 8 hands went up. "Let's talk." The vets went off by themselves. Jeff wanted to help so badly. His daughter was in there and he had a rifle, but only two magazines of ammunition. Even if he only got one of terrorists it would be worth it to him.

The vets had returned from their huddle. "Folks, I'm Army Infantry, we have a Marine here, and an Army truck driver who is game. We are going to scout out the situation and return. We are going to do our damn best to get our kids out of there. If you want

98

to help us out, the other vets will stay here with you and help get this thing organized. When we get back, we will work out the plan and do it."

The scouts started their reconnaissance of the area. There were three items of interest to the scouts. How many jihadis and where were they. Where were the possible entrances to the school. Which possible entrance was going to have the beat chance to allow them to approach it with the least possibility of observation by the jihadis. By this time there was no doubt that it was jihadis that held the school.

Jeff immediately volunteered to help. The vets were forming the men into teams based on the weapon they carried and how good they thought they could shoot. One team was composed of scoped rifles and heavier caliber weapons. This team would be responsible for trying to engage the watch, or any other jihadis observed at far range. The other men would be in the breaching and assault teams. The call went out for axes, hammers, or any tools that might be useful in defeating locks or barricades.

The scout team returned. They had decided on the entrance that they wanted to try. The Marine approached the lead police officer. "We are going in to get our kids. We're not going to wait for SWAT to arrive. I might die of old age before that happens. Are you with us or not?"

The officer realized he was about to lose control of the situation. The number of armed men was now over 100, and the officers were outnumbered eight to one. "Let me make one more call. If SWAT is not here in 15 minutes we won't try to stop you. It will take you that long to get in position in any case. And best of luck to you"

"Deal" said the Marine, and the men got underway. They were briefed along the route. "Once we get to the building, take everything slow and easy. We can't risk shooting our own kids, and if one jihadi gets behind us, many of us will get shot. Watch for booby traps, they have been in there all day and wires are dangerous. Stay away from wires or packages as much as you can."

The lead officer called dispatch and let them know that there was a group of armed civilians that intended to storm the school and the officers on scene could not stop them. "Either SWAT arrives in the next 10 minutes or send ambulances." He was told that he could probably get some ambulances. There wasn't much for the ambulances to do at the sites of the downed bridges and most of the ambulances had been needed at other locations, such as what was now likely to happen at the high school.

Jeff was with one of the follow on assault teams because he was too light on ammunition, and would need to save his fire for inside the building. When the time came, the long range guys opened up on the watch jihadis they could identify which started the action. The other teams then rushed for the entrance, the first assault team laying down fire to try and make any jihadis in the area be afraid to engage the breach team as they battered on the door trying to enter the school.

The door gave way, and the first men entered. Then the first bomb exploded as one of the jihadis detonated his suicide vest. Four of the men in the first assault team went down with the jihadi. More men poured into the entrance. One of the vets was toward the lead, directing men into each of the classrooms as they worked their way down the hall. Three or four jihadis appeared at the end of the hall and started to fire at them. A man went down. Jeff thought the

100

whole scene was so surreal, the bullets making a different and louder sound by virtue of the firefight making its way down the hall.

Jeff was a little bit more than halfway down the hall when he thought he felt before he heard the sound of more bombs going off. The fire from the jihadis at the end of the hall slackened or stopped. Jeff couldn't tell which, but the mass of the armed parents moved forward. Reaching the end of the hall, Jeff's instincts told him to turn right toward the gym. It was obvious that the gym had taken the brunt of the explosive force. There was smoke, rubble, blood, bodies, and body parts everywhere. Jeff gained a new insight on the phrase "a scene from Hell."

Then a glint caught Jeff's attention. Sticking out from a pile of rubble was a girl's hand and forearm. On the girl's wrist was a gold bracelet with an Alamo charm on it. At that instant, Jeff knew that he had failed to rescue his daughter and his heart broke. He got down on his knees and started to clear away the debris covering Julie's body. As more of the debris gave way, Jeff saw that his daughter was naked. He tried not to imagine what those animals had done to his beautiful Julie. He had not made it in time to rescue Julie. His life was ruined and those responsible would pay. Not only the animals who did this to Julie would pay, but those who let those animals have free reign on the country were also responsible.

Jeff took off his jacket and tried to cover Julie as best he could. He gently picked her up in his arms, and now wondered where he should take her. Jeff wanted to take Julie home, but then he didn't want his wife and son to see Julie like this. As he headed toward his SUV, he thought that maybe he should take Julie to a hospital. It wouldn't look so bad then when the other family members saw her. By now, Jeff had exited the school and was outside. He noticed ambulances were arriving, and EMT crews already exhausted from the day's prior toll, now had one more disaster on their hands.

A couple of EMTs and one of the police officers approached Jeff. "It's OK, we will take care of her now."

"Nobody can take care of her now. I was too late to save her and nobody else did shit." Jeff cried.

As the day was turning into evening, more parents of students had arrived, and had become aware of the scale of the carnage. Many of the men were armed, and were talking among themselves. They arrived at a consensus. It was clear who was responsible for this, and it was past time for some payback. The Islamic Academy run by the school district and the mosque a few blocks down the street seemed like good places to start. When Jeff and his new found friends were done, the Islamic community would wish they had never heard of Texas.

Over in Fredonia, Jim told Lise of the mobilization order and that he was going first to Austin, and probably would be back the next day.

She said "Be as careful as you can." when she kissed him goodbye.

"I'm at the level now where all I do is sit around and talk on the radio." Jim reassured her.

She knew that was probably a lie, but it didn't matter.

Roberts decided to travel in uniform. In a chaotic situation, it could be helpful in smoothing things out along the way. Fortunately, the only Interstate he would have to cross would be I-20 in an area that was not affected by the attacks as far as he knew. Camp Mabry was to the west of Austin's I-35, so whatever mess was going on there could be avoided. He decided to take back roads, and top off the tank when it got below 3/4ths full. Given the as yet unknown scale of damage to the transportation system, and sure to be panic, gasoline was likely to be in short supply very soon.

He took in the best available news sources on the current situation and asked his militia XO to call him every hour on the way to Austin with updates if possible. As of now, it appeared that somewhere between 200 and 250 bombs had been set off at Interstate intersections across the United States with some loss of life, but tangling up traffic in major cities as the major consequence. Additional bombs in the major subway systems on the east and an elevated train or two in Chicago had also been detonated. This was then followed by a series of armed attacks on various schools across the country. It was unknown who the attackers were or if the attackers made any demands for hostages.

Roberts concluded at this stage the first bombings were the diversion to stretch out the "first responders" to the breaking point to leave the targets intended for maximum damage open. Attacking schools had been a tactic of Islamic Arab terrorists for years. And the model was the Paris attacks, but on a larger scale. Similar events had happened in Europe.

Roberts wondered about a few points. What were the bomb types and delivery methods. Vehicle bombs either suicide or command detonated made sense as not being noticeable in morning traffic. The school attacks had a similarity to Beslan and that school massacre. With any luck, there would be a briefing from the Intel section of the Department of Public Safety in Austin. Of course, all of this assumed that Texas was really going to try and work the militia movement into the Texas Military Forces, and there was not some other agenda. Looking at the numbers it made sense. The Texas Army National Guard was two brigades and it might be federalized and unavailable to the state. The State Guard was less that one brigade in real Army terms and unarmed. That left the heretofore private militias as the only credible (at least theoretically) military force at the ready for use by the State of Texas. If so, the worm had turned.

Updates along the way indicated schools were indeed being targeted, and there was considerable loss of life. The US Government was urging everyone to keep calm and not blame the events on the peace loving Muslims in the US. That was all the confirmation Jim Roberts needed. He asked for some research to be sent to him prior to the 1800 meeting. Identify all of the practicing Muslims you can in the Department of Homeland Security, especially Senior Executive Service members.

Roberts arrived at Camp Mabry and was told the briefing would be held at 36th Division HQ. Roberts spent a few minutes working to put some slides together for the anticipated PowerPoint marathon based on what came in and a vision he was going to try to sell. He went in the headquarters building and his seemingly out of date uniform and unrecognized unit patch drew some attention.

When Roberts entered the briefing room he recognized the General and nobody else. "Good to see you sir, although under almost the worst of circumstances."

"What do you make of the situation?" the General asked Roberts.

"I think we are dead in the middle of a game on jihad. One wild ride is going to happen. I assume the situation is desperate enough that we have been called in? I was hoping we would get some briefing from what is laughingly referred to as the intelligence community." was Roberts's assessment.

"I asked for you. I can use you to say things I can't." the General said.

"I could be looking forward to that at least, sir." replied Roberts.

The meting began with the Adjutant General of Texas. He outlined the actions so far, first was a call up of the National Guard as a Title 32 call pending a decision from the Department of Defense to make the Call up a Title 10 order, which would then transfer control of the Guard to the Federal Department of the Army. The State Guard had been activated and the Governor had signed an order arming the State Guard. And as an additional measure of meeting anticipated needs, the Reserve Militia was being utilized, with retired officers being recalled to duty and existing militia units being recognized, new units organized and being incorporated into the Texas Military Forces.

Each of the component commanders then gave an update. Guardsmen had been delayed in reporting due to the traffic tie ups across the state. As some Guardsmen lived as many as 100 miles from their units, the Guard was only now being able to bring units online and would be able to deploy tomorrow. The State Guard was in a similar situation plus hampered by the fact it had done no training as an armed unit, and would have to start that tomorrow. It was anticipated that the State Guard would get an influx of volunteers probably exceeding the current 2500 members that would be a challenge to in process. Next was the General, who had been appointed commander of the Reserve Militia, which answered one question in Roberts mind. They were not yet being merged into the State Guard, but remained a separate reporting channel to the Adjutant General. The General estimated a brigade could be raised in the next week, starting with a battalion online tomorrow.

"Are you sure about that General?" the Adjutant General asked.

The General pointed at Roberts "There is the battalion commander right there. Want to ask him?"

Next was the situation brief on what was known to have happened during the day. Department of Transportation highway camera footage was being reviewed to try and identify the vehicles or persons used to set the bombs in place and detonate them. The schools targeted seemed to be in suburban and somewhat upscale districts.

Then was discussion on the deployment plan. The idea was to have the National Guard units to cordon off affected areas, so the police would be freed up for reducing the terrorists at the schools via their SWAT and tactical teams. The State Guard would take on a similar role in smaller communities while it armed up and started in on tactical training. The Reserve Militia would be mobilized and personnel taken in to state service as available and used like the State Guard, and reinforce other operations.

Finally, Roberts had all he could take and broke in. "Sir, there isn't time for that."

The Governor had entered the room during this part of the meeting "Roberts, explain yourself."

"Sir, the plan recognizes that there really is not much we can do for the existing hostages. But we need to prevent more hostages from being taken. We can work on that two ways, try to protect every potential target or go after the insurgents support structure. We are in the middle of an insurgency, please look at this slide from our friends at the Special Warfare Center. The armed component is only a small part of the total effort directed against us. The auxiliary support structure, and underground are much larger and generate the resource used for the armed part. If we keep chasing after the armed guys, we will be 24 hours and thousands of bodies behind. We need to generate pressure on the enablers of the armed component."

The Division Commander of the 36th Division said "I see your point. But it almost seems like you are asking us to operate like we did in Iraq."

"Sir, that is what happens when the US Government brings Iraq here. Someone might check this list of Department of Homeland Security Officials for known to be practicing Muslims and compare that with a list of people at DHS who are not helping us." Roberts suggested.

The Governor asked "What are you suggesting Roberts?"

"Internment of enemy aliens. Shut down every Mosque, round up the Muslim population and inter them pending being expelled from Texas." Roberts proposed.

"We can't do that." said one of the aides to the Governor.

"They are not US citizens. I recall there is a court case about this relationship of Texas vis a vis Washington, DC underway. Given the number of deaths that have occurred or are currently in progress, I suspect the public may demand it." Roberts said.

"I'll consider your advice." said the Governor and thus ended the participation of Major Roberts in the meeting for the rest of the evening.

The Governor decided to reconvene the meeting in the morning. "You may have seen the news reports from last night. There have been several instances of known Muslim properties being set afire and destroyed. It would seem that the feelings of support of such actions are widespread across Texas. We need to modify the plan from yesterday."

It was now a given that non citizens were going to be detained and probably expelled from Texas. The Governor would act under the authority of the US Constitution Article I, Section 9: "The Migration or Importation of such Persons as any of the States now existing shall think proper to admit, shall not be prohibited by the Congress prior to the Year one thousand eight hundred and eight, but a Tax or duty may be imposed on such Importation, not exceeding ten dollars for each Person."

The task allocation became the TXARNG would assist in the clearing and securing of attacked locations, the State Guard would operate the detention centers, and the Reserve Militia would conduct the detentions, in conjunction with sheriffs and police.

Chapter 9

Such Persons as the States Shall Think Proper to Admit

LET US CONTEMPLATE OUR FOREFATHERS, AND POSTERITY, AND RESOLVE TO MAINTAIN THE RIGHTS BEQUEATHED TO US FROM THE FORMER, FOR THE SAKE OF THE LATTER. THE NECESSITY OF THE TIMES, MORE THAN EVER, CALLS FOR OUR UTMOST CIRCUMSPECTION, DELIBERATION, FORTITUDE AND PERSEVERANCE. LET US REMEMBER THAT "IF WE SUFFER TAMELY A LAWLESS ATTACK UPON OUR LIBERTY, WE ENCOURAGE IT, AND INVOLVE OTHERS IN OUR DOOM," IT IS A VERY SERIOUS CONSIDERATION ... THAT MILLIONS YET UNBORN MAY BE THE MISERABLE SHARERS OF THE EVENT. – SAMUEL ADAMS

The consensus among the militias was clear. Illegal aliens and in particular practicing Muslims were going to be expelled from Texas. For some, the question of what about the rights of citizen Muslims came up. Their status would be a question for the legal system. And any support of the attacks on Texas should be considered treason and treated as such. Any person found in a Mosque or Islamic center would be considered constituting probable cause for detention.

Roberts had been assigned a sector and as he left Camp Mabry, made a call back to the Borden County Militia. "Prepare to move, we are going on an expedition later today. We're taking everything we've got, including the black projects."

"Where are we going sir?" the XO asked.

"You will get the details when I arrive, but it will be to the metropolitan area where I used to live." Roberts replied.

"Do we have rules of engagement?" the XO was still curious.

"Carthago delenda est." stated Roberts.

"Carthage must be destroyed, roger that sir." the XO understood what the Romans did to their enemies.

Roberts retraced his route back to Freedonia. Gas was still available is a few towns, so Roberts had three quarters of a tank when he arrived in Freedonia. The fragility of the infrastructure of Texas was briefly discussed with the General before he left. Attacks on pipeline terminals, electrical transformers, and other points would be easy and crippling. There were not enough units, men and organizational infrastructure available in the Texas Military Forces to defend every vulnerable node of the public infrastructure. It was one of the reasons Roberts thought it was vital to go after potential attackers and their support network. They had to be attacked and destroyed before they did the same to Texas.

The people of Texas had realized that, even if the politicians didn't. Once the scale of loss became clear, it was probable that tens of thousands if not well over 100,000 school children had been murdered across the United States. And those children were not just indiscriminately targeted, but in neighborhoods where the demographic tended to be culturally western. One of the weaknesses of western civilization was that the westerners were not making enough babies to keep that western civilization going. The attacks were designed to accelerate current population trends in place in addition to the terror aspect.

The Borden County Militia had one advantage over the other militias and even the State Guard. As a result of the bail bond forfeitures of the federal agents who failed to appear in court after their arrests, millions of dollars had been made available by the county for militia equipment. The Borden County Militia via the State of Texas, had gone on a shopping trip to the Sierra Army Depot for vehicles, tentage, generators, field kitchens, and fuel tankers. Much of the military equipment of a light infantry battalion was on hand, and now was going to be put to use. The militia still needed the ammunition, food, and fuel to flow in order to operate but a base level of operational equipment was there for them. Others had to make do with civilian pickup trucks, and vans.

With the population growth in Freedonia, the Borden County Militia was the nucleus of a light infantry battalion. They had two almost full strength rifle companies and a headquarters company for support. Roberts expected to fill out the other two rifle companies as the operation got going. They would get either other militias assigned to them, or as what had tended to happen in the past, volunteers who appeared along the way.

The battalion had the vehicles loaded and was ready to move on order as Roberts returned from Austin. He told them to stand down as the move out would take place at 1900 after the evening meal. Another few hours wasn't going to matter.

"But sir, there are still hostages out there." the XO said.

"You have to consider anyone taken hostage as already dead. If we get one back, that is a bonus. In any case we are hours away from our objective. Let's get on with the OPORD." Roberts ordered.

Roberts now had the battalion staff, company commanders, and the county emergency board assembled. "First off, the Governor has ordered the detention of all non US citizens in Texas for internment and probable repatriation out of Texas. This is to be conducted primarily by Texas peace officers with assistance from the National Guard, State Guard and reserve militias called into the Texas Military Forces. Thus, we will be interested primarily in situations that occur when local police or sheriffs can not accomplish the task with their own resources.

The National Guard units are tasked with supporting hostage recovery, and public infrastructure reconstruction. The State Guard is now to be armed and operate the internment camps. Our task is to assist in the round up and handover of detainees to the State Guard. Once Austin realizes, if they haven't already, that all of the support units needed to make this operation go are in the Army Reserve, and the Governor can't call them up or issue orders to them, we will have the issue of sustaining the operation. Either the feds support it and call out the Army Reserve, or we just have to deal with the supply issue, and maybe the feds, too.

Our area of operations is the Dallas / Ft. Worth region. We will move from here with Start Point time of 1900, S-3 will provide a less traveled road route so that we are moving into the area during darkness. This is to make it less obvious that an operation is underway before the public announcement tomorrow. We are maintaining a platoon here in Freedonia of those not going for maintaining local security under control of the county emergency board. We can at least operate for three days with supplies on hand, after that we either have logistics, or we have to pull supply from here.

We are going to move to the north east of the metropolitan area and commence operations south down US 75 in McKinney, A Company to the east of 75, and B Company to the west. From there we take it as it goes. I plan for us to end up at the Joint Reserve Base Carswell, which should be where we would also draw logistics support if this gets sorted out. We know of heavy concentrations of Muslims along 75 all the way south to Richardson, through east Dallas, into Arlington and south Irving. That then leads us to the Ft. Worth sweep.

Rules of engagement: use of force authorized to ensure compliance, and use of deadly force authorized to protect life and property.

We will use our generated CEOIs, pending Austin picking up the ball on commo. We will also primarily use the PRC radios for commo, but also make sure the HAM radios are packed for travel as we will need them, too. The fewer the people who can listen in on our radio traffic the better I like it.

We'll release people for a couple of hours of family time before we get going. Questions? I hope not many, because you now know about as much as I do." Roberts ended the briefing.

Lise was home as Jim finally returned, and was now going to pack his gear for the deployment. Jim's gear was always packed and ready to go, but every time he took it, he inventoried it again just to be sure nothing was missing. They drove to the assembly point, and families were gathering, just as they have done from time immemorial, when they send their men off to war. Lise hugged Jim and whispered in his ear "Come back to me."

"I will. Like I said, all I do is sit around and talk on the radio. And go to meetings" Jim promised.

"I know you're lying to me, but it's all right." Lise said.

A loudspeaker system had been set up so that an old American military tradition could be revived. As the convoy of vehicles started to leave Freedonia, the speaker system was playing the tune, "The Girl I Left Behind Me." Until now, Roberts favorite lines of the song were "many a name our banner bore of former deeds of daring, but that was in the days of yore of which we had no sharing". This time Jim Roberts was leaving a girl behind.

The convoy route avoided the Interstates, with the exception of crossing I-35 north of Denton. Then the convoy stopped for the night, to resume the last two hours travel to time arrival north of McKinney to coincide with the morning announcement by the State of Texas pertaining to illegal aliens and aliens of hostile nations – those nationalities were to be detained pending repatriation out of Texas.

The announcement was made at 9 in the morning by the Governor and companies A and B moved in on the Mosque and Islamic center immediately thereafter. When they arrived, several Texans already had the locations under siege. Shots had been traded back and forth. As the schools had finally been cleared, the police presence was shifting to the locations where Islamic activities were under observation by vigilant citizens making certain that no further terrorism should take place. The procedure used by the militia was the same at each location.

One of the unit officers would identify himself to the senior police officer present and ask if he was aware of the Governor's order. This changed the orientation of the police from being the buffer between the two groups to now having a responsibility to do something. Or, as it turned out, to get out of the way, as local police had no interest in trying to arrest any number of Muslims who were not being cooperative and also armed. They were happy to turn that problem over to someone else, because it looked like it was going to be dangerous.

Without the police presence, the citizenry had no hesitation about trading fire with the Muslims who had sought refuge in their Islamic community facilities. The citizens on site seemed curious about what was going to happen, mixed with relief that now their losses of both lives and property were finally being taken seriously by the government of Texas.

The A company commander arrived on the scene. The senior police officer asked him, "Are you guys going to storm the Mosque."

"No, I've got no interest in getting our own people killed." replied the company commander.

"So, you took over just to stand and watch like we did?" asked the police officer.

"No." said the militia captain.

"What are you going to do?" further inquired the police officer.

"Just watch." said the A company commander.

Roberts was in the battalion TOC when the call came in that the first mosque was surrounded, and the occupants refused to leave and submit themselves to detention. It also hadn't taken long after the announcement from Austin, for reporters to come looking for the Borden County Militia. Roberts now had two reporters and camera crews in tow, and more were on the way. A militia that had made a practice of arresting federal agents was notorious, and the fact that it was now working for the State of Texas was news.

Roberts asked the S-3, "Mortar platoon ready?"

"Yes sir, we have a section supporting each company." Affirmed the Operations Officer.

Roberts then turned to the reporters, "Come along with me and you will have the visuals you need for the news." The scene had been set for the visuals so that the reporters would add to the reputation of the Borden County Militia. It would be so spectacular, that they had to air it.

The media circus and Roberts arrived at the location where the company commander was supervising the cordoning off of the area around the mosque. The two mortars had been set up about a half mile to the west of the mosque, just off the street that ran east and west past the mosque. The intention was to try to avoid having the

116

flight path of the mortar rounds go over a house or business. They really wanted to avoid the possibility of dropping a round in someone's living room.

Roberts then approached the company commander "Got a safe place relatively speaking, for the cameras and reporters to set up?"

"One block south of the mosque should do, sir." the company commander told Roberts.

Turning to the reporters, Roberts said "Let's go." And to the company commander he said "Go ahead Captain."

The senior police officer was briefed that he should try to get word to the mosque that they had five minutes to surrender or be destroyed. The press had just finished setting up, as the approach was made. Roberts had the radio on, so the reporters could listen to what was happening over the radio net. The soldier accompanying the police officer reported over the radio that there was no answer from the mosque.

Five minutes later the company commander was heard over the radio. "Adjust fire, over." Giving the map location of the mosque.

The mortar platoon sergeant was acting as forward observer. He repeated what the company commander had said over the radio and added, "HE in effect, variable time, height of burst five meters, danger close. Direction to observer one five eight zero mils."

"Round out" came the call from the fire direction center.

"Splash over" They were now five seconds away from the explosion.

"Splash out."

The round exploded slightly above and to the west of the main dome of the mosque. A jagged hole was torn in the dome and the onion dome of a minaret was torn off. That brought cheers from the onlookers. Those in the mosque were given five minutes more to consider their position. Still no response.

"Three meter height of burst, fire for effect." This time, two rounds came in and exploded near the roof, causing part of the roof to collapse. Two men came running out of the building and were immediately shot down. At this point the message was clear. Either surrender to the Borden County Militia, or be destroyed. Word would get around quickly because two TV stations had it on film.

Without assistance from the State, it would have been hard to build the mortar platoon. It had been part of the shopping trip to the Sierra Army Depot. The transfer had been difficult, because while the states have the authority to buy military equipment from the Department of the Army, none had ever done so before. They had been content to let the federal government loan military equipment to the National Guard, which was still owned by the national government and not the state. Texas had fronted the transaction for the Borden County Militia. This set the ATF into an apoplexy, because the weaponry would be in private hands, requiring registration and payment of the destructive device tax.

But, individuals, were not going to own the weapons, they were property of the militia. It had been over 100 years ago, and before the ATF even existed that a militia had been sold material from a national armory or arsenal. There was no regulation or agency determination as to how the transaction could happen. The ATF could not stop Texas from taking possession, and thus the transaction took place. The ATF took solace in the fact that the manufacture of ammunition for the mortars would require ATF approval.

ATF approval to manufacture mortar rounds was the last thing on the mind of anyone at the Freedonia Army Ammunition Plant.

Even the Freedonia Army Ammunition Plant has its limits, and mortar round production was not an activity of high volume. The battalion didn't have that much mortar ammunition to repeat the show for very long. Fortunately, the images shown on TV were compelling, and not every building full of individuals decided to die in place.

The number of detainees was growing rapidly, and the next question was where could Texas ship them. There were no volunteers stepping forward from the federal government or other states to increase their non native population.

The action by Texas quickly drew the ire of the US Government. As a first measure in dealing with the crisis, the National Guard was federalized, taking away command authority of the Texas National Guard from the Governor of Texas. By now, the school massacres had ended, with loss of life in the tens of thousands, and still not yet totaled as to the total extent of the loss of life. Michigan, and in some of the other locations with very large Muslim populations were suffering from copycat attacks. Texas had not seen any follow on activity yet, but there was another huge problem in progress.

There were not enough facilities to house the detainees, and without the National Guard, not enough guards. The guard problem started to solve itself. As the operation went underway, and units such as Borden County were able to reduce the hold outs without loss of life to the unit, Texans volunteered to join the militias and the State Guard. Roberts initially solved the problem of incorporating volunteers by splitting each company in half, and filling in with volunteers to have a full strength battalion. The volunteers kept coming. A fifth company was created, and then each of the companies went from a structure of three rifle platoons to four. That structure was stretching the headquarters company ability to provide logistical support past the breaking point.

The Houston battalion was in even worse shape. It had more territory and people to cover, and less military equipment on hand. The retired Army officers were working as a brigade headquarters to run all of the activity, with a battalion for a region of Texas. The situation reminded Roberts of a quote from the Quartermaster General of the US Army during the Mexican War, when the needs were so overwhelming the capability of the Army. "I find myself needing to literally pay for time, in order to try to meet the requirements of the service."

Texas soon found out what the real problem with the immigration system was. Once found, the issue was that the people were difficult to expel because no other political entity would take them. Without government provided resettlement money, "charitable" organizations in other states had no interest in taking the aliens off of the hands of the people of Texas and taking them in themselves. The US State Department refused to contact the countries of citizenship of the aliens as well. The holding areas became over crowded.

Ultimately, the Muslim organizations paid to resettle their people in other states. Roberts assumed that the Islamic jihad figured on taking over the rest of the US, and then would come after Texas after the rest of the United States had been subjugated. A battle had been won, but it was only a temporary respite from a lager battle to come later. At least western civilization was winning a battle. For too long it had gone the other way.

While it was far better to win battles than lose them, there was still the war to be won. That was going to require much more effort in order to achieve success.

Chapter 10

United States v Texas

I HAVE SPENT ALL MY LIFE UNDER A COMMUNIST REGIME, AND I WILL TELL YOU THAT A SOCIETY WITHOUT ANY OBJECTIVE LEGAL SCALE IS A TERRIBLE ONE INDEED. BUT A SOCIETY WITH NO OTHER SCALE BUT THE LEGAL ONE IS NOT QUITE WORTHY OF MAN EITHER. – ALEKSANDR SOLZHENITSYN

The civil trial of the century was coming to a close. As the Solicitor General of Texas assumed, in this case the jury selection would be vital. He had made every effort to have jurors serve who had no direct connection with the federal government as an employee, contractor, or lobbyist. That seemed to rule out over 99% of the population of Washington, DC which was the source for the jury pool.

The US argument had been all about federal supremacy. A state can not contradict the federal government. On the other side, Texas had argued the text of the Constitution and supporting documents from the convention through the federalist papers. From the point of view of Texas, those laws were beyond the authority of the federal government, and thus a power reserved to the states or to the people. Which way the jury saw it would be critical. Jurors who benefited from that federal government behavior would be unlikely to find for Texas.

The other unknown was how the terrorist attacks would play into the feelings of the jury. There could be a reflexive look to the federal government for security, or a perception of lack of security because of federal government indifference could be considered a factor. As every good trial lawyer knows, the case was decided when the jury was chosen. This case was no different.

There was a great deal of tension in the court when the jury returned. The Chief Justice asked if the jury had reached a verdict. The foreman answered in the affirmative. The foreman was asked for the verdict. "We find for the plaintiff." The ninth and tenth Amendments to the US Constitution were no more.

National media outlets were quick to hit the airwaves with the news. The Federal Government had just completed a rebuke of Texas. All was now right in the world of the Boston to Washington corridor and its Los Angeles annex. The court having announced the decision, the question to be asked was now what would happen to the Texans who had defied the US Government while the State of Texas had stood by and watched the whole affair.

Coverage of events by Rampaging Elephants Radio had been constant concerning the proceedings. The morning host got Roberts on the phone for an interview. "Jim Roberts what is your reaction to the Supreme Court?"

Roberts was prepared with an answer. "For many years, the USA has been a land in which two groups of people exist. A group dedicated to individual liberty and a Constitutional government inherited from our founders. The other group is intent on using governmental power to accomplish whatever ends that group sees as desirable. Those two views of government can not exist together. It has to be one view or the other is the operating principle under which we live. Therefore, one of three scenarios happens going forward.

One scenario is a return to a federal system. The states operate under the principles its citizens think best. Some states would gravitate toward an individual liberty and protection of individual rights set of principles. Other states would be free to implement such socialist models as they think fit. The key principle being that the federal government is out of the way, therefore those key decisions about the laws under which we live, are to be decided at the state level. People then have the ability to live in the state which they find most suitable to their happiness.

That was the surest way to resolve our differences peacefully, and maintain the idea of the United States. The actions of the federal courts, and agents of the federal government itself, are now closing the possibility of this happening. This increases the likelihood of another scenario which will fundamentally transform the nature of the United States.

The next scenario is that of the two groups contesting for control of our political future, one of the two will become dominant in each state. This ultimately leads to the breakup of the United States, as the ability of the federal government to enforce its' will on millions of people unwilling to submit and backed by a state government is minimal. Certainly that ability is almost non existent under any peaceful course of events.

The most painful scenario is one where one of the two factions, or possibly both, refuse to allow the other to go its' own way peacefully. At this point a civil war is fought, and the victor will be able to impose whatever form of government it thinks best on the vanquished. Past experience in the history of humanity indicated that such an event would have repercussions for generations. Hard feelings would remain on the part of the losing side, which would manifest itself in many unpleasant ways.

We will now find out if Texans believe in liberty or submission. The choice can not be avoided much longer. Who is elected in November to go to Austin will probably decide our fate."

Roberts' views were representative of the Rampaging Elephants audience, Free Texas members, the Lone Star Party, and a substantial number of Texans. The decision came just a few weeks before the November elections and every candidate for office could only take one of two positions. Texas was going to obey the Supreme Court and the federal government no matter what they decided to do, or Texas was not. Negotiations were no longer a viable option.

In one sense, politics in the state was now made easier. If you believed in the absolute sovereignty of the US Government, you were a Democrat. If you believed in limited federal sovereignty based on enumerated powers specified by the US Constitution, you supported the Lone Star Party. If you were confused, you were a Republican. Every state wide office holder was a Republican, and media outlets were keen to know what the State of Texas was going to do next, or more to the point, what action the Governor was going to take. Fortunately for the Republicans, there were few state wide offices open in the November elections, but the entire State House, and half of the State Senate was in the midst of campaign season.

The stakes were high because of the importance of the election for US President. The President would appoint one or more Supreme Court Justices. Between the Supreme Court and a President willing to act unilaterally, the candidate who won that office would have the potential to ruin or save the country. It all depended on your point of view.

The Governor scheduled a press conference. He had been taken by surprise by the Supreme Court outcome. He had staked his politics on using the court system to get controls put in place on the federal government. He was now completely undercut, and even more so because of his actions in using the National Guard without federal permission after the terrorist attacks. He had also used the Guard for detention and expelling alien populations. This press conference would likely determine his political future.

The press conference began with the statement from the Governor. He started off with the recollection of the traditional method of resolving differences between interpretations of the Constitution, which was to have the matter adjudicated by the courts. This had worked reasonably well throughout history, but the system had failed, just as it had in 1798 leading to the Kentucky and Virginia resolutions. The Governor reminded the listeners that because Jefferson had been elected President in 1800, the point of contention addressed by the resolutions had become moot, and the mechanism by which states could declare federal actions unconstitutional had never been brought to a clear resolution.

The Governor continued to state that the present circumstances now brought this issue back on the table. After the elections in the next month, the Governor would call a special session of the Texas legislature to convene on the first Tuesday in December to consider taking up where the state resolutions in 1798 began. He hoped that other states would join in the effort and propose an Amendment to the Constitution to clarify the power of states to void federal legislation or acts. This would be the best way to solve the problem without undoing past case law.

The governor ended his statement by calling on the President to leave the situation as it was until after the election. As he had done previously, the Governor chose a path of trying to avoid direct conflict with the federal government, but it was now clear that position was not one that could be held much longer.

The press conference was the evening's topic of conversation in Freedonia, as it was elsewhere. Free Texas and Lone Star Party frustration with the Governor was starting to boil over. Ed McMasters was the first to make a statement about the situation. "Screw the Governor, it is past time to resolve this and get the feds under control. He never solves the problem."

Roberts took the situation more calmly. "I think he is playing his hand petty well. He knows there is a good deal of discontentment, but how much sacrifice will people make to be rid of oppression, balanced by uncertainty and some active opposition."

Ed wasn't mollified. "Democrats will never vote for him anyway. Why should he care about them?"

"Ed, they and the Republicans are firmly entrenched in the capitals. Their surroundings operate to give the impression that both of them have more support than they really do, and the opposition is weaker than it really is. The need for bribes for anyone who wants the government to do or not do something in the form of lobbyists only strengthens that perception." was Roberts reply.

"Where do we go from here Jim?" McMasters asked.

"Win some elections." Was Roberts advice.

The decision by the Supreme Court was greeted with unrestrained joy by over 90% of the population of Washington, DC. It was now a given that there were practically no limits on any power the government of the Unites States might choose to exercise. Meetings were scheduled to solve the Texas problem, and to shut down those rogue operations defying the federal government freely in Texas, violating several federal laws and an untold number of regulations.

The FBI was the lead agency to identify the key leaders in the criminal enterprises, study their travel patters, and determine how best to effect arrests and seizures of property. This matter had the personal attention of the President and his staff. They wanted this resolved before the President left office after the election. Time was short.

The first action taken by the US Government was not that unusual. The National Guard of all of the states was called into federal service. The Adjutant General of Texas notified the Governor of the action.

"Is the call under Title 10 or Title 32?" the Governor asked.

"Title 32, they know how to play the game to give themselves control of the Guard while still claiming they are in a state status performing law enforcement." was the answer.

"Well, General, I suppose it is a bit late to start asking where everybody's loyalty is, isn't it?" asked the Governor.

"Sir, our loyalty is to Texas. I think of it as now the feds are signing our checks, but until we receive an order to do something we shouldn't to let it roll." advised the Adjutant General.

"I give them about 12 hours until they tell you to stop the deportations. We need to get the camps under control of the State Guard and militias. Start the calls to the militias." ordered the Governor.

The terror attacks and resulting deportations were already taking the state budget past the breaking point. Some of the money could be recovered via the federal disaster, but that money could not be seen to be funding the State Guard and militias. If the feds found out about what Texas was doing, Texas would get cut off from federal funds. As most of the bridge bombings had been of Interstate highways, that money was going to come out of the federal budget as well.

Rampaging Elephants Radio was trying to interview every candidate for the Texas House, Senate, and the open state wide offices. Those media people were not afraid to ask the questions the typical politician did not want to answer. After a Rampaging Elephants interview any voter would know if the candidate deserved your vote – or not.

News of the militia call was fast to make the rounds of Freedonia. The Borden County Militia was spending so much time on missions that Roberts now considered the under strength battalion about as good as one of the better National Guard units. As long as Texas was paying for the active duty time, it was just more cash into the economy of Freedonia.

After the election, Rampaging Elephants Radio was moving its operations to Freedonia, and would probably start video production. There would now be an information outlet directly associated with Freedonia and the liberty movement across Texas. Roberts considered that media outlet as key to the success of the effort. It is vital to have a media outlet on your side of the issue to get your message out to a sympathetic audience.

That messaging had been a struggle. It was relatively easy to do internet broadcasting, and there was no shortage of people willing to broadcast their opinions. The audience for such shows tended to be small, until the broadcasters got an editorial focus and really put shows together. That was the key to get listeners to return – a predictable format that brought real information about Texas politics and pending governmental actions.

The residents of Freedonia were also certain about one thing. This decision was likely to give federal agencies the idea that they could now take on the businesses and residents of Freedonia for violations of various acts and regulations. Therefore a degree of extra vigilance was required to be able to prepare a proper reception for uninvited guests. When leaving the county, the Freedonians would travel in groups for additional self protection.

The executive directors of Free Texas were considered especially important targets for the feds, and additional security measures were taken for them. If a Free Texas Executive Director left the county, he was to be accompanied by a Personal Security Detail. There was not going to be a repeat of a tactical error made by other groups that allowed their leadership to be in a vulnerable position subject to arrest. The stakes had grown too high to allow for a mistake on the part of the Texans.

While most of the country was focused on the Presidential election in the United States, the Lone Star Party was focused solely on Texas. The LSP had made the move from a nobody to the third largest party in Texas. A few Republican state office holders had bolted from the Republicans to join the LSP. But the strength of the LSP was now at the county level, where many rural county and local office holders were members. Often, party sympathizers were not officially office holders because of the non partisan nature of those offices. The LSP was now trying to expand its influence by moving in to the State House and Senate.

The election would show how much strength the Lone Star Party really had in Texas. The election would also probably determine the future of Texas.

Chapter 11

The First Tuesday in November

DEMOCRACY IS THE WORST FORM OF GOVERNMENT, EXCEPT FOR ALL THOSE OTHER FORMS THAT HAVE BEEN TRIED FROM TIME TO TIME. – WINSTON CHURCHILL

Turnout for the November election was predicted to be extremely heavy. The future of Texas was going to be decided. While most of the country was focused on the contest for President due to the contrast between the candidates, the Lone Star Party was focused on the Texas Legislature. Those State Representatives and State Senators would be the key to the future relationship between Texas and the US Government. The Lone Star Party leadership considered the terror attacks staged by Muslims, and the subsequent public reaction to be very favorable for the candidates of the LSP.

Much of the LSP leadership was gathered at the Green Dragon Tavern in Freedonia. Most of the media coverage was on the very tight race for president. It was important for the Texans who won, because a win by the Democrats would mean increased and more acrimonious tensions with the US Government. A Republican victory could lead to a more amicable negotiated settlement. For this reason, they left the television channels tuned to the national results as they came in.

As the night continued toward midnight and the Presidential race was still undecided, attentions turned to see how the Texas races were going. The tension from the results for President mirrored the vote count for the Texas State House races. The first good news to be had was that the LSP was holding the seats of the Representatives who had switched over to the party. The name recognition of incumbency did matter. With the exception of El Paso, almost every office up for election west of Interstate 35 was going for the LSP. The Democrats were holding the big cities, and the fight was on for the suburbs. Republican candidates had played on the fear of not voting Republican would lead to disaster in Texas. Tonight would show how well that strategy worked.

The economic message of freedom and jobs being created as a result of that freedom seemed to have gotten some traction in traditionally Democratic precincts. A few seats had been taken from the Democrats, who were now down to 46 seats in the Texas House. A few suburban seats went Lone Star, which in addition to a few more making the move in rural east Texas, gave the LSP 32 seats. The Republicans were now down to 72 seats in the Texas House. No one party had a majority of the Texas House. The next session of the Texas House would be an exercise in coalition building and the art of politics.

The state senate races were much tougher for the LSP as only half the seats were up for election. The LSP only ended up with three seats, taking one away from the Democrats and two from the Republicans. The Republicans no longer had the 20 of the 31 seats needed to end debate and force votes in the Texas Senate. Some accommodation for coalitions was necessary in the Texas Senate as well as the House.

There would be no one party rule in Texas for the next two years. Everybody was going to have to make deals to get anything done. In this environment, even the LSP were now players that had to be considered in any political calculation. And the LSP was going to head to Austin ready to play.

It was late into the night when the race for President was called for the Republicans. The news was greeted in Freedonia with relief. While the hard core Texas Independence supports thought this would take some of the energy out of the movement in the short term, additional time would now be gained to better prepare Texas and Texans for the inevitable. The Free Texas Executive Directors had a short chat before heading home from the election party at the Green Dragon.

Ed McMasters was feeling good about the results. "I feel good for the country even if this sets us back a little bit. We are going to get there."

Jim Roberts was more cautious. "It is still a long road to travel. At least we are on the playing field in Texas and can't be ignored. The dealing in Austin is going to be intense. Nationally, we still have three months before anything can change. We really don't know what that change will be, and how all of this plays out in the Republican Party. Nobody in Washington circles wanted that guy, and he may have to fight everybody for anything he wants to get done. Not much may change, no matter his intentions."

McMasters was now becoming a bit more reflective "I'm much more worried about trying to negotiate for independence with him.

He knows how to negotiate, and I'd rather have dealt with the other one on that."

"I doubt they would negotiate. It would have to be done the hard way. In any case, the road starts in Austin, and that is where we have to go." remarked Roberts.

As the world was focused on the next President of the United States, and what that was likely to mean for them, only a small subset of the political class noticed that something very unusual had happened in Texas. A small third party had survived an election and increased the number of party office holders. Not only had the party survived, it was now positioned to be a power broker in Texas politics. The election was a peaceful revolution in more ways than one.

The election results had also created a dilemma for the Republican party of Texas. They no longer had a majority of the House seats, and if the Speaker of the House was going to retain his position, either Democrats or Lone Star Party members had to vote for him. Of course, it would be easier to deal with the Democrats, as the Republican Party had always done. But it was clear that such actions had now cost the Republicans support from their voters. Many formerly solid Republican districts had gone Lone Star, and as long as the Lone Star Party survived, that would be a problem unless the Republican Party made changes.

Recent events had not helped the Republican Party of Texas. Attempts to blame the Supreme Court Decision on the Lone Star Party had failed in the election cycle because everybody in Texas knew that the Republican Governor had run on a platform of taking the US Government to court in order to control the federal government. The Lone Star Party had forced him to do exactly what he said that he would do. One of the disadvantages of spending huge amounts of money on political ads is that the voters tended to remember them.

The Muslim terrorist attacks should have been to the advantage of the Republican Party as well, but too many voters had remembered the failed promise of the Republicans to keep the Texas border secure. Those voters who decided that they had nothing more to lose voted for Lone Star Party candidates. It made the Lone Star Party difficult to deal with in the political sense. The Lone Star Party had shown limited willingness to make deals unless the LSP also got part of its platform enacted. Republicans would have to do things, their remaining supporters would rather they didn't if deals were made with the LSP.

All of the terrorist related events across the United States had benefited the Lone Star Party as the party which was strong on border security and limited immigration. The LSP had been able to portray itself as the party that would have done more of these things to prevent terror attacks had they been in power. That message had traction among the voters.

There was other good news for the LSP. The candidates backed by the LSP had done well in county elections across west Texas and in several counties in east Texas. The major metropolitan areas were still firmly in the hands of Democrats and Republicans were strong in the suburbs. Politically, Texas was separating on the basis of geography. In this regard, politics in Texas mirrored that at the national level.

From the perspective of the Lone Star Party, there was one imperative for the next meeting of the legislature. It was time to put the following question to the people of Texas. Should Texas remain in the United States or go its own way? The question needed to be asked, the debate should be had, and the people of Texas express their wish. Almost anything else was negotiable, but the price of support from the Lone Star Party was a referendum.

Back in Washington, DC, the President's staff was very agitated. The President was insistent that something be done about the Texas situation before he left office. Most of the regulatory agencies came to the conclusion that about all they could do was to implement more regulations that the Texans would continue to ignore as they had the other regulations. But there were still many agencies loyal to the President. The Department of Justice was working on a plan.

There was the risk of FBI and other agents operating in Texas being arrested by state or local law enforcement as previously. To mitigate this possibility, the FBI would hire security contractors, and engage them to arrest the Executive Directors of Free Texas and other leaders of the rebellion in Texas. The non agents had a much better chance of getting into Texas and setting up the operation undetected. They would not be facing arrest in Texas for their previous actions while in the employ of the US Government. This was the advantage to performing the operation outside of the usual channels.

The White House approved the plan. Security contractors were hired and deputized as US Marshals. A surveillance order was approved by a federal judge to intercept communications of the targets. Based on previous experience, they would not attempt an arrest in Freedonia, but make the intercept of the targets while traveling elsewhere. That would be part of the real value of the intercepted communications – to know of any travel plans. If there was enough advance warning, the arrest could be effected via vehicle roadblock or where the targets spent the night.

The Attorney General and Director of the FBI were just as keen as the President to get payback for a major embarrassment to the US Government. They just needed those targets to be at the right place at a time before the next President became aware of what was happening and might decide to stop it. At this point, the contractors were waiting for an opportunity.

The election results did have several consequences for Freedonia. The massive inflow of funds and silver into the Freedonia Transaction Company took a pause. The assumption was that the new President would lead to policies creating a more business friendly economy, and the security hedge represented by the silver account was not as urgent as it had seemed previously.

The pause was much needed by the Freedonia Transaction Company. While the FTC itself was not accepting US currency, other member institutions of the Texas Financial Network did. Those institutions needed the FTC Promissory Notes to put into circulation in order to cover those deposits or account credits. To obtain the notes from the FTC, the institution either had to deposit silver with the FTC or take out a loan. The institutions had reached the point where they needed the silver coinage on hand to meet demands, and were taking out loans from the FTC to get the needed Promissory Notes.

This left the problem of obtaining the silver coinage reserves with the FTC to solve. The demand was starting to affect the market for what coin dealers refer to as junk silver. Already silver dollars were trading at a Federal Reserve Note price above that of two halves, four quarters, or ten dimes in silver coinage. The demand was getting to the point that silver coins were now trading above the spot price of silver. If the pause had not occurred, the exchange rate of TXD to USD would have to be unlinked from the price of silver. This would be one of the first signs of inflation for the USD, or expressed differently, deflation for the TXD.

For now the problem was avoided, but Beth Dunwoody and Jim Roberts had discussed the issue in detail. Not having silver reserves to back the notes was not an option. Limiting the number of notes in circulation to the reserve would be disruptive to the economy they supported. That left the option down to accepting silver not in the form of pre 1964 US coinage to meet reserve requirements. Neither liked that idea because it put the Freedonia Transaction Company in the silver trading business.

They decided that there was just one option left. The Freedonia Transaction Company would operate a mint as a subsidiary, which would purchase silver and pay in FTC Promissory Notes. In order to meet reserve requirements, pay outs of redeemed Promissory Notes would still be made in US coinage so as to maintain confidence in the value of the currency, but the mint would melt down the purchased silver and then produce Texas Dollar coins of the same content as the pre 1964 US coins. There would also be in copper a small half cent, large cent, and five cent piece. That coinage would be held in reserve until they were forced to announce the fact and circulate it, or circumstances allowed for circulation that would not shake confidence in their financial system. Due to the court case with the IRS and the defense to be used by the FTC, the implementation date for this program would be put off as long as possible.

In order to move the IRS issue toward resolution, the legal counsel for the Freedonia Transaction Company filed a motion to dismiss, claiming the Legal Tender Act precluded the IRS claim and that the question at issue had already been adjudicated by the Supreme Court. The Federal District Court scheduled a hearing on the motion.

There was one other need that was not being addressed sufficiently in the liberty movement. The intended move of Rampaging Elephants Radio to Freedonia would serve as the base for a plan. The Freedonia Broadcast Institute would strive to produce visual and sound only programming to support the Lone Star Party, Free Texas, and more liberty in general. The existing messaging by these organizations was being distorted by too much reliance on other media outlets to provide information to the people of Texas in their opinion.

It was the opinion of the LSP and the executive directors that the movement needed a tighter editorial focus and a more attractive mass market presentation to gain audience. Most of the programs to date were in the talk radio format. That meant the listeners tended to be those who liked the hosts personality, and whatever the host selected for program content. There needed to be a news format that would attract audience share from other media and entertainment outlets.

This was the central problem of modern mass communications. There were any number of information outlets, and most of the audience was concentrated in some half dozen visual channels and a few dozen radio networks. Ideally, the top programming produced would enter one of those media content bundling channels, and the alternate channels run by the Freedonia Broadcast Institute would at least break even if not make a profit by providing an editorial focus that could win a market share.

That last point was crucial in the minds of those who had founded Freedonia. The businesses located there were profitable. Without that profit, the whole project would not have been viable. The challenge to get the whole project underway in the first place had been the ability to convince businessmen that there was an opportunity to create profitable enterprises in a no regulation environment. Once that hurdle had been overcome, the rest was merely the willingness of the population to literally pull a trigger to defend it.

That had led to the current political situation in Texas to where the central issue in Texas politics was the relationship between the state and federal governments. Or stated differently, does the US Constitution matter anymore? That led to the next logical question of how the Constitution is to be enforced. The Freedonia answer is that everyone everywhere was responsible for that enforcement. Every where the founders had put government in place, there was always an alternate means to protect the rights of the people. The idea that only the Supreme Court could determine what the Constitution permitted or did not permit was expressly rejected by the founders via the Kentucky and Virginia resolutions.

The situation in Texas also had one other difference from many other locations in the United States. Muslim terrorist activity in Texas and a few other western states, where a counter reaction by the population had been provoked, was almost non existent. In other states that were governed by those practicing tolerance toward the supposed religion of peace, periodic violence continued. Refusal to acknowledge that fact was a contributing factor to the victory of the Republican candidate for President. If the government couldn't recognize enemies of the United States, much of the citizenry could do so.

Likewise, a solution to illegal alien deportation was needed. Action had started in Texas to move the illegal aliens to sanctuary cities surreptitiously. The plan was to give the advocates of such policies the logical implication of what they had advocated for others. The plan had been debated in the Texas Military Forces. Some thought it immoral to subject fellow citizens to the risk that such a population posed. But the argument that those who voted for a policy deserved the consequences of their choices, won the day. It was the only way those advocates were likely to learn from their choices.

The Borden County Militia benefited from these actions, so that the personnel could return home from guard duties, which were now being rotated among other units. It was hoped that within a year, the population of Texas would consist only of those legally entitled to live in the state.

Jim Roberts approved the creation of an Information Operations section supporting the Borden County Militia. This team would work with the Freedonia Broadcast Institute to create an image of the movement to be distributed on social media to influence public opinion. The tasking for one team was to get the message of the Lone Star Party and Free Texas spread to places where likely sympathizers could be found. The goal was to increase membership and strengthen both organizations. And there was another and more secret team. This team had the mission of masquerading as leftists, infiltrate leftist social media to obtain information and plant disinformation that would benefit the Texas liberty movement at the appropriate time.

The stage had been set for an exciting special and regular session of the Texas legislature. While most of the country was waiting to see what the new President would do, Texas was going to see what would come from the politicians in Austin.

Chapter 12

Here Be Dragons

TROOPS WOULD NEVER BE DEFICIENT IN COURAGE, IF THEY COULD ONLY KNOW HOW DEFICIENT IN IT THEIR ENEMIES WERE. – ARTHUR WELLESEY DUKE OF WELLINGTON

In 2015, the Central Committee of the Communist Party of China restructured the Peoples' Liberation Army. A fifth branch was created, the Strategic Support Force, to be responsible for logistical support as a public mission and cyber warfare as a non public mission. The reorganization was the result of adopting a new national military strategy outlined in the publication of "Unrestricted Warfare" in which the Peoples' Republic of China adopted as the operational model for conflict.

Future conflicts were not only to be waged by armed struggle using conventional and rocket forces, but all means of utilizing national power could be employed against an enemy. This power included economic damage to an opponent, and exploiting information systems vulnerabilities. These actions were to be decided and coordinated at the highest levels.

Every opportunity was used to exploit weaknesses in the United States. The United States was deindustrialized and its production capability moved to mainland China whenever possible. Then, the sales of Chinese produced goods produced revenue that allowed for the purchase of US Government debt. The process had been amazingly easy, as US businessmen and government officials only looked on a short term horizon of one to four years in making decisions, and the Chinese considered 10 years out to be short term planning.

Other US business outsourcing activity provided additional exploitable opportunities. Not only manufacturing of hard goods, but software production, technical support, importing engineers and software developers, all provided cover for the Strategic Support Force to plant agents capable of stealing valuable research and engineering information. This saved the PRC companies billions in costs they did not have to bear and resulted in usable technologies and products that could undercut the prices of their western competitors for the same item or capability.

Information systems were another strategic area to be exploited by the Strategic Support Force. As with manufacturing, US business practices made it even easier for the People's Liberation Army to target a future opponent on the world stage. Much of the software code writing was outsourced to companies based outside of the United States, and when possible, even technical support was outsourced as well. Business executives became convinced that almost any technical problem could be solved by an English speaking person with the most basic education, reading a script, with a telephone and remote access to the supported system.

Each of these factors provided opportunity for the PLA to gain access into foreign information systems. Once inside the targeted computer environment, data could be copied back to China for analysis and spy software planted to enable continued access to targeted systems. It was also possible to plant software that could be activated in the future to perform actions such as destruction of data, open network connections for security bypass, and other effects. Over a number of years, almost every data center had been hit and data had been stolen. Such hits were not limited to private enterprise, but included the US Government, which had the information pertaining to every security clearance granted in the last 20 years stolen.

The Peoples' Republic of China was well positioned to cripple large numbers of information systems in the US and Europe at a time of its choosing. The election of a future President seen as hostile to the interests of the PRC created such an occasion. The Central Committee of the Chinese Communist Party met to evaluate the current world situation, the probable strategy of the US under a new President, and the actions China should take in response to these developments.

It was considered likely that US policy would become more aggressive in the Pacific. There would be a probable increase of support and aid to US allies in the region. Such actions on the part of the US and Japan in the South China Sea could lead to an unacceptable loss of "face". Thus, action should be taken to humiliate the US before the new President took office. Such events might lead the new President to realize the strength of the PRC and consider the weakness of his own position. This could lead to the new President having to recognize the dominance of the PRC in the Pacific region. The results of exploiting a temporary weakness in the US Dollar and Treasury Bonds had looked promising.

The decision was taken by the Central Committee for use of the Strategic Support Force to create disruption in the US technology sector, to be a warning to Europe and Japan, and provide assistance in a move to occupy bases in the South China Sea that would enforce territorial claims of the PRC. If necessary, the PRC would then use negotiation with the new President to create a new "normal" in the Pacific region.

Early Sunday morning, several data centers in the US noticed latency in Internet traffic. It was taking too long for data to transfer from place to place via the Internet. Remote clients were having difficulty accessing servers in the data centers for information. Some Network Operations Center personnel noticed more traffic to and from Asia than was usual. Some of the more curious engineers started to try to trace the origins of the traffic, which seemed to be using proxy machines in the United States.

At the top of the hour, servers started to crash. The situation was serious because they were hardware failures, and not limited to a single machine, but now most of the servers in the entire data center were failing. Unknown to each data center, the same sequence of events was occurring in other data centers across the United States. Data Centers started escalation procedures for outages, which consisted mainly of notifying managers and additional engineers. Or at least notifying the engineers who were local to the data centers, as the support staff in other countries was now unreachable, due to some problems also occurring with telecommunications.

The widespread hardware failures cause the first set of challenges, as there were few extra sets of servers just sitting around doing nothing. The trend toward virtual servers meant that less hardware was needed to perform more computing tasks and a number of notional computers servers now shared the same physical server hardware. If a task became unsustainable, the same hardware server was used to create another virtual instance of a running server that in reality was nothing more than a server software running on a machine running many such software notional servers simultaneously. Not only could another new server not be created, the backup copy of the data needed for a restoration was located on another set of now non functional hardware servers or storage devices.

Individuals getting on the Internet now found that they were unable to reach social media sites, or shop online. The support calls started, or at least for the support that was performed in the United States. Outages now spread to cell phone service, and the remaining bandwidth for data transmission was getting choked with the number of devises trying to work around service disruptions. By noon on Sunday, most of the data centers realized they were in the midst of a major event.

Then the power stations throughout the US went off line. By now, the US Government Computer Emergency Response Team had been made aware of events and concluded there was an Internet based attack on US infrastructure. It was necessary to disconnect electrical power plants from the grid to get them back online. First priority was to provide power to nuclear and government facilities. Business and consumer electrical needs would have to wait until a way could be found to communicate with the various meters and switches that communicated via transmissions over lines that were now suspected in either being intercepted, or the transmission protocols themselves had been breached.

It did not take long for the effects to be felt. Not being able to shop online, use social media, or email were only minor inconveniences compared to the electrical and data center outages. Most people in the United States were now without power, there being a few exceptions. Data centers and commercial enterprises frequently had generator backup which was now functioning. But the loss of the ability of corporations to use their information systems was being felt.

While airports had backup power, the ability for airlines to process reservations, issue boarding passes, and manage flight operations was dependent on now unavailable information systems. Scheduled flights had to be cancelled, and no new reservations or rebookings could be made. Air travel was effectively grounded just as it had been in September of 2001.

Those businesses that were able to open even with no power or under power provided by generators, were not capable of processing credit card transactions. Gas stations were dependent on power to operate gas pumps, so people could not refill vehicles. Phone systems, requiring computer software to route calls had limited outages. Those phone calls that were not dependent on computer software running at data centers had a chance of being completed. However, the number of calls being made by people trying to communicate with relatives or friends soon crashed the functioning phone networks.

As a rule, the only now functioning communications were broadcast radio and HAM radio operators. Commercial radio was reporting that electrical and computer outages were widespread across the United States. The cause of the outages was unknown and it was uncertain when power and computer systems would be restored. The Department of Homeland Security was advising everyone to remain home and shelter in place until further notice.

The events of the day were only a minor immediate concern in Freedonia. The water and power systems in Freedonia were operated by Freedonia Utilities, a department of the town of Freedonia. In fact, other than contracting out for streets to be built, operating the utilities was just about all that the town of Freedonia did. If not for the legal requirement by Texas to do so, there would not even be the mayor, two council members, and the Secretary. The main reason the town even existed, was to prevent the territory from being annexed by some other political entity. The town was financed by a 2% sales tax and the providing of utilities. Other political entities imposed a property tax, but not the town of Freedonia.

Providing utilities had been an economy of scale decision on the part of the original residents of Freedonia. Most of the residents were of the "prepper" mindset, so they wanted water and power independent of existing systems that would be vulnerable to disruption. The 100,000 gallon water tower had come in at just over $300,000 USD, or about $20,000 in TXD terms. The sales price in each of the 400 quarter acre lots had allocated $1000 USD for the Freedonia Utilities, which had provided the capital for water system construction. As money had come into the Freedonia Transaction Company, Freedonia had sold municipal bonds for the financing of construction of the water and power systems at tax free returns to investors. Freedonia bonds paid 2.5% interest. All in, water and sewer had cost Freedonia a good $1 million in USD. Power had been another adventure as bidders tended to follow government regulations, and another $2 million USD had gone into a 2MW power plant.

Although Freedonia had issued $250,000 TXD in 30 year bonds paying 2.5% interest, the project made economic sense. An individual family, trying to have independent well water, septic system, and solar power could easily spent $30,000 to achieve that degree of independence. Doing the job as a community had cut the cost to one third, and at one half Texas cent per kwh, Freedonia Utilities generated about $125,000 TXD in revenue per year once

150

the population had expanded to some 5000 people. For all practical purposes, the whole town of Freedonia was "off grid" by building a grid of its own without a single smart meter. All Freedonia Utilities cared about was how much electricity and water you bought. What you did with that electricity and water was your business, not theirs.

Except for not being able to access Internet sites, loss of TV and radio stations, and some individual computer services such as email, the loss of electricity around the rest of the country was merely an object of curiosity in Freedonia. There was certainly some interest as to the cause of the outage, as the community was well aware of the implications of such an event. It being a Sunday, the Green Dragon had attracted a crowd for lunch. The crowd had grown larger than normal, due to the lack of external entertainment from television, and there were no more tables to be had at the tavern. When the crowds got this big, the people who didn't have seats, would order at the bar, wait around for the order to be prepared, and then take the food and drink outside on the sidewalk or into the town square. When done, the dishes and glasses were returned to the bar.

Such doings would have greatly annoyed the Texas Alcoholic Beverage Commission had any of its agents dared to visit Freedonia and the Green Dragon. That such a visit had never taken place showed unusually good judgment on the part of the TABC. Word might have already gone around Austin that trying to enforce a state regulation not approved of by Freedonians tended to result in one or more government agents establishing residence at the county jail. It was embarrassing to call your boss with news of your arrest while doing what you thought was your job. The other reason that the TABC may never have visited, is that the Green Dragon had never applied for a permit to sell the beer and wine that was being carried around the town square by armed individuals in violation of several other TABC regulations.

Jim and Lise Roberts, along with Ed and Sarah McMasters and some of the McMasters family occupied a table at the Green Dragon. The discussion was unsurprisingly about the loss of power and information systems across the rest of the United States. Nobody thought it was a spontaneous event. Sarah McMasters asked Jim what he thought was happening and who was responsible.

Jim's reply, "As of now I'm guessing it is an economic attack designed to try to somewhat cripple the US economy. The goal would be to either make us less able to compete economically against an adversary, or inhibit our ability to respond to the attacker's actions somewhere else in the world. It will take more information to determine who is behind it and why. We just can't know yet."

Sarah was interested to know what Roberts thought would happen next. "Jim, what can we expect to happen next? Will it be the EMP?"

Roberts noted that Sarah, like many in the "prepper" movement were focused on Electro Magnetic Pulse effect, which needed a nuclear weapon of about a one megaton warhead size detonated about 100 miles above the Earth's surface to generate an electrical shock wave that would probably fry a number of transformers and electrical components in a 1000 mile radius from the explosion. "Sarah, I'd expect they are going to make an assessment of how successful their actions so far have been. Then they will probably try to interfere with our recovery attempts to prolong the effect. The challenge will be how well our side can bring power back

152

online, and deliver power to people who are now cut off. Restoring computer systems will be needed to prevent further loss of business capability or even try to operate certain businesses at all."

Sarah wanted still more information. "When do you think they will do the EMP?"

Jim replied, "I'm not sure there will be one."

Sarah persisted "But ..."

Roberts interrupted her, "But there has to be one? Why? We shouldn't impose our expectations or operational template on an opponent. A good bit of the country is fairly well crippled at the moment."

"They are going to want to take out our electrical grid and set us back 100 years." was Teresa's response.

Roberts decided to conduct the strategy lecture. "The concept is called non attributional warfare. You conduct offensive action against an opponent who can't be 100% certain as to who is responsible for the act, and it gives the attacker a veil of deniability. We will eventually come to a reasonable conclusion as to who did this, but it will come down to our accusation on our part, which will be denied. As to the EMP, popping nukes leaves a really good indicator as to who is responsible. Not just anyone can perform a successful EMP strike. In theory a non government group of computer nerds could have pulled this stunt. In terms of effectiveness, that main difference in what we now have and an EMP strike is time to repair. In theory, the current damage is reversible to a large degree if it can be repaired swiftly enough. In the far out realm of possibilities, you might not destroy an electrical grid that you intend to use yourself."

The last point got to Sarah. "Do you think that somebody might invade us? Who?"

Roberts said, "My assessment is nobody has the capability to successfully invade us, but as I said before, I'm not going to impose my operational template on an opponent."

Now Ed got into the conversation. "Jim, I have a son and his family in Mississippi. I think we need to go get them, and bring them here."

At this juncture, Roberts interceded. "Ed, you can't go. If it comes to that, we will send a team, and Sarah can go with them. It is a minimum of two days travel each way, and we can't let a Free Texas Executive Director incur that amount of personal risk. You are too important to what is happening here." Jim didn't want to rebuke a friend like that, but the facts were that if the country was possibly going to go a bit sideways, rescue attempts needed to be done, if at all, by people with some real deal military experience.

McMasters wasn't going to argue with Roberts, but Ed was disappointed to hear Roberts say what he did. "Jim, you know I'm in this for my descendents. If they don't get any benefit from it, that will really hurt me."

Roberts tried to reassure McMasters, "Ed we need the leaders to lead and manage the effort. We have plenty of guys with rifles willing to rescue the family of someone important to us."

"They have to move to Freedonia. They should have already done so." Ed decided.

154

"OK, Ed. I'll start planning on how we are going to get them here and who we should ask to go on the mission. For the same reasons you can't go, neither can I if that helps." Roberts said to his friend.

Chapter 13

SOS

ROMAN CIVILIZATION FELL DUE TO THE LOSS OF THE WILL TO CONQUER; SATISFACTION WITH THE 'STATUS QUO'; AND HIGH TAXES, WHICH DESTROYED TRADE AND PRIVATE ENTERPRISE. THESE CONDITIONS EVENTUALLY FORCED PEOPLE OUT OF THE CITIES. THE CYCLE IS RETURNING. – GEN GEORGE S. PATTON, JR.

While the attack on the Internet connected networks, government and business computer infrastructure, and data centers located in the US was being fought, the consequences of those attacks in reality in addition to cyberspace were very real. By early Sunday afternoon, the staff at the Freedonia Technology Company had gathered enough information to make a preliminary assessment of the nature of the attack. One of the computer user IDs used for remote access into the Freedonia Technology Company's data center had planted software that had tried to connect to a computer system in the Peoples' Republic of China. Firewall rules in place at the Fredonia Technology Company had prevented the connection from taking place.

Analysis of the planted software found it was a script designed to run on any machine using Adobe Flash Player. The code would allow for capturing ID information from the infected computer and installation of additional software from a remote computer. If a data center allowed unrestricted outbound access for machines, and there were other versions of this software written for Javascript, Active X, and Silverlight, a data center could have any or all of its computers compromised. Depending on how long the code had been in place, and if all backups were stored on computer hardware, and not removable media, it would be very difficult to restore clean uninfected data.

The Freedonia Technology Company had avoided serious damage by having all remote access to one server in an isolated security zone and firewall rules designed to generally prohibit or restrict connections to and from computers outside of the United States. The remote access server had been shutdown, and only inbound web browser, email, and Lotus Notes connections from outside of the local area network of the Freedonia Technology Company were being allowed. The remote access server was shut down, and was being further analyzed to gather additional information.

These findings were reported to Roberts, who then shared his assessment with the Free Texas Directors. Roberts asked the staff at the Freedonia Technology Company if they could set up an isolated area to let the compromised remote access server to run for the purpose of trying to identify what was happening in the other centers around the United States, with the goal of attempting to learn what software was being planted, what that software did, and then see about how to negate its effects.

Roberts than notified his established Personal Security Detail of a probable mission, and then called Ed McMasters. "Ed, I think we have the preparations made to get your family out of Mississippi. I'm going to guess that this won't be resolved in the next 24 hours. Do you have any way to reach them that is still working?"

"No I don't. Maybe the text or email will get through at some time." replied Ed.

Roberts wasn't surprised by that answer. "Sarah will need to go, so there is someone with them that they will recognize and trust when they show up. I'll call back when they are ready to go."

Planning was well underway for the trip to Mississippi. The main constraint was gasoline. If electrical outages continued across the area to be traveled, there would be no way for filling stations to pump gas, except by generator. For that reason, and considering that any functioning filling station would be barren by now, they would need to carry all of the fuel they might need with them. That meant using a pickup in addition to two SUVs. And that meant 50% more fuel had to be carried for the additional vehicle. A six man security detail was going on the trip, and that was the absolute minimum. It was a two day trip from Freedonia, and Roberts did not want them to stop at a motel on the way, or spend too much time stationary in one location.

That was going to tire out the security team. There could be rest once they arrived at the destination, but the vehicles and fuel would have to be guarded. If you were going to have someone awake on guard, the group might as well be moving. All of those difficulties across the country also meant that there should not be much traffic encountered, except in towns. That was going to be a hard five days, and Roberts started to think about the possible need to rescue the rescue force. At least they would be equipped with HAM radios, and one of the detail members being sent on the mission was a General class HAM operator. That would allow them to transmit and receive on frequencies better suited to long range transmission. Not that Roberts expected the FCC to be worried about unlicensed amateur radio operators under the current circumstances.

Meanwhile, the staff at the Freedonia Technology Company were working to try and document what was used to conduct the attack on the computers, and how that attack operated. The compromised server gave the first clues. The malware used the Windows updating service to contact a computer in the Peoples Republic of China, which then installed another software than ran a control that launched Internet Explorer in order to run an Active X control. The control was used to wipe data off the hard drive of the server and shut the server down. The server would not start when turned on.

This gave the technologists a start point which seemed to replicate what was happening elsewhere. If they had been successful in capturing a copy of the downloaded code, they might be able to start to unravel the mystery of why efforts underway to restore service were not successful. One team went to work to analyze the malicious code, while another tried to bring the remote access server back to life. To some degree the server team had the easier task, as if enough parts are replaced, an operating computer is the end result.

Once the main board, which contained the main processors was replaced, the computer would power on. However, the hard drives did not work, and they had to be replaced as well in order to have a functioning hardware server. The Freedonia Technology Company, like most other data centers only had limited amounts of spares. If this happened again, there was now only enough spare parts to repair one more computer. A data center that had a substantial number of computers taken out of service, would not be able to come back online until sufficient spares could be procured. Work would continue by the technologists to see if the non working hardware could be repaired.

The results of this effort were communicated to the county officials, Free Texas Ddirectors, and the board of directors of the Freedonia Technology Company. There was considerable overlap among the three groups. Jim Roberts also had the most technical background of the group, based on his post Army experience in the IT sector. Roberts was asked what he made of the information obtained up to now.

Roberts made his assessment, "I'm thinking out loud, and my preliminary guess is that we are likely dealing with widespread hardware damage, which is why server related technology is still unavailable this many hours after the initial events. Available hardware will probably be used to get the data centers themselves functioning, and then Internet related infrastructure such as functioning DNS servers. Any hardware left over from that will go to try to bring back online the most important customers.

That takes us through the next 12 to 24 hours. That 24 hours is critical because the disruption is sure to hit transportation and other logistics companies. The ability to place orders, pull orders to create a logistical load for train, truck, and more importantly emergency air shipment, if not air travel itself, is heavily dependent on technology. By tomorrow afternoon, shipments are going to be delayed or cancelled, until some workaround is put in place. Just for planning purposes, let's say that takes the rest of the week to figure out what organizational tasks IS systems were currently doing.

Just in Time inventory management is now going to break on everything, from computer parts to groceries. Truth be told, that is

160

why airline flights resumed and ports had to be reopened in September 2001 before the desired security measures were put in place. In cities and towns, grocery stores may run out of stock starting Wednesday. That is the day that the electrical grid has to come back, or data centers and commercial buildings will run out of generator power, and everything drops out again.

So, that tells us where the first priority will be out there. Whatever computers and related software that manages the electrical grid has to be sorted out and soon. Some larger companies will have disaster recovery plans, and if they can avoid the malicious software getting into the standby infrastructure they could come back quicker depending on ability to recover data. That is the wild card at the moment, if they had backups sitting on hardware that got destroyed, and that is typical these days due to lower cost, then the standby infrastructure may not have all of the data needed to resume operations without disruptions.

Summary is that the nuts and bolts that make a good deal of modern life possible have come undone. Wildly optimistic scenario is a week of doing without, it is probably a good 30 days, and maybe longer depending on how much computer hardware has been made inoperable, because that may rely on production and shipment of which a good percentage of that takes place outside of the United States."

Ed McMasters asked "Is there any good news?"

Roberts said "It depends on your perspective. The team to get your family out of Mississippi should be ready to go, and we should send them now. The Freedonia Technology Company is fully operational, so anything internal still works, and has a caching DNS servers, so many web sites still online can be found. We have not heard of any similar outage in Europe, so there is the possibility some of the load can be picked up from there. Our power generating plant is online, so Freedonia Utilities is not affected. The disaster could be good for local business."

Ted Greenlow added "I would not want to still be living in the Dallas area after all of this in the past 90 days."

Ed McMasters replied "That is just one of many reasons why we are here. Jim, as soon as Sarah is ready to go, can the team head out to Mississippi?"

Jim said "By Wednesday sundown, they need to be on the way back. Life could be really exciting by then if things go bad."

Sunday evening began the influx of people who had decided not to wait for the situation to correct itself. Many of the arrivals had crazy relatives who lived in Freedonia. Somehow, those relatives living in Freedonia didn't seem that crazy anymore. At the Green Dragon Tavern, there were no more rooms at the inn – it was full. The next step would be to have the militia put up tent city in the town square.

Rampaging Elephants and the Fredonia Broadcast Institute were still on the air. The reports from around Texas and the rest of the United States were a contrast with the continuity of life in Freedonia. That coverage may have been the spark for those who could make the trip to Freedonia to do so. Freedonia was in the farm and ranch country of Texas, so the food stocks that would have been sold for shipment elsewhere happened to be on hand to feed the extra mouths in the county or on the way.

Late on that Sunday evening, HAM radio operators were passing along the first stories of looting in major urban centers. Grocery and liquor stores were reportedly being raided. Unknown was if the actions were a pre-emptive strike by those not going to chance hunger, or the frustration of those who found their electronic benefits cards were no longer working. By Monday morning, the conservative media outlets still broadcasting, were picking up on the story.

Monday morning also started the first reposts from the leftist oriented press concerning these events. Right wing extremist militias were suspected of attacking the electrical grid and the Department of Homeland Security was investigating. When those reports made their way to Freedonia, they were laughed off as being totally out of touch with reality.

Jim Roberts was quick to point out the seriousness of the accusation. It was sure to make the situation more volatile and the looting would proceed to riot. And then there would be targets selected for retaliation. If those selected targets were approved of by the federal government, there was going to be a great deal of misery in possibly every major city in the United States.

Roberts suggested that if you had relatives that you liked, getting them to Freedonia would be a good move. Unfortunately, the convenience store in Freedonia had pumped its last gallon of gas awaiting shipment of a new supply. Freedonia was not totally insulated from reality. If only there had been the time and resources to build a small refinery. That was a 100 year old technology, so it couldn't be that difficult to do.

As of Monday evening, a rumor was being circulated on the leftist media that utility companies were intentionally lagging in restoring power in order to get regulatory approval of higher rates and suspension of EPA regulations. Freedonians weren't able to pin down the source of the rumor, but the law of unintended consequences soon kicked in. The rioters started to target some utility infrastructure, including a few power substations. Some neighborhoods were now going to be without electricity for weeks at a minimum.

As Jim Roberts remarked, "You don't have to destroy a country when you can get the country to destroy itself."

Tuesday morning there was a message for Roberts from the security detail. They had crossed the Mississippi River at first light, and expected to arrive at the destination toward the end of the day. The news was relayed to Ed McMasters.

Meanwhile, the technologists at the Freedonia Technology Company had been busy with software code analysis. They had found something that was well planned and deliberate. The software code was very unlikely to have been created and put in place by someone just out to get a vicarious thrill from causing haphazard damage. The malware on the remote access server served three functions (A) To poll an IP address in the Peoples Republic of China at 4 in the morning Greenwich Mean Time and check for another program there, and if present to launch a web browser with an executable plug in to run that software (B) capture admin IDs in use on a windows network, and transmit that information as part of the polling contact, and (C) replicate itself on any other computer that would accept the security ID of the ID currently being operated.

It was the software that had been downloaded from China and executed that caused the real problems. That code tried to wipe the hard drive of the machine where it was being run and overwrite the file allocation table to make data recovery more difficult, and with the next set of instructions which tried to identify the hard drive on the machine and its processors for the purpose of disabling their ability to operate, effectively killed the machine.

This was evidence of a deliberate effort to gain unauthorized access to computers and destroy the data on them, while rendering the machines themselves inoperable. This was effective cyber warfare. Any remote access to a computing environment entailed risk. The adage in the security field was – if you can get in, so can anyone else. When your business model relied on your customers having remote access to their servers, there was an enormous amount of risk.

The Freedonia Technology Company was spared the disaster because it discouraged remote access to servers. If absolutely necessary to have remote access, a security token architecture ensured that only the person authorized who had the token on the connecting computer could get in. As demonstrated in the cease of the compromised remote access server, not even this was foolproof, as an authorized machine could be infected with a computer virus which could be transmitted to the remote access server.

What had spared the Freedonia Technology Company from disaster was the next step. The remote access server was separated from the rest of the computing environment so that there was no direct connection possible from outside the Freedonia Technoogy Company to a server in its data .center. A separate user ID was required inside the data center environment, so that the remote access server could not share uninspected data directly with the rest of the data center. The security design had met the challenge this time. The external and internal firewalls had contained the damage.

That settled the issue in the minds of Jim Roberts and the others. The Peoples' Republic of China had deliberately crippled the computer and by extension, the electrical infrastructure of the United States. But the question remained, why was it done, and why now. The timing made sense in terms of demonstrating power to the new President. But, demonstrating that power was at cross purposes with an attack mode that was designed to be deniable by the government who conducted it. What else that was happening around the world was an unknown to the Freedonians.

The next report came in from the security detail. Ed's family was safe and they would try to cross the Mississippi heading west before nightfall tomorrow. Jim Roberts and Ed McMasters would feel much better about the situation once they were safely across the Mississippi River. If they got into difficulty on the east side of the river, there was no realistic way they could help. There was additional support available in Freedonia, but gasoline was limited, and given the situation, a three vehicle convoy was out of the ordinary in the current circumstances. More vehicles and people would attract too much attention – it would be assumed there was something valuable there in that convoy which was worth stealing.

News from Europe and Asia gave insight into the reason for the cyber attack on the United States. The Peoples Liberation Army had landed on and occupied the Senkaku Islands and were in the process of fortifying them. The Peoples' Republic had claimed the islands as Chinese territory, Japan claimed the islands as Japanese territory. The International Court and the United States recognized the islands as Japanese. Japan considered this action an invasion of Japan, and the Japanese Self Defense Force was being mobilized.

To the extent the United States was paying attention to anything happening elsewhere in the world, there was no reaction from Washington. The Japanese were reminding the US Government that it had treaty obligations to defend Japan and Japanese territory. As the President was just a few weeks away from leaving office, and had a domestic crisis on his hands, he had no interest in the United States being a participant in another war. The President Elect was in favor of a more forceful response.

The picture was now clear. A United States focused on an internal domestic crisis might be too paralyzed to respond to the Peoples' Republic of China expanding its power in Asia. The Japanese and the US would either be embarrassed, and shown to be weak, or they would have to engage in conflict with the Peoples Liberation Army, Navy, and Air Force in a remote location that few would westerners would think of as a strategic interest to either opponent. All other Asian countries would realize the United States was no longer a Pacific power. The Peoples' Republic of China was now a world power, and all in Asia and the rest of the world were now on notice of the fact.

The whole story was incredulous to Ted Greenlow. "Why have I never heard of the Senkaku Islands?"

Roberts replied, "No real reason, unless you are a student of recent Asian history. They were Chinese territory until the Sino – Japanese War of the late 1800s. The treaty ending that war meant they became Japanese. The Chinese want the islands back. Most of recent Asian conflict is an attempt to erase Japanese gains from those turn of the 19th century wars."

Ted asked "Do you know what the people living there want? How do they feel about being part of one country or another?"

Roberts reply shocked Ted. "The islands are uninhabited."

Greenlow was still in disbelief. "We could have a world war over an uninhabited pile of rocks in the middle of nowhere?"

Roberts replied in a very even tone. "When there is going to be a war, any excuse will do."

Within 24 hours the security detail had returned with Ed's family members. Power was in the process of being restored across much of the country in places where rioting had not destroyed transformers. Shipments of goods were still somewhat disrupted, but whatever was now being done manually was starting to take effect. With some social media sites now being hosted in Europe, even with loss of data and a different look to the sites, selfies could again be posted on Facebook. Half the US population seemed to whine that the government needed to do more to help sooner, and the other half thought the government was to blame for the mess in the first place.

Chapter 14

Blood in the Streets

A LEADER IS A DEALER IN HOPE. – NAPOLEON BONAPARTE

In deciding what it perceived to be threats to the United States, the US Government's choice of targets had become increasingly bizarre. It acted as if there was no threat anywhere outside of the borders on the United States. For years, the focus had been on domestic groups who believed in a government of limited power or groups who believed in an armed citizenry were the primary threat to the United States. Government officials had confused threats to their power to be threats to the United States. Any perceived threat to unlimited government power was to be negated. Among such groups were those centered around Freedonia.

After the Supreme Court victory over Texas, several sealed indictments against those who led those efforts that were embarrassing to the US Government were obtained. That had happened in Washington, DC because grand juries based in Texas had refused to indict. That was only a minor irritation for the Department of Justice to get the indictments returned elsewhere.

Based on past experience, attempting to make arrests in Freedonia was considered impractical. In fact, history had shown that it had gone the other way with the federal agents sitting in the Borden County jail by the end of the day they had arrived in Freedonia. By listening in on phone conversations and trying to intercept email, the FBI hoped to learn when the targeted criminals would be away from Freedonia.

As an extra precaution, the arrests would not be made by agents, but by security contractors. In the opinion of the FBI hierarchy it was considered likely there would be a firefight, and employing ex military people for the task would provide skills that the agents did not have. Unexpressed by the supervisors in the FBI was the belief that there would be losses on both sides, and they would rather not have to deal with the consequences of one or more dead agents. Nobody would care what happened to the contractors for more than five minutes of a news cycle and the ability to add murder charges to the rest of the accusations to be made against the suspects would be a plus.

The crisis had been good for business in Freedonia. Rampaging Elephants and the Freedonia Broadcast Institute had not missed a single program and had been able to cover the events using all of their normal resources. Both media outlets gained audience as a result. The Freedonia Technology Company had come through unscathed, and some businesses that thought having their data in a more secure computing environment found the idea of employing a company that had successfully come through this incident care for their systems to be desirable.

There was a voice mail on Roberts' phone after he returned from lunch. The Governor and the Military Affairs Committee of both houses of the Legislature intended to revise the statutes relating to the State Guard and Militia. Roberts and others were invited to come to Austin for a working session with the committees and Adjutant General's Department. A reply was requested.

Roberts phoned in and said that he would attend. He was given the meeting date and location. Roberts said that he appreciated the opportunity to provide the lessons learned from his experience. He was also told that the assessment in Austin was that given the number and scale of the incidents so far, the conclusion was made in Austin that a more robust militia and State Guard capability was required to keep Texas secure and to prepare recommendations accordingly.

He was told that those in Austin were looking forward to seeing him. The FBI agent listening in on the conversation was sure that some of his superiors would be looking forward to Jim Roberts' trip to Austin as well. The FBI contractors were notified of the projected date of Roberts' trip to Austin. They started to plan for the intercept, considering possible routes, and intercept points on each of those routes for a team to be positioned to make the arrest.

Roberts met with his Personal Security Detail to let them know that the next trip to Austin was going to take place. They started to plan the route – it would be a different route than the one Roberts took the last time. The group would take two vehicles and seven members of the security detail would accompany Roberts. As this was an official meeting with the state, they would travel in uniform as members of the Borden County Militia.

As the meeting started at 9 AM, Roberts and his escort would leave from Freedonia the previous day. They left Freedonia shortly before 10 in the morning, and as they left town, all of the mobile phones were switched off. There would be no further planned communications until the group reached Austin.

When Roberts turned off his cell phone, that was all confirmation the FBI needed that Roberts and possibly others who had also turned off their phones were on their way to Austin. Roberts did not use a smart phone, just an older generation GSM phone, so about all the FBI could do was plot his location when the phone was on and listen to his conversations. None of the backdoors from smart phones and the apps loaded on the phone were available to the FBI.

If the previous attempt to capture Roberts and his fellow rebels had failed due to FBI overconfidence, this time the FBI was taking no chances. Aerial surveillance was in place to try to identify the vehicle in which he was traveling. It was not difficult to pick up the two SUVs leaving Freedonia, and heading south out of Borden County. The intercept points were closer to Austin, as the FBI did not know what route Roberts intended to take, but they did know the destination and a time window of when he was likely to get there. Too close observation until Roberts and his gang got closer to Austin might be detected, so there was no need to keep the vehicles under constant observation until later.

Roberts and his crew had been watching to see if they were being followed, and their opinion was that so far, they were alone. That belief persisted through lunch, They were back on the road by one in the afternoon. There had not been much traffic at all on the route, and that was one of the reasons why that route was selected. Anything unusual would be obvious. For twenty minutes, they had seen the only two vehicles on the road when they saw a motorcycle rider approaching them from the other direction. The rider waved at the vehicles.

Roberts' driver wondered aloud "Why do you think he waved at us."

"Noticing things like that is why you are on my security detail Phil." Was Roberts reply. A few minutes later, he said "Phil, there is a picnic area ahead on the right. Let's take a stop there and stretch our legs."

Phil answered, "OK sir." but remarked to himself that was out of place for Roberts. On every other trip, Roberts was only interested in stopping for gas, food, or sleep. After a couple of miles, the picnic area sign was visible, and Phil turned on the right blinker, so the chase vehicle would know they were going to pull off the road.

"Phil, pull up to the last covered table." said Roberts while reaching for his stack of maps that he was carrying with him.

Phil did as instructed and both SUVs were alone in the picnic area. Everyone got out and followed Roberts to the table. Roberts set down the maps and his Coke can on the table. A couple of the guys took seats at the table with their drinks while the remainder stood nearby or made a quick scan of the area. Roberts was feeling around under the table and soon produced an envelope. He opened the envelope and studied its contents. Now all seven members of the security detail were now under the roof covering the picnic table.

Roberts sorted through his stack of maps, and pulled one of the maps out of the stack. The security detail saw that is was a military 1 to 50,000 scale map and the map was of an area some miles ahead on their route. Roberts then let them in on the secret. "Gentlemen, there is a roadblock set up here." Roberts pointed to the position on the map. "I am informed some dozen armed people are the reception committee. It looks to be set up so that this hill hides them from observation by us until we get around this bend in the road. We will use that to our advantage because it also hides

173

us. The first vehicle will stop just as we make the turn and observe the roadblock. We'll then un ass the SUV and lay down the base of fire to keep the reception committee fixed in place. The chase SUV will stop behind the hill here, where they can't observe you while you work your way north and then hit them in their right flank and roll them up. Got it?"

Phil asked "Why get ambushed? Couldn't we just drive around it?"

Roberts replied "Fair question. Here is why we are going into it. First, we are fortunate that our spy network has provided us with this information. If we avoid this ambush, there will be another one on another trip we take and we may find that out the hard way. Which leads to the second reason, that if we avoid this ambush they will assume it was compromised, we found out about it and start looking for the source of the leak. I want to protect our source. Third, the reason there are only about a dozen there is they have other routes blocked in case we go another way, by defeating this ambush, we break through their defense line and can probably make it to Austin. Fourth, another failed operation where we emerge victorious enhances our reputation and makes the feds look bad again. That is very much to our political advantage."

"Jim, I get your point, but you should be with the assault force and not with the bait. You are the probable target more so than us." Phil suggested.

Roberts had the final word. "I have to assume that there is a drone up there now keeping us under observation. We can't do anything that may cause them to suspect we have advance warning. We all have to get back in the vehicles in the same places we got out before taking this rest break to make a final look at our planned route. When we do just as they expect, they won't know something

174

has gone wrong with their plan until the first vehicle stops too soon, and we bail out weapons ready. By then action will be under way, and they won't have time to think about where is that other vehicle."

All eight men got back into the two SUVs and the vehicles returned to the road, heading southeast toward Austin and their destiny. While on the way, everybody stripped their kits down to just weapons and ammunition. Nothing else was going to be needed until after the shooting stopped. At least with the advance warning there was an opportunity to put earplugs in. That was going to help tremendously.

They were now at the critical spot where the road ran mostly south with the hill on their left and were approaching the left turn that would bring them into the kill zone of the ambush. The trail SUV had slowed to increase the distance between the two vehicles and remain at the point where it would stop and the four team members would get out and on the ground.

Phil took the turn slowly and as they were facing east, they saw the vehicles blocking the road 300 meters in front of them. Phil punched the accelerator like he was going to speed up and pull up to the checkpoint, when he swerved to the right just off the road and stopped. All four doors of the SUV were already open by the time the vehicle stopped with the engine block of the SUV positioned to put it between the mass of the roadblock and Jim Roberts. Meanwhile Roberts and the rear passenger were out of the SUV and into the ditch on the right of the road. The man to his rear had immediately moved ahead of Roberts in the ditch.

Phil and the rear driver side passenger had exited and were trying to get to the rear of the SUV when the firefight started. Just has Phil had made it to the rear of the SUV, he went down.

"Phil's been hit!" shouted the man who had been riding behind Phil. Roberts moved back to assist him in dragging Phil to the ditch and hopefully better cover. Fortunately the SUV would help hide them as they crawled over to Phil. He had been shot in the right shoulder which was serious but probably not life threatening. They had Phil in the ditch, and Roberts was almost in the ditch himself when he felt a hot sting a bit below his left knee.

As he slid into the ditch, Roberts said "I've been hit, too. I'll take care of Phil. Go back up forward and keep that sniper busy. It seems the quality of our opposition has improved since last time."

The first aid kit meant one more trip out of the ditch to the SUV, but the two other men on the team were now putting out covering fire. The hop to and back from the SUV wasn't too bad which meant probably no serious breaks in the lower leg bones. The throbbing was really uncomfortable because Roberts couldn't elevate the wound above his heart.

The sniper had been pleased with his work. His first shot had been rushed when the driver had done the unexpected, but he had still put the driver down and the driver wasn't going anywhere. His next shot had not been a clean shot because the target was making good use of the SUV to conceal his movement. But he had just now had a round come back at him uncomfortably close. It might have been a lucky shot, but with the leaves falling off the trees, there was a chance his sniper hide was no longer working and he either had to move or take a chance that it was just a random shot. He didn't have a good target view from his current position anyway, so he decided to adjust his position. It was a fatal decision.

The two men on Roberts' team now providing the base of fire had not concerned themselves much with the men on the ground behind the vehicles constituting the roadblock. They did not have clear shots as long as they stayed behind the vehicles, and if they came forward, even at 300 meters, the shot would not be that difficult to make to take them down. The concentrated on possible sniper positions. After one shot at them, there was observed movement. The sniper had been found. For any trained soldier, 300 meters is not a difficult shot. The men had Trijicon scoped ARs which for all practical purposes were M16A4s.

Allowing for the possibility the sniper also had body armor, the aim point became the man's pelvis. The resulting scream and thud of the body hitting the ground cause several of the men manning the road block to turn around. The agents at the road block had little time to meditate on the singularity of this occurrence when they received another surprise. Unexpected gunfire was heard from the right of the road block position and four agents were down followed soon by a fifth. The remaining agents now realized that the second vehicle they had been expecting was missing and it was now accounted for. They were now outnumbered and caught in a cross fire.

It was soon over. Ten agents on the ground dead or dying, and two surrendered. The two who had surrendered were brought to Roberts. He addressed them. "FBI I assume?"

One of the men replied, "Yeah we work for the FBI."

Roberts didn't like the answer. "I have yet to meet a fed not quick to point out that he is a Special Agent. You guys are either Federal Agents or you aren't. Which is it? And you might as well cough up the ID now."

"We're FBI contractors." was the reply

"Contractors as in Private Military Company?" queried Roberts.

"Yep, we were hired to take you guys down."

Roberts was getting annoyed. "Then you know the custom among Soldiers of Fortune I presume?"

"You mean you think we are mercenaries?" asked the smarter of the two.

Roberts told him "Yes I do. You are not members of the military and not police personnel. You have been captured under arms while engaging members of the Texas Military Forces while on their official duties. Do I make myself clear?"

"But we're just contractors!"

Roberts told them their fate. "Due to the fact you just slightly shot me and I'm still alive, I'm feeling generous and you get a choice. You can have a bullet at the base of the skull, which I am told is the fastest and least painful way out, or through the heart, which will take a bit of time for you to bleed out, but your family can have an open casket funeral."

"Damn, Jim, that's cold blooded!" exclaimed Phil.

Roberts glared at Phil.

"Sorry sir, I mean is it really necessary?" Phil asked meekly.

"When you joined our band of merry men, the laws and customs of war were carefully explained to you and everyone else. This standard of conduct is taken seriously by all professional military organizations around the globe. There is also a mercenary tradition, which by the way is an honorable profession among those true professionals. They never allow themselves to be taken alive. That is part of the custom." explained Roberts.

"But do we have to?" persisted Phil.

Roberts answered "You don't. This will send a message to the government that hired these men. Do your work yourself or face the consequences. Everybody else go get the vehicles ready and let's get out of here. Disable their vehicles, collect weapons and ammunition. I'll stay here with these two. Leave me some stuff to splint up my knee."

The second SUV was brought over to the first. The first had sustained too much damage, so one of the functional road block vehicles was taken and loaded with the contents of the first SUV. While work was under way, the men heard two pistol shots in rapid succession, and Roberts hobbled over to them.

"We might as well crank up all of the gadgets now. The FBI must know we are here. We're going to divert to the nearest hospital. I'm concerned about Phil, I've got to get my knee elevated before I do an Albert Sidney Johnston at Shiloh, and I have lots of phone calls to make." ordered Roberts.

The nearest large sized medical facility appeared to be in Georgetown, so that became the destination. On the way, Roberts made phone calls. Freedonia was told of the incident and the militia battalion XO decided to send A Company to guard Roberts and the hospital, while the rest of the battalion would prepare to defend Borden County in case this was the first shot of a federal invasion of Texas. The General was notified of the incident and Roberts delayed arrival at the meeting. Media outlets in Freedonia were notified, and the first reports of the US Government invading Texas were soon circulating.

And then Jim called Lise. "We had some trouble and you are going to hear about it on the news."

Jim could hear the concern in Lise's voice. "What happened?"

"There was a small battle and I got a little bit shot." Was Jim's attempt to reassure her.

"You told me that you just go to meetings and talk on the radio." Lise was almost crying.

"Well I was on my way to a meeting when it happened. I have to go now, we are at the hospital." Was how Jim ended the conversation with his wife.

As the two vehicles arrived at the hospital, Fox News and Breitbart News were there. The reporters wanted to know what happened.

Roberts gave them a statement they were sure to carry. "Today the US Government engaged elements of the Texas Military Forces while engaged in duties serving Texas. As a result of this unprovoked attack, the US Government has one week to vacate Texas. And any agency of the US Government who remains, without proper authorization from Texas, will be forcibly evicted from Texas. I myself, was shot by personnel in the employ of the FBI and am now here for medical treatment. Thank you."

Roberts then went into the Emergency Room.

Roberts' phone rang. Although a doctor was working on his wound, he answered the call because it was the Governor on the phone. It very likely did not take long for his remarks to the press to reach the Governor. Undoubtedly, the Governor would have something to say.

Indeed, the Governor was irate. "You really exceeded your authority this time when you told the US Government it had one week to get out of Texas. Half the time I'm glad you are on my side, I think. The other half of the time, like now, I'd like to fire you. But, we both know that I can't do that. What were you thinking when you said that?"

Roberts knew that now the Governor was boxed in. "Sir, you have the opportunity to clarify the meaning of my remarks by dialing some of it back. You could clarify that the ultimatum does not apply to the Department of Defense, Veterans Affairs, the Border Patrol and Immigration and Customs Enforcement. I suspect you will have popular support in ridding Texas of the IRS, EPA, and every other regulatory agency."

The Governor was still annoyed. "I don't know how I'm going to get out of this. It reminds me of the first time I met you and you said I was going to be the last Governor of Texas. You're really trying to make that happen aren't you?"

Roberts replied "Sir if you remember the rest of that conversation, I also said you could be the next President of the Republic of Texas. Which way do you think events are going?"

"Roberts, I'd hate to think that you were after my job." The Governor was still miffed.

"You won't have to worry about that sir, the news reports will eventually come out that I summarily executed two mercenaries working for the FBI. That could cost me votes even in the Lone Star party."

The doctor said to Roberts "Not everybody takes a local and chats with the Governor while I'm working on them. You a skiier?"

"Why do you ask and how's the other guy doing?" Roberts responded.

"He'll end up OK, but I don't know how you managed to walk on that knee before you got shot. Your skiing days are over. You can go ahead and schedule the knee replacement." Was the doctor's conclusion.

"I don't think so. I have a meeting in Austin." was Roberts' conclusion.

Chapter 15

The Legislature Meets

GUARD WITH JEALOUS ATTENTION THE PUBLIC LIBERTY. SUSPECT EVERYONE WHO APPROACHES THAT JEWEL. UNFORTUNATELY, NOTHING WILL PRESERVE IT BUT DOWNRIGHT FORCE. WHENEVER YOU GIVE UP THAT FORCE, YOU ARE INEVITABLY RUINED. – PATRICK HENRY

The inability of the US Government to provide any internal security whatsoever against attacks both physical and virtual, had been the last straw for the Governor. Even worse, was the probability that the US Government by its actions had enabled those attacks was especially angering Texans. He called for a special session of the Texas Legislature. The special session was timed to start one month in advance of the regular session, so in reality the legislature was being called into session one month early and would be exempt from the usual time restrictions on how long it would take to pass legislation.

It was clear that the three major political parties in Texas would have differing agendas for the session. The Democrats would try to keep kicking the can down the road on almost every issue to be brought up. The Republicans would try to prevent any major changes in the relationship between the US Government and Texas unless approved by the new President. The Lone Star Party represented the Texans fed up with the US Government and its overwhelming incompetence to keep the United States safe and its citizens free from governmental tyranny.

Although the party with more seats in the legislature than any of the others, and all of the state wide offices, the Republicans were in a very difficult spot. A deal would have to be made to retain control of the House by reelecting the Speaker. A deal would have to be made to get the 20 votes needed to prevent a Senate filibuster. It was very likely that the Republicans would then be considered responsible for whatever results came out of the state government.

The objective of the Lone Star Party was simple. Make a deal for a referendum on Texas self determination. That choice of language was considered an easier sell than Texas independence or Texas secession. Whatever it was called, the result would be the same. The opportunity for Texas voters to say they had enough of the actions of the US Government, and Texas would go its own way.

The Democrats went into the session with the objective of keeping things as they were. Any changes would provide opportunities for either opponent to gain strength. Like at the national level, the party was a coalition of extreme leftists, and ethnic voting blocs intent on maintaining their influence in government and government largess for their constituents.

The first decision by the House, the choosing of the Speaker would set the tone of the entire session. The Speaker seeking reelection was a nominal Republican, who had support from the Democrats to keep the rest of the Republicans in line and prevented him from being replaced by more conservative Republicans. Continuing this strategy in the special session and following regular session, would now cause a problem. He could only get re-elected with support from Democrats and the vast majority of the Republicans, or with support of the Lone Star Party and a vast majority of Republicans. The question was how many Republicans would be willing to be seen as allies with another party on the first vote to be taken.

Some of the Republican office holders had survived challenges from the Lone Star Party, and there was more than one close call. Those Republicans would almost have to vote with the Lone Star party or face another and potentially better challenger in the next election. Some of the more moderate Republicans who had been somewhat friendly to the Democrats had been defeated, and this made the negotiations with the Democrats more difficult. The Speaker himself had to be seen as part of the negotiating team, and this drove away a few more Republicans.

The deal offered by the Lone Star Party was to move the self determination referendum toward the end of the session, enact most of the Republican Party of Texas Platform, and increase the effort on security, while making reductions in federally financed programs to pay for the change in priorities. This offer was announced publicly, and emphasis was placed on making this offer known to traditional Republican suburban voters. This was an effort to put pressure on the conservative and precarious Republicans to make a deal with the Lone Star Party.

The Speaker clearly wanted to make a deal with the Democrats. The Lone Star Party was going to exercise its prerogative and force a public vote for Speaker. The Republican House members were going to be forced to cast a vote allied with one of the other parties. Republicans now had to ask themselves, given the results of the recent national elections, could they afford to be seen as governing with the help of Democrats, or would such an appearance of old parties working to keep the new party out of power be fatal to the remaining Republicans.

If one considers the primary motivators of a politician to be more power and reelection, which option entailed the least risk to those objectives would be a good predictor of behavior. The LSP had tried to frame the problem so that the least risk for most of the Republicans, except for the Speaker and about a dozen of his key Republican allies would be to deal with the LSP. Could the LSP seal the deal by supporting a conservative Republican house member as an alternative to the current Speaker.

An understanding was reached. The Lone Star Party would run an announced candidate for Speaker. As nominations were made, there would be a third, and therefore surprise nomination of one of the conservative Republicans. The Lone Star Candidate would then announce his support for the conservative Republican. Then the vote would take place between the two Republicans. It gave the conservative Republicans the cover they needed to operate with the current Speaker until the vote took place. If it somehow went bad, and the vote lost, the conservatives could claim they needed to vote in this manner to win reelection. Any politician would understand that.

Press coverage was intense. The rules for the special session limited bills to be considered to those subjects outlined by the Governor, which had been Defense, Homeland Security, State and Federal Power and Responsibility. All three issues were Lone Star Party key issues, and major parts of the Republican Party of Texas platform. The special session set up the opportunity for the LSP to get its issues addressed, and save the cram downs for the regular session.

The legislature was called into session for the first day of the special session. A motion was introduced for the election of a Speaker. As this was understood to be a means to only hold one election for both the special and regular sessions, the motion passed and the floor was opened for nominations. Politicians like it when it appears that everyone can work together. It was no surprise when one of the Speaker's Republican allies placed his name in nomination. There was little surprise when a member of the Lone Star Party was nominated as the Don Quixote candidate to show token opposition to the Speaker. It was a great surprise to the Speaker and the Democrats when another Lone Star Party member asked to be recognized and nominated one of the other Republicans. It was a shock when the current Speaker got only 73 votes to the other Republican's 77.

The Democrats in the Texas House of Representatives were now virtually powerless. The Lone Star Party and conservative Republicans currently had a working majority and moderate Republicans had no choice to play along or be forced to become Democrats in word as well as deed. Lobbyists that had no use for the LSP less than 24 hours ago, were now keen to extend invitations to LSP members of the legislature and schedule meetings. While the world had turned upside down in the House, there was little change in the Senate.

Special Committees were formed to handle each of the three areas for the special session as outlined by the Governor. As the majority party, the Speaker appointed known conservative Republicans to chair each of the committees. This was expected and welcomed by members of the LSP. That there was not even one of the committees chaired by a Democrat or moderate Republican demonstrated how politics in Texas had just experienced an earthquake.

The Special Committee on Defense took up the organization, equipping, and duties of the Texas Military Forces. The Federalization of the National Guard had presented a problem in that recent events demonstrated that the force available to Texas had been insufficient to meet the defense needs of the people of Texas. This had caused undue death and suffering among the population. Texas needed a larger military to meet these security challenges to Texas. Everything pertaining to the National Guard was in essence dictated by the federal government, so Texas could make no changes pertaining to organization or what equipment may be appropriate to place in the hands of the National Guard.

The Texas State Guard and Reserve Militia were entirely within the purview of the Texas Legislature. A proposal was entertained to quadruple the size of the State Guard, taking existing organized militia units and using them to achieve this objective. The existing units would now be joined by the organized militia units to form two infantry brigade combat teams on the same organizational structure as the US Army.

Somehow, someone in the Lone Star Party had worked out such a proposal, and introduced it the first day the committee met. There would also be a militia branch of the State Guard that would undertake to organize militia companies in every county in Texas, and in counties with over 50,000 population entire battalions, while in counties of over 1 million population, brigades would be organized. The objective was to start a system for incorporating an armed population into the issue of defense of the people of Texas, In short, the means by which the people could defend themselves.

Over in the Homeland Security Committee, the Lone Star Party was working to derail the momentum in place. The LSP was opposed to a larger Department of Public Safety and more uniformed police personnel. LSP members thought that too often, these personnel were being used in ways that did not advance public safety, but rather increase the power of state and local government to create and enforce regulatory schemes of little use to real security. The LSP would rather that this committee should take up different subjects.

One of the LSP Representatives submitted a resolution stating that the US Constitution Article I, Section 9 clearly left the subject of admitting aliens to the states, subject to what restrictions the federal government chose to make viz: "The migration or importation of such persons as the states now existing shall think proper to admit". Thus, Texas would determine what immigrants it thought proper to admit with such legislation the remit of the Homeland Security Committee.

The Democrats on the committee were livid, hurling charges of racism and subverting the authority of the federal government. The LSP replied that was exactly what Democrats were doing with sanctuary cities legislation. This would be one more area to lead to a split in the Republican Party between contributors and many TEA Party supporters. In a close vote, the resolution passed.

This encouraged the LSP to further restrict immigration. One of the proposals was a bill to limit property ownership in Texas to US citizens only. All foreigners would have six months to sell any real estate owned in Texas. Foreigners would have to provide evidence of legal residence to rent property. The accusations of xenophobia and worse were made at supporters of the bill. The LSP and its supporters were tired of terrorists and criminals being given too much cover under which to operate. The bill also passed on a close vote.

The LSP was having good success on its secondary objectives, which would make the landscape in Texas less favorable for those who intended to use immigration laws to place subversive populations in Texas. In the regular session, the LSP would try to reduce federal subsidies and entitlement programs. If the LSP was successful, Texas would be a less friendly place for someone unwilling to get a job.

The real excitement for the special session was saved for the LSP referendum on self determination. As with the previous referendum, the language used would be the key to passage and the Republicans who had deposed the previous Speaker staying on board with the deal. The Governor had stayed out of the line of fire on the other items in the special session, but there was an expectation that he would be involved in the machinations regarding this subject.

In the end, the simple language approach won out. In part that was because of the built up pressure from the citizenry. The terrorist attacks and turmoil around the world had the people of Texas worried that the country was falling apart and their lives were in jeopardy. That strengthened the power of the Lone Star Party and while most of the media were not friendly toward the LSP, the fact was that the LSP could not be ignored. They had support and any politician that tried to stop the LSP agenda was running a risk that most politicians would rather avoid.

The people of Texas would vote in May on a very simple statement: "The State of Texas should resume its former status as the Republic of Texas." There was enough ambiguity to leave room for negotiation all the way around, while being clear that the choice was between remaining a state in the United States or not. Like the other votes, it was close but passed.

The question was whether the Senate or Governor would dare to oppose any of the measures that had passed the House. Contrary to the House, there had only been a slight shift in the direction of the Lone Star Party in the Senate. This would make the negotiations more intense, as the Democrats still held 9 seats, and two more Senators joining with them would stop a measure from Senate consideration.

Many of the more moderate Republican Senators would be up for election in the next elections. Those Senators had to consider if another year would be enough time for the state of the country and Texas to heal to a sufficient degree that any actions they took to stop the efforts coming from the house would be forgotten, or their votes would be considered the reason and thus responsible for further disaster. The Lone Star Party tried to play to this fear, and the probability there would be further challenges to Republican office holders from Lone Star Party candidates in the future.

A different strategy was employed with the Senators. Just put the referendum out there and let the vote occur. If as was anticipated by the Democrats and Republicans, there was not enough support for the referendum to pass, let the voters reject it. If the Republicans and Democrats wanted to kill the Lone Star Party, the failure of the referendum would be a good start. The LSP was playing a high stakes game for its future. As the well entrenched political class was certain of the failure of the referendum, and that failure would possibly be fatal to the LSP, it was passed out of the Senate.

Now attention shifted to the Governor. Would the legislation passed by the House and Senate be signed into law. As with every other state wide office holder, the Governor had campaigned on a platform of fighting against federal government over reach into areas that should be legislated by the state. Not signing the bills were probably a signal that the Governor had no intention of running for re-election. The bills were signed and the referendum was set for the same time as municipal elections in May. This would be just after the scheduled close of the legislative session.

Now the legislature would move into the regular session. The Democrats and moderate Republicans expected to stage a counter to the success of the Lone Star Party in the special session. The method they intended to use was the Texas constitutional provision requiring a balanced budget. All of the military related and security proposals passed in the special session would now have to be funded. The Democrats and moderate Republicans expected that the LSP would either fail to find the money or there would be enough votes to block additional funding sources.

The first ploy was to go back on the deal in electing the Speaker of the House, and call for a vote to elect a Speaker. The 77 to 73 margin held, and the Speaker remained in place. This session in the Texas house was going to be unlike any other in recent memory. No Democrats were appointed as committee chairs. Every committee of the Texas House was now chaired by a conservative Republican, with support from the Lone Star Party. The LSP provided the votes to prevent a rebellion by the moderate wing of the Republican Party assisted by the Democrats.

Bills were now referred to the committees that would change the way the government of Texas was run. Government programs and agencies were on their way to being cut or eliminated. Bills were introduced for eliminating the requirement to have a license to carry a handgun, to eliminate vehicle inspections after purchase, ban red light cameras, eliminate toll roads, allow parents to send their children to the school of their choice, and other measures to bring more freedom to Texas.

There were other proposals to restrict the use of federal funds that would prohibit the use of federal funds by any organization chartered by the State of Texas to settle refugees, teach school courses in any language other than English, or provide any funds by the State of Texas for a federal program other than Medicare.

This was the conservative Republican and Lone Star Party answer to how the Texans would pay for its military preparations. When the resulting controversy was being stoked by much of the media with the able assistance of Democratic Party operatives, the chair of the Lone Star party offered the following comment. "If you don't like the direction in which Texas is headed, move." It was his sincere hope that many such individuals who had no intention of obtaining gainful employment, would heed his advice.

There were anecdotal stories of such population shifts. Some people were moving to Texas in hopes of more independence from the federal government, and some were moving to other states where federal programs were better funded.

Chapter 16

The Bear Awakes

WAR IS THE PROVINCE OF CHANCE. IN NO OTHER SPHERE OF HUMAN ACTIVITY MUST SUCH A MARGIN BE LEFT FOR THIS INTRUDER. IT INCREASES THE UNCERTAINTY OF EVERY CIRCUMSTANCE AND DERANGES THE COURSE OF EVENTS. - KARL VON CLAUSEWITZ

For some reason, almost incomprehensible to learned observers, both Russia and the United States seemed intent on returning to the days of the Cold War. Both Russia and the United States shared the problems relating to an insurgent Muslim population threatening their populations. However, Russian actions in Eastern Europe threatened the stability and growth of governmental institutions in nations who had formerly been members of the Warsaw Pact. This lead to a concern on the part of those former Warsaw Pact countries who were now members of NATO regarding Russian motives.

Russian foreign policy objectives seemed to be a combination of fighting Islamic terrorists, establishing Russian influence over Eastern Europe, and negating Western European and American policy by controlling the supply of natural gas and other forms of energy to continental Europe. As had also been true of the old Soviet Union, this policy was accompanied by an implied military threat evidenced by large numbers of Russian troops stationed or conducting military exercises close to the borders of neighboring countries.

Like the Peoples' Republic of China, Russia had revised its military doctrine to make provision for more modern technologies to assist in the attack of adversaries and influence the opinions of target populations. In this regard, Russian military doctrine now more resembled US Unconventional Warfare doctrine. Observers considered Russian actions in the Ukraine that resulted in Russian annexation of Crimea to be a trial run of this military doctrine. Certainly assisting this successful Russian action was the ambiguous and timid response of the western countries.

Historically, Crimea had been Russian for some 100 years before being placed into the Ukraine by the Soviet Union. This made claims of Crimea belonging to the territory of Ukraine to be doubted by the western countries. Combined with instability and the perception of widespread corruption in the government of Ukraine, this paralyzed western response to Russian actions.

Similar instances of a pattern matching the initial stages of the conflict in Ukraine were now happening in the Baltic States. These small countries which were annexed by the Soviet Union in 1940, regained their independence after the collapse of the Soviet Union. During the Soviet occupation, ethnic Russians moved into these countries, and their descendants were now present in these countries post Soviet collapse. Russians were fed a series of media reports in their press about the mistreatment of their ethnic cousins by these countries, using the Russians descendants as targets for their ill feeling toward Russia.

Along with the geographically isolated Russian territory of Kaliningrad (formerly the German city of Köningsberg) as a base of operations, ethnic tensions were being stoked in these small republics. The Baltic Republics were NATO members and made an appeal to NATO alliance members for support. This request made obvious the weakness of western land power. The US had two brigade sized units stationed in Europe, who also rotated out to the war in the Middle East; Germany had an army of three divisions, the Dutch had sold their tanks to Canada, the British Army no longer had troops stationed on the continent, and the French Army was busy patrolling the streets of France.

When Roberts had been stationed in Germany, the US had over 5 divisions, or about 17 combat brigades in Europe. The Germans at that time had 10 divisions or 30 brigades. In total, NATO had almost 60 combat brigades on hand to stop the Warsaw Pact forces. On a good day, NATO could now put 15 brigades in the field in Europe, and that depended on the new NATO countries such as Poland to scrape up that much force.

The peace treaty ending World War II and putting Germany back together, and allowing for expanding NATO, also encouraged disarmament. As part of the agreement, NATO and Warsaw Pact forces had limits on the number of conventional weapons such as tanks and artillery pieces that could be located in Europe. Every time NATO added a former Warsaw Pact member, such as Poland, or the Czech Republic, or Hungary, their military equipment now counted against the total permitted NATO, and was subtracted from the total that now counted against Russia. As a result, NATO powers such as the US, Germany, the UK, Netherlands, and Canada either removed units from Europe, or cut the size of their land forces.

Russia had also made changes in the former Red Army of Workers and Peasants. The then over 100 divisions were reorganized into brigades, and more reliance was made on career soldiers who were supplemented by draftees. When the reorganization was complete, the Russian Army would have some 40 divisions (120 brigades) and be the dominant power in Europe. Russian military doctrine now emphasized the utilization of the entire spectrum of conflict. Action might start with establishing groups designed to promote economic and political instability in the target country. Next would follow escalating civil violence, transforming into insurgency warfare and then revolution, followed by the entry or attack by conventional Russian forces. The idea being that by the time the targeted country realized that it was in a conventional war with Russia, it was too late to marshal the resources needed to successfully resist.

The Eastern European countries which had lived under the control of the Soviet Union were well aware of what was happening on or near their borders. They began to rearm, buying US or German military hardware. Except for small arms and ammunition, none of these countries were capable of manufacturing heavier weapons, and were dependent on their NATO allies for first rate aircraft and armored vehicles.

The Eastern European countries tried to get the attention of the US to counter the Russian build up on their borders. The US was engaged in the Middle East, and when attention could be paid to Europe, would send a couple of companies of infantry or maybe a heavier battalion of troops as a show of strength. In the days of the Cold War, the US would send another Armored Division to Europe for a month to make a point that in ten days, another 5 divisions (15 brigades) could be present in Europe. The US no longer had that capability to project force.

Into this sensitive situation in Europe blundered the Texas independence movement. For the most part, the Texas independence organizations tended to be not particularly interested in geopolitics. Their frustration with the US Government led to a single focus of breaking that chain, by any means possible.

To the extent the organizations considered a potential Texas foreign policy, it was in the context of thinking in terms of gaining international recognition for an independent Texas. A couple of the organizations started to try to make contacts with other international organizations or even governments. Their thinking seemed to be that there was a good opportunity to gain recognition for an independent Texas, and possibly even assistance from countries that would be hostile to past US foreign policy. One of the Texas independence organizations was seen with the Russians and another organization was trying to work the United Nations.

This issue had caused one of the few splits that happened among the Directors of Free Texas. A couple of the Directors thought the concept of the other organizations had merit. Roberts and the others were adamantly opposed to talking to any other government or even entertaining the idea until after there was a decision on the part of Texas to split. This had been the subject of more than one discussion at the Green Dragon Tavern in Freedonia.

Ed McMasters thought the idea worth exploring. "There are a number of countries that would like to see the US taken down a notch or two and I bet would be willing to help us."

Roberts was on the other side of the issue. "Other countries operate on what they think of as their own self interest. They may talk about poking a finger in the eye of Uncle Sam, but if it costs them to do so, no action is taken that risks the cash flowing from Washington for foreign aid."

Ed persisted "The Russians really want to stick it to the US. Some of them even were talking to the Native Texas Movement."

Jim responded "The Russians want to keep the US from spoiling the Russians plans for Eastern Europe. They are saving their conflict with Washington over the pipelines running through Syria. They want to control the flow of gas and to the extent possible, oil to Western Europe. They are not going to waste their time on Texas independence. The only interest the Russians have in Texas independence is the possibility of gaining control over the Texas oil industry. Controlling more oil production gives them more leverage in the market."

Ed wasn't convinced "There is no way they could get control of our oil."

Roberts tried to explain "Many of these guys are ex KGB and have no conscience at all. I've met any number of guys from Texas who went to Moscow after the break up of the Soviet Union to do oil exploration deals with Moscow to get oil out of Siberia. Guess who owns the oil and the wells today? You are not dealing with amateurs here. They will just use the Texan groups as a distraction and cover for the real operation that they will pull while using their own people to run it. If they get involved in a Texas independence movement, it is in order to control Texas resources. The Russian security service had an operation recently to take over one of the small Balkan countries. The plot using the natives dealing with the Russians was easily discovered. That was just a sham operation, and the real one was discovered only by luck. We need to stay away from those guys."

Ed still wasn't entirely convinced. "Are you sure they could do that?"

Roberts continued "Ed, there are Starbucks locations in Dallas where I can listen to a couple of guys jabbering away with their cell phones in a Slavic language. One of my more adventurous friends tells me they will do a hit on your ex or some other non important person for $5000 and have put the Italian mafia crime families out of business. Just another reason why we need to be careful about who has the privilege to live in Texas."

Ed was looking for a way to make the idea seem workable. "If we got support from another country without any conditions?"

"Foreign aid is a means of buying influence. Do you think an independent Texas would be interested in selling oil to continental Europe? I think we would. What if selling that oil meant diplomatic conflict with Russia? So you think Russia will spend money it doesn't have to help an economic competitor? We need to look at the world as a highly competitive environment. We like to point out the size of the Texas economy as a selling point for independence being realistic. The other large economic powers see a potential competitor. How often in business have you subsidized your competition?" summarized Roberts as a conclusion.

"I see your point." Ed said.

In the mind of Jim Roberts, this conversation had been the entire restoration of liberty movement in a microcosm. There were a number of great people involved, but their focus was too narrow, not taking into consideration the wider implications of their actions. The fixation on Texas independence as the solution to a number of problems, many to be solved later, could lead to counter productive decisions. As Roberts saw it, solving the problems of the loss of liberty and government strangulation of business, produced the probable result of Texas independence. Having the independent nation of Texas throw you in jail for an illegal knife or a pile of scrap lumber on your property was not a win.

Such was the state of the world when the new President of the United States took office.

Free Texas, the Freedonia Technology Company, and the Borden County Militia had been working information operations since the widespread computer attack took down much of the Internet infrastructure in the United States. Restoring these systems provided an opportunity to create fake people as Internet personas to be used to plant ideas in the communities online in which were target audiences. Most of the effort was aimed at the leftist / progressive social media presence.

The initial effort was at creating IDs and personas that in the scramble to bring the communities back online, would allow for the establishing of credibility that would be difficult to verify and research. Over time, as the chatter on those sites increased, the IDs became credible members of the community. At this stage it was important to merely parrot what was being said among people of similar opinion. Care was taken not to introduce new ideas, or to engage in any conversation critical of liberal policies or ideas. It was important to become part of the mob in order to later influence the direction of the herd.

Over time, opportunities would appear that would provide a way to influence thought and potentially start to emerge from the crowd as a thought leader that might be able to influence others. Part of the fun for the information operations personnel was to find the most outrageous ideas and plans from other leftist sources, and post the same or similar content as the contributions from the fake people. Another source of fun was to see how often the contributions from the fake IDs were repeated and referenced by others.

Shortly after the Presidential election, a prime opportunity presented itself. Some Californians got the idea that they should launch an effort for a California referendum to exit the United States. This was a perfect setup for the information operation underway. The fake IDs picked up on the idea, and much of the preparation work for Texas independence, could be used and was well known to the people conducting the operation that could apply to this effort. An independent California would have one of the world's largest economies. California would be able to admit as many refugees as needed to be resettled. California court decisions would not be reversed by the Supreme Court. The fake IDs could speak well and authoritatively on the subject based on their knowledge of the Texas independence movement.

This was the key to the success of the effort. Ideas and opinions published by the fake IDs started to get traction on other leftist sites. When necessary, some of the fake IDs were used to agree with and lend credibility to other of the fake IDs. It became a game in Free Texas to have a leftist alternate personality to boost the reputation of the fake "thought leaders".

This particular operation had three objectives: (A) Boost a California secession effort as a possibility of diverting effort from national efforts to impose liberal policies (B) Set a trap so that those supporting California secession would have difficulty in later opposing a Texas secession effort (C) Soften national opposition to Texas secession by the possibility of the loss of both a liberal and

202

conservative state. Thus, Texas alone would not be the cause of the breakup of the United States.

Setting the date for the referendum in Texas, which was thus now operating on a faster timeline than California, had led to some liberal push back on their social media. Now was the time to use the previously established credibility to make the case that the United States would be better off without a state full of haters that had forced refugees out of the state. Texas was full of racist haters, and any progressive person needed to get out of "the state of hate" and move to a more welcoming and inclusive society.

Progressives everywhere found the phrase "the state of hate" fiendishly clever and started to use that phrase to refer to Texas at every opportunity. The phrase became a joke inside Texas. In Texas, the phrase "the state of hate" was a reference to the attitude of a liberal when trying to engage in a conversation. It all depended on your frame of reference and sense of humor.

The last time the United States had been so divided politically was in 1860. In that election, four candidates had won Electoral College votes. Only Stephen Douglas got Electoral College Votes from a slave state and a free state. All of the other candidates got votes only from free states or slave states. In the 21st Century, the split was urban vs. rural. Every city with more than one million population voted Democrat. As most of the population lived in counties of more than one million population, politics had become fractionalized.

By a narrow margin of victory, the Republican Party held the Presidency, Senate, and House, at the federal level. While Texas was reliably Republican, the margin of victory was narrower than usual. There had been almost no change of office holders at the federal level. Tension was high to see what the new President would be able to do.

The President Elect had ruffled feathers all the way around. He had people working in his team that apparently knew the way the government operated very well. They were asking the kind of questions the bureaucracy did not want to answer. The kind of questions that could identify people who would be fired and programs eliminated.

The conservatives had also been put on notice that federal procurement was also going to be examined for efficiency. That was going to make federal contractors unhappy. The way the game was supposed to be played was that you contributed money to your Congressman in order to get your contracts, and then nobody questioned contract performance or the price charged the government. The President and his team were not playing by the established rules. A large number of people with connections in Washington, DC were going to be very unhappy.

Chapter 17

Munitions of War

LOGISTICS COMPRISES THE MEANS AND ARRANGEMENTS WHICH WORK OUT THE PLANS OF STRATEGY AND TACTICS. STRATEGY DECIDES WHERE TO ACT; LOGISTICS BRINGS THE TROOPS TO THIS POINT. – ANTOINE-HENRI JOMINI

Building a modern military from next to nothing is a formidable task. As the Texas legislature had approved of the steps necessary to build up the Texas Military Forces as a credible deterrent against potential threats and to secure the border of Texas with Mexico. And failing deterrence, to be able to conduct war as necessary, a survey was underway to catalog that military capability within Texas. Ultimately, the goal was to be able to arm and equip the Texas Military Forces from suppliers located inside Texas. The results of the initial survey were discouraging.

Jim Roberts had been one of the officers charged with completing the survey. He had been brought into the project based on his experience in equipping his and other militia units. Those units had spent much of the last year in service to Texas. This led to an initial hope that much of the required industry was already located in Texas. Roberts had one comment about the idea that Texas was well positioned to meet its defense needs and summed up his experience with the issue. It only took him two words to express his conclusion "We suck."

It started with underwear, T-shirts, and socks. The military procured items were not made in Texas, and while there were any number of possible suppliers, the items would be made elsewhere and imported. What annoyed Roberts the most about these items was that the military bought them from the federal government. The US Bureau of Prisons ran its own manufacturing operation and sold the products to the US Government at market price. That price was then passed on to the GIs who bought the issue items. And that wasn't all. Prison labor made helmets, bunks, and other military items, too. Texas couldn't count on the US Government as a source of supply.

Uniforms and other clothing to include the wet weather gear were made by a few manufacturers located primarily in the southeast US. The traditional boot manufacturers were located in the northeast and midwest. Rank insignia and unit patches were also sourced outside of Texas. In fact, Roberts himself had unit patches made in China, not by choice – that is where the supplier had the factory. And the quality control was poor. Soldiers had been unhappy with the uniforms since the 2005 pattern change. At least sourcing all of this from inside Texas would be an opportunity to fix some issues.

The rest of the field gear faced the same problem. For helmets there were three suppliers. Two were federal set aside contractors, and the other one was the conglomerate that made most of the equipment to be had because they had bought almost every manufacturer of military equipment. There were two suppliers of vests and pouches for canteens, ammo magazines, and other accessories. There seemed to be only one manufacturer of sleeping bags. None of the production facilities were located in Texas.

The small arms picture was not quite as bleak. There were three small manufacturers of AR style rifles in Texas that could be used for military style production. Only one manufacturer of handguns was in Texas, and most of their parts production was actually made in the Philippines. The final assembly was a Texas product. None of the facilities could turn out the number of weapons needed to equip an army.

Only Fabrique National produced 5.56 and 7.62 automatic weapons, and that was at their plant in South Carolina. The .50 cal Browning Heavy Machinegun, entering service in 1919, had a number of parts suppliers, and one company working with complete weapons in addition to the Anniston, Alabama Army Depot. Cannon were arsenal production, and not in Texas.

At least some small arms ammunition was made in Texas. In addition to Roberts' Freedonia Army Ammunition Plant, there were a few other makers. Only Freedonia had the equipment to turn out military specification ammunition. That was critical for operations in humid or wet environments to prevent moisture from getting into the powder of rounds carried in magazines as part of the combat load. In setting up the Freedonia plant, Roberts had insisted on that capability because it was so important. Roberts personally had fired 60 year old military ammunition and the rounds worked because of the military specifications which were designed for long term storage in hostile environments. At maximum capacity, Freedonia could turn out 100 million rounds per year, which was 8% of the capacity of the Lake City Army Ammunition Plant in Independence, Missouri.

The same story repeated itself for mortar ammunition, anti – tank missiles, artillery rounds, air to air, ground to air, and just about every other type of ordinance. It was produced somewhere else, except for the Lone Star Plant near Texarkana. At least there were hand grenades made there, but not mines. They were produced somewhere else, too.

The military combat ration, the Meal Ready to Eat (known as Meals Rejected by Ethiopians to GIs) had three producers, and one of the packagers was located in south Texas. Roberts figured that abomination needed a better solution anyway.

Radios had components made in Texas, the same suppliers also making night vision equipment. Final assembly on the radios was done out of state. Batteries for the radios and the chargers to charge the batteries came from a plant in upstate New York. Much of the night vision and thermal imagery equipment was assembled in north Texas, so at least one bit of critical combat gear for the 21st Century was a Texas product, even if final assembly of sub components happened elsewhere.

Body armor with the military lighter weight plates had two producers. One was a subsidiary of 3M, and the other belonged to the other major defense conglomerates. Roberts noted that item also as not made in Texas.

This was the challenge just to put fighters in the field with quality gear able to hold their own in a defense. True, that degree of equipage should enable dominance over the cartels, or any non military opponent. But, one does not always know what the future will bring. One thing was for certain, if Texas was going to need an army, there should be some business opportunity there for someone who could meet the needs of that military.

Roberts moved on in his survey to vehicles and heavier equipment. While GM had an assembly plant in Texas, there was nothing military related produced by that factory. Pickup trucks were the heaviest type of vehicle the plant was capable of producing. The lighter wheeled vehicles tended to be AM General procured items, or heavy wheel vehicles for fuel and major loads from Oshkosh production. That included trailers for water, kitchens, or other uses such as generators.

Then there was the problem of tracked vehicles. The line that had produced the M113 and Bradleys for FMC had been bought by BAE and was located on the west coast. The US Army had the production of two tank factories for the M1 series. One of the factories had been shut down at the end of the Cold War and mothballed. The other plant was at Lima, Ohio and did not produce new tanks, but rebuilt M1A1s into the M1A2SEP version. The same factory produced the M88A2 tank recovery vehicle.

Artillery pieces of various kinds and rocket launchers compounded the problem of where the components were manufactured and where final assembly into functioning weapons with some form of mobility. This was a microcosm of military procurement, whenever possible, as many companies in as many congressional districts as possible were involved in production. It kept the federal money rolling into those procurement programs and campaign contributions into the campaigns of incumbent Congressmen.

The military aviation situation was less dire. Bell helicopter in Ft. Worth had produced the UH-1 transport helicopter, the AH-1 Cobra attack helicopter, and the OH-58 recon helicopter. While the current Blackhawk was a Sikorsky product, and the Apache a Boeing product, the older models of helicopters were still capable machines. In theory, the production lines could be reopened; the challenge was how much institutional knowledge in the minds of the workforce that had built those helicopters by the thousands had been lost to the ravages of time.

General Dynamics in Ft. Worth was the home of F-16 fighter production, and the Texas Air National Guard still flew some of those F-16s. While the production line had been shut down, the same solution as with helicopters was possible. With the new President in office, the Air Force procurement of the F-35 had become an issue. This was a case of the problem going the other way – The US and every other country buying the F-35 was buying a plane assembled in Texas, The President was not happy with the program cost and management, which had implications for the future of the program.

Provision for a Texas Navy was the most problematic issue facing Texas. The only real naval facilities were near Corpus Christi, and Galveston. There was no ship building capability in Texas, and certainly not anything that might be used to construct warships was located anywhere in the state. The Texas coastline was essentially undefended, except by air intercept.

However Texas did have what poker players referred to as a hole card. Pantex, near Amarillo, was the only production facility for nuclear weapons in the United States. Every US nuclear weapon constructed in the last 50 years was built at the Pantex facility. If nothing else, that gave Texas a unique possibility compared to any other state in the United States. Theoretically, Texas could have nuclear weapons built for the Texas Military Forces. The issue would be turning that idea into a credible threat.

Roberts and his contemporaries from the putative Air Force and Navy summarized their findings for presentation to the political leadership and the senior staff of the Adjutant General's

Department. The General asked for an advance brief from Roberts before the presentation was to take place. This would help Roberts frame the issue for the "dog and pony show" and be prepared for what the likely reaction would be to what he was going to say.

The General summed it up. "The inventory of where we are is going to frighten the politicians. You are going to have to show our leaders the way forward to lead them out of the swamp. Otherwise, they will fall in the muck and drown themselves in fear."

Roberts understood. "Yes sir, by the time I'm done with them, they will be thinking about how to get the new factories located in their districts and how much money they can get out of the owners in campaign contributions."

The formal brief on sourcing material for the future Texas Military Forces took place for the Governor, Lt. Governor, House and Senate committees, Adjutant General's staff and the command and staff of the Texas State Guard, which would be implementing the statute organizing the Reserve Militia into the Texas State Guard structurally. Roberts was to give the land forces portion of the brief, followed by the air and sea components. The presentation slides were loaded and the title slide appeared on the screen as Roberts began his portion of the briefing.

"This morning we are looking at sourcing the equipment needed to create credible units in the Texas Military Forces on the model used to create the militias which have been conducting operations unofficially or as in the past few months officially in response to major threats directed at the people of Texas. In the original militia model, each soldier is responsible for procuring his own kit, and retains ownership of his weapons and equipment. Certain items, such as body armor, night vision, and communications equipment are either restricted sales by federal law, or very expensive. Thus, some of the gear which we managed to obtain informally, is not a workable option to get that gear into the hands of our fellow citizens with more modest means, or in considerable quantity by citizens with greater financial resources.

We were able to stockpile some gear via our Quartermaster. For the most part, these items are individual uniform and field gear. As time went on, and we grew and obtained additional resources, we could expand the inventory of supplied items to include helmets, ammunition, rifle magazines, first aid kits, etc. Still, these were not high dollar items or restricted sales items. Additionally, our procurement went into the hundreds of items, and then other units copied our approach. While a few thousand personnel have been equipped via this method, it has reached its limit, and can not be expanded further.

To fully implement the militia plan outlined for Texas, that would result in a Texas Military Forces of over 2.5 million men who would need to be equipped. It should be noted that this amount of manpower exceeds the uniformed personnel of the US Department of Defense active duty and reserve component. This represents a considerable challenge, not only in terms of purchase of equipment by individuals and the Military Department, but also in terms of production to meet demand, and thus the opportunity.

As you see in your briefing packet, we have listed individual clothing and equipment items, and their current suppliers to the US military. You will of course, note that these items originate and are made throughout the United States, with almost no items directly connected to Texas. Thus, in the short term, we are dependent on suppliers of uniforms and field gear located almost entirely outside of Texas. Our supplies are subject to disruption, or on suppliers that lack required capacity to supply the quantity of goods needed. To encourage local supply, if we give preference to purveyors inside Texas, we may encourage suppliers to build their additional capacity in Texas in order to supply the Texas Military Forces. Just in uniforms alone, we will have a projected need for over 500,000 sets per year for the foreseeable future. Or stated differently, we will increase the demand for uniforms by over 2000 sets per working day over the current US military requirement.

In the next section of the briefing packet, you see a similar situation for field gear. Fully equipping a universal militia requires production for over 1000 sets of field gear per working day. By way of comparison, it took over 10 years to equip US forces with new helmets. Again, we are requiring industry to more than double current production in order to meet our needs. It is not unreasonable to think that a businessman would locate that additional production close to a customer that buys 100% of that additional production capacity. Especially so, when all of the right economic incentives are in place.

In the next section, you see the hard to get items that are individual use. Unlike the previous sections, you see that the night vision systems have a strong Texas provenance. It is my assumption, that initially, we will not be able to procure these items in quantity due to three factors. The first is budget, they are expensive, and there is no budget for them. Procurement at this time will rely on various fund raising mechanisms. Second, there is probably limited capacity to expand production. Third, the federal government limits who may buy some of these items. Even if you office holders pass a law permitting purchase of these items in Texas, each supplier runs a risk of federal prosecution if he sells equipment to us. For the short term, these should be unit issue items to deployed individuals who must return them to unit stores at the end of the deployment.

This brings us to the unit gear section. Here we see the sources for tents, field kitchens, generators, light wheeled vehicles for general purpose and transportation / cargo. Currently many of these items are surplus to current US needs, and thus as a rule, available for sale by the Department of the Army to Texas. In this case, the good news is the bad news. The Army may refuse to sell this equipment at any time. As with the previous section, due to expense, and number of items that might be procured, this would be a rotating stock of equipment for use by deployed units.

This brings us to the heavier engineer equipment and wheeled vehicles. Most of that has final assembly in the midwest, but parts come from everywhere. There is only one assembly line for medium tracked vehicles, which happens to be in California. The US had two tank factories capable of building the M1 series. The factory in Lima, Ohio still does rebuild work, while the other has been mothballed. Should we be able to move the mothballed plant to Texas that would give us some advantage in meeting our defense needs."

The Governor broke in. "Roberts, that is the thing about you. I can't tell when you are serious and when you are joking. Who would try to buy a tank factory and move it to Texas?"

Roberts took up the challenge. "Sir, as you probably know, I already own an ammunition factory, and a tank factory would compliment that nicely."

Now the General was curious. "Do you have the financial resources for that?"

214

"I might be able to get a loan from the Freedonia Transaction Company." and Roberts was finished with his portion of the briefing.

The brief from the Air Force and Navy was short. There was air frame manufacturing capability, although with older model air craft. As for a Texas Navy, there wasn't going to be one using only Texas resources. A Texas Navy would have to come out of the ships mothballed in the US Navy reserve fleet or take ten years or longer to produce ships.

One of the Congressmen commented "Texas Navy? What would we need that for?"

Roberts decided to take the issue head on. "We have a coast line to defend, and it is a good idea to provide all of the buffer zone that we can. We expect to trade and ship goods to other countries. A navy is a statement that we will protect our shipping. And there is the possibility that we may engage in conflict before the fight gets to Texas. If so, the navy protects the sea lanes to the war zone, and gives the army a ride to where the war is."

The Governor commented, "Well Roberts, it looks like your friends in the Lone Star Party have been just a bit too ambitious in thinking we can build our own military. We're dependent on the rest of the United States."

Roberts was prepared with the rebuttal. "Sir the rest of the United States is just as stuck with the same situation that we are. They depend on Texas to have a functioning military. And that mutual dependence is the basis for negotiation."

Chapter 18

Referendum

HOWEVER [POLITICAL PARTIES] MAY NOW AND THEN ANSWER POPULAR ENDS, THEY ARE LIKELY IN THE COURSE OF TIME AND THINGS, TO BECOME POTENT ENGINES, BY WHICH CUNNING, AMBITIOUS, AND UNPRINCIPLED MEN WILL BE ENABLED TO SUBVERT THE POWER OF THE PEOPLE AND TO USURP FOR THEMSELVES THE REINS OF GOVERNMENT, DESTROYING AFTERWARDS THE VERY ENGINES WHICH HAVE LIFTED THEM TO UNJUST DOMINION. – GEORGE WASHINGTON

The adherents of the secession is illegal argument always pointed to the White v Texas Supreme Court case. Few of them, if any, had ever bothered to read it. Had they done so, the conclusion would be obvious that the Supreme Court had said the issue was the use of the proper mechanism of secession and not secession itself as the legal disability in the case. In modern politics, the truth was seldom an impediment for a seasoned advocate engaging in public discourse.

With the referendum scheduled for May, much of that debate was over. Contributing to the shift of focus as factors had been talk of California secession, and information operations mounted via the

Free Texas organization. This had helped to shift the debate away from the issue of self determination, which had now become the phrase used instead of secession or independence. The delay of the referendum was to the advantage of both the Lone Star Party and the Republican Party of Texas. The new President would have been in office over 90 days by the time the referendum took place.

From the point of view of Republicans, opposing the referendum was a matter of giving the new President the chance to fix the country. The gamble was that 90 days into the new administration there would be plenty of optimism that the United States could be turned off the path to disaster and the future would seem brighter than before. Texas independence would not be a theme as long as things looked better for the United States as a whole.

The Lone Star Party thought the delay would help them. There would be the ability to glean just how much change was going to take place with the new President in office. The question would be if this iteration of "give the Republicans a chance" would turn out differently than the others. That was a topic of discussion in Free Texas as well as the other Texas independence organizations. If the various Texas self determination movements had their differences with each other, they all agreed on one point. The people of Texas should have the opportunity to vote on their future. That opportunity to have their voice be heard was now just weeks away.

Friday night dinner in Freedonia at the Green Dragon had become an informal Free Texas Executive Directors meeting. Many other Free Texas members and friends of the movement were inclined to attend as well. Phil was almost recovered from the shoulder wound and finally had his left arm out of the sling. Ed McMasters started the conversation. "Jim, where do you think we are on the referendum? Are we going to make it?"

Roberts was thoughtful in his response. "We are about to see what happens when the unstoppable force of the President and his appointments meets the immovable object of Washington, DC. The resulting collision is where we are likely to win or lose. If the President has trouble getting his team in place, it will be impossible to make any real structural change in the federal government. That would have devastating implications for the Republicans.

The other wild card is the California petition effort for secession. The more successful that appears to be can go both ways for us. The Republican spin will be that without California, it will be easier to save the United States. If California appears on its way out, that clears out the structural objections to Texas leaving. With both California and Texas out, there is about 20% of the population of the US, and over 25% of the US economy.

What is the more interesting to me is that just the discussion illustrates that the idea of the United States breaking up is no longer the taboo it once was. It may be that our information operations have been helpful in this regard. That could be very important depending on how the vote goes. If Texas votes to stay, that perception about the permanence of the United States will be a factor in bringing up the issue again, should that be necessary.

If Texas votes to leave, it would be helpful to have Democrats and others wanting to push us out the door and try to apply that pressure on the President. He will realize what the loss of Texas means to the US, and will work to prevent that.

Between now and the vote, we need the party organs as the communists would say, working to send our message that western civilization is under attack. This view will be validated via some of the other conservative media sources. We won't have to look hard to find news that will support this presumption. Our editorial focus of federal government incompetence should also be played up as we need to show that the new President can't turn it around. The Freedonia Broadcast Institute programming will reflect this, and I suspect Rampaging Elephants will provide the needed Texas twist on all of that.

Then we have the fear factor of the unknown. Free Texas has to be there with the answers of how Texas as a nation will finance itself, and there will be more focus on our ability to keep or modify the effects of federal programs. We can defer some of that concern to the all of that is to be determined at the Constitutional convention answer – but we still have to have a point of view that we advocate. More than ever we have to sell that vision of a free and prosperous Texas.

It is going to be a near run thing to quote a famous general."

Because the Texas referendum was going to take place before any possible referendum in California, the attention was focused on Texas. In some ways, this referendum was bound in some respects to be a replay of the last one. How many of those that had voted to have Texas do something about federal over reach would be mollified by the election of a new President that gave the appearance of addressing some issues important to Texas was the key unknown. The President was clearly sympathetic to the measures taken by Texas to limit the resident population to the native born.

On the other side of the equation was the continued ability of enemies of the United States to mount attacks throughout the country. US Government efforts at defense against such attacks were perceived as ineffective as the number of dead and the resulting economic damage testified to that fact. Could Texas do a better job of defending itself and its citizens than the US Government had done to date was an important question.

For their part, the Democrats and associated leftists played on the "state of hate" theme. This vote for independence would result in the ending of taking in refugees, most social services, nobody would have health care, Jim Crow laws would return, girls would be forced to have babies they didn't want, and homosexuals would be subject to public floggings.

For its part, the Free Texas information operation played on the Democratic party line to urge all people in favor of social justice to leave Texas before the disaster occurred and risk being trapped in the "state of hate". Given the disarray in which the left of the political spectrum was in after the Presidential election, it was possible to spread that fear of the referendum would appeal to the bitter clingers unable to comprehend the virtues of social justice due to their lack of intelligence.

As the date of the vote drew closer, the media coverage, nationally and internationally intensified. The possible break up of the United States was an even larger story than the failure of the European Union to maintain cohesion among its member countries. Underneath, the issues driving both populations desire to rid themselves of a government from which they felt alienated was the same. Throughout the west, was the desire for living under a government that respected local culture, protected the lives and property of its citizens, and defended their ability to have the best possible standard of living. In summary, a substantial percentage of the population wanted a government that benefited the citizenry, and not any other interest.

220

Everyone knew the vote would be close. To the extent anyone cared about what the polling data showed, it confirmed that the vote was probably a toss up. Nobody wanted to predict the outcome in advance. Nonetheless, in Freedonia the consensus was a narrow win like the previous referendum was the probable outcome. Those favoring the referendum were considered more motivated to come to the polls and vote. One of the information operations was spreading the idea in the liberal communities that the vote didn't matter because the courts would disallow Texas from leaving the United States. The Lone Star Party was depending that the recent events which had shown the federal government to be weak and unable to prevent various attacks on the United States, and the inability to stop the actions taken to date that challenged federal authority, would also work in favor of the referendum.

Finally the date of the referendum had arrived. In Freedonia, the day took on a festive aspect, being almost treated as a public holiday. The weather was good, and the Freedonia Broadcast Institute was broadcasting over loudspeakers in the town square. Once again, the Green Dragon was the Free Texas watch party central. Reports during the day were of moderate to heavy turnout in the rural counties, and moderate turnout in the more populous counties. This gave the Texas independence organizations reason to hope for a favorable outcome. What could be done had been done, and now was the time to wait for the polls to close and the votes to be tabulated.

Those opposing the referendum had worked on the message of putting fear into the population. There would be no Social Security, no Medicare, no government help for the needy. When interviewed on the point, Roberts had responded, "The point is which fear is greater. The fear of a life without the federal government, or a greater fear of what the federal government has become and will do to you in the future."

The first results reported in Freedonia was the vote total in Freedonia itself. The result was 2758 votes in favor and 0 opposed. That announcement got the party started in Freedonia. The County total was then announced as 4005 votes in favor and 9 opposed. This caused Ted Greenlow to turn to Ed McMasters and remark "I thought we got rid of all the lefties in the school district?"

Tabulations from across Texas started to arrive. Everyone assumed they were going to be in for a long night, so not much attention was paid to the early tallies. Those would be from counties with small populations, and would generally be in favor of the referendum. Success or failure would depend on the populous counties and voter turnout there. As Roberts remarked to those assembled around the table, "One of the most difficult things a leader has to do is wait for additional information to arrive. There is a natural urge to take action, but every useful action has already been taken."

Those remarks were picked up by many of the major media outlets, which had descended on Freedonia "in the manner of locusts" according to one member of the Borden County Militia. The referendum was big news as a comparison to the United Kingdom voting to leave the European Union. However it turned out, Freedonia, and many of its prominent citizens that had led the effort were in the spotlight. There were also reporters camped out in Austin for reaction from the Governor, and in the cities where Texas independence organizations called home. Whatever the outcome was, it was going to be the news story of the week, and possibly longer if the referendum passed.

Roberts had a camera shoved in his face for the first time in the evening by CBS news. "You must be happy so far with the result." The reporter said more as an accusation than as a question.

Roberts responded, "It is too soon to tell, although it looks promising so far." mindful not to say something that would later look stupid was the first rule in dealing with a hostile press. As annoying as those reporters were, there was no way they could be avoided this evening. It was just part of the public spectacle that deciding the future of Texas had become.

A reporter from NBC took after Roberts, asking "Do you think those voting in favor of secession will show how much of an anti government sentiment there is around here?"

Roberts coolly replied, "I am reliably informed that people shot at by the FBI tended to support the referendum."

Rampaging Elephants Radio was on the scene in Freedonia doing a more in depth coverage of the referendum. They were profiling the key players in the Texas independence movements and the Lone Star Party. No matter what the result, just the fact that the vote was taking place was historic, and Rampaging Elephants was there to document it. The Free Texas Directors were much more relaxed with the morning host, who was one of the early residents of Freedonia and used the Freedonia Broadcast Institute studio for his program.

As the evening continued to 9 PM, the results from large population counties started to add to the tally. The easy margin of victory was tightening as expected. The lead by the FOR vote had narrowed to 60% in favor, and 40% were opposed. Roberts was trying to compare vote totals between the referendums. He was looking to determine if the same pattern as the previous referendum was holding, or whether this vote was doing better or worse than the previous referendum.

Toward 10 PM the attention being paid to the vote totals became more rapt. The gap was narrowing, but the vote was still in favor by a margin of 56% to 44%. By 10:15 in the evening the updates started to slow down. The turnout of voters in the metropolitan areas had not been that high, and the Freedonians started to sense victory, and the reports were starting to talk Brexit repeated which was now being referred to as Texit.

Major network reporter unease was making itself manifest by the new line of inquiry, a probable Democratic Party spin effort. Roberts was asked, "If the result stands, does this mean that Texas has repudiated the new President?'

Roberts knew the answer was going to make it around the Washington circuit and to people that Texas would need to negotiate a solution to the situation. The reply was "No, I see it a conclusion that the President and federal government can not reverse the trends now in place. The situation can not be saved from economic disaster by even the most talented management. When a company is so deep in debt that payments can't be made, it has to go into bankruptcy. Texans have concluded that $20 Trillion in debt is too far gone to climb out of the hole."

By 10:30 PM, it looked as if almost all of the precincts were in. Some 55% of the voters had voted to bring back the Republic of Texas.

Most of the town of Freedonia was ecstatic. A dream was being realized, and the champagne bottles started to appear. Jim Roberts sat at the table deep in thought. Lise Roberts started to ask what was wrong, but decided not to. Ed McMasters brought a bottle of Dom Perignon to the table and poured a glass each for Jim and Lise. Ed said to Roberts, "We've done it. All of that hard work has paid off, and we won."

Jim Roberts looked at Ed solemnly, "The really hard work has just begun. But, for this moment, I'm going to enjoy some very fine champagne."

There was now a scramble to get reactions from various politicians to the result of the vote in Texas. The news was breaking around the world that Texas had voted to leave the United States.

The reaction of the Governor was a combination of disbelief and intrigue at the idea of being the President of a potential world power. Many Republicans were shocked at the prospect of losing a major part of the party and its key supporters. Suddenly, the Republican Party went from poised to rule the United States for the near term to potential breakup.

Washington reaction tended toward disbelief. The line most often repeated was that a state can't leave the United States. The President would have a statement the next morning.

Democratic Party reaction swung between everybody get out of Texas now, to contemplating the probability of gaining control of the rest of the United States for the foreseeable future, to send in the Army to arrest all of those haters in the state of hate.

Elsewhere around the world was shock and wonder at what would happen to the United States. The financial markets put the US Dollar under pressure, as the US might potentially lose some 10%

of its economy. The exception was the UK Independence Party in Great Britain which welcomed the news and expressed hope for the possibility for a future free trade agreement with Texas.

One of the thoughts that occurred to Jim Roberts was when the British Army surrendered at Yorktown, they marched out to the surrender while playing the tune "The World Turned Upside Down" Another thought was what mixed feelings there must have been on the part of those who left their old lives behind when moving to North America. Did they realize that they were never going back when they got on that ship crossing the Atlantic Ocean. Texas and the United States had forever been changed.

Chapter 19

Without Recourse

WHENEVER THE LEGISLATORS ENDEAVOUR TO TAKE AWAY, AND DESTROY THE PROPERTY OF THE PEOPLE, OR TO REDUCE THEM TO SLAVERY UNDER ARBITRARY POWER, THEY PUT THEMSELVES INTO A STATE OF WAR WITH THE PEOPLE, WHO ARE THEREUPON ABSOLVED FROM ANY FARTHER OBEDIENCE, AND ARE LEFT TO THE COMMON REFUGE, WHICH GOD HATH PROVIDED FOR ALL MEN, AGAINST FORCE AND VIOLENCE. – JOHN LOCKE

The actions of the Supreme Court, US Government, and Texas Legislature had created an impasse. Thrown into the mix was the demand for the US Government to leave Texas, which had been considerably walked back by the Governor. While the two governments were seemingly at an impasse, the referendum results now tipped the balance toward the government of Texas. That vote gave the State of Texas the moral authority to push forward with the expressed will of the people of Texas.

The Freedonia Transaction Company got some good news. The IRS action was dismissed in Federal District Court. The arguments presented that had been summarized in the press release won the day with the judge. He found that the Supreme Court had previously ruled on the question at issue and additionally noted that the Freedonia Transaction Company position was also supported by the following section of the federal code: 31 U.S. Code § 5103 - Legal tender - United States coins and currency (including Federal reserve notes and circulating notes of Federal reserve banks and national banks) are legal tender for all debts, public charges, taxes, and dues. Foreign gold or silver coins are not legal tender for debts.

Thus, payments made in United States coins specifically designated as legal tender by the Coinage Act of 1965 had the face value specified on the coin when tendered as payment for a debt or obligation of contract. The IRS filed notice of appeal to the 5th Circuit Court in New Orleans. It seemed that the federal government hope was that a court outside of Texas might take a different view of the matter. Like all of the other pending issues, court decisions were becoming less important than the question of enforcement.

As Jim Roberts remarked after being informed of the decision and IRS appeal, "Doesn't matter anymore. Unlike the IRS, we are capable of enforcing our edicts."

This decision, with a combination of other factors led the Freedonia Transaction Company to approve of minting coinage to supplement and eventually replace the US silver coinage currently in use and being held as reserves. The new Texas Dollar series would be ten sided coins to easily distinguish them from existing coinage and facilitate the use of the coins in machines. The coins featured prominent figures of the American Revolution:

One Texas Dollar – Haym Salomon
50 Texas Cents – Benjamin Franklin

25 Texas Cents – George Washington
10 Texas Cents – James Madison
5 Texas Cents – Thomas Jefferson
One Texas Cent – Patrick Henry
Half Texas Cent – Christopher Gadsden

It would cost the Freedonia Transaction Company too much to continue to print the fractional currency promissory notes for denominations of less than one dollar to meet the increased demand for Texas currency. Coins lasted many years longer than the banknotes that were handled frequently in commerce. As the portion of the Texas economy using Texas Dollars grew, and that was certain to be the case given the referendum result and the pending decision by the legislature on making the Texas Dollar the official currency of Texas and legal tender, there would be the need for expanded production of that currency.

The five cent, one cent, and half cent coins would be copper, and unlike United States coins, have a real value. A sandwich and a soft drink could be had at the Green Dragon for fifteen cents in Texas Dollars. This plan would make the Texas Dollar copper coins a different size, and ten sided to make then readily distinguished from US coins. The Freedonia Transaction Company could now exchange the silver ingots and silver tokens and coins that customers brought in wanting Texas Dollars in trade.

The legislature did take up the matter of legal tender in Texas, as post referendum the legislature was now meeting full time. This was in marked contrast to the normal schedule Texas kept as a state legislature which met for 140 days every two years. The legislature defined the Texas Dollar to be 371.25 grains of pure silver. This standard recognized pre 1965 US silver coins and the coins produced by the Freedonia Transaction Company as Texas

Dollars. The statute would also allow for other entities to mint Texas Dollars if they chose to do so. A true free market in currency and coinage was to be had in Texas.

The demand for the federal government to leave Texas had not been enforced, and may have played a role in the outcome of the referendum. Some functions of the federal government continued unimpeded. Others, particularly those pertaining to enforcement actions tended to be rather shy about operating. Militias and some sheriffs around the state, were making it a practice to prevent seizures of assets or property by federal agencies. This tended to keep most federal government employers in their offices and hesitant to risk arrest or possibly being shot.

On the other side of the equation were several federal indictments of State Government officials and militia leaders, including warrants for murder naming Roberts. Nobody in the US Marshals Service was willing to try to serve any of the warrants. The request for service went to the FBI, who knew that would be yet another armed encounter with the Borden County Militia. Having lost the previous two encounters, and not certain about having the support of the President to take on an entity that seemed to be operating with the tacit if not explicit approval of the State of Texas, nothing happened.

The longer it took to resolve the situation, the more uncertain life would get for Texans and US Government employees living in Texas. Any Texan that traveled to another state could be subject to arrest by the US Government if the Texan did not comply with government rules and regulations, while employees of the US Government were increasingly likely to face arrest in Texas for performing their assigned tasks. It would be a short time until either the US Government was indeed removed from Texas or

Texans would be back to being subject to the whim of any government agency.

Some of the Lone Star Party legislators, Free Texas Directors and LSP executive committee members took a weekend break in Freedonia. North of the town square near where the churches were, a new sign had appeared. It announced the pending construction of the Synagogue of the Maccabee Congregation. Roberts looked up one of his Jewish friends in town. "I presume you now have ten Jewish men in town and have started a congregation?"

The inquiry was answered in the affirmative. There were conservative Jews who were just as tired of the endless socialism being imposed on them as were their Christian friends and decided that resistance to tyranny had called them to Freedonia. Roberts though it good for the movement to help show that liberty is good for everyone.

The situation in Austin became the subject of a Lone Star Party and Free Texas informal conference. This was a matter of strategy, and the movement had a few strategic thinkers. It was time to ask for suggestions, and the chair of the Lone Star Party caucus looked at Roberts. "Jim, what do we do?"

Roberts considered the question and replied, "We need to get to the Point where the President calls the Governor or the Governor calls the President, and they decide that the way out of the impasse is to have a negotiation on the role of the federal government in Texas. More specifically, which agencies will function in Texas, and which agencies will not operate in Texas, pending the resolution of this independence matter. Our task is to create the conditions that make that conversation take place as soon as possible. If the legislature were to create a provisional national government and start to put national functions in place, that would probably make that conversation happen sooner. General, what do you think?" Roberts asked the General.

The General said, "I agree. Demonstrating independence will get the attention of Washington, and I think the President will prefer negotiation to confrontation. We need to get the feds to the negotiating table before some bureaucrat does something stupid."

The Lone Star Party members took the idea back to the Republicans who were allied with them. Support in the House was close, but there was not enough support in the Senate and with the Governor and Lt. Governor to start on forming a national government. Continuing down this path would destroy the Republican Party. The national Republican Party without a strong Texas component would be at a disadvantage against the Democrats at the national level. Party loyalty was still strong among some Republicans.

The independence supporters arranged for Roberts to be present at a gathering of Representatives in his role on the military staff. They would bring up the conflict between the Republicans on the need to press forward with creating a national government for Texas. That would allow the opportunity for Roberts to remark "If you are worried about the future of the Republican Party, you might want to consider how many of your party supporters voted for the referendum. And if the Governor ever thought he might one day be President of the United States, he needs to think again."

That was designed to play to what was always the unspoken threat of the entire militia movement. There was the possibility of a change of government without the use of the ballot box. That particularly annoyed Democrats, who never seemed bothered about revolutions led by leftists, and one of the Representatives targeted Roberts with the statement "You can't help threatening violence when you don't get your way can you?"

Roberts reply was "As every good Communist knows, finely targeted violence is highly effective. It was Chairman Mao who stated political power comes from the barrel of a gun. We just happen to be better at it than your apparatchiks are."

One of the moderate Republican house members overheard the conversation between Roberts and the Democrat. "Most Army officers show more respect to their legislators." he directed at Roberts.

"I can't imagine why," retorted Roberts, "You people need to hear it straight on. And by the way, I'm not Army. I'm a militia officer, so you don't get to vote on my rank."

One of the Lone Star Party House members sensing that things with Roberts were getting animated and had come over to see what was happening. He had caught the last part of the conversation. He then said to Roberts "And they really don't understand why you military people have utter contempt for politicians."

"If the politicians were like you, we wouldn't." Roberts told him.

Word soon came back that the Governor was starting to think that being the President of the Republic of Texas might not be such a bad thing, after all. The legislation to create the provisional Republic of Texas got unstuck and started to move forward. All the Governor had to do to become the Provisional President of the Republic of Texas was to sign the legislation. He wouldn't even have to stand for election or campaign for office until it became a permanent presidency. What was not to like about that.

In fact, the Governor did conclude that the will of the voters should be respected, and signed the legislation creating the Provisional Republic of Texas.

Chapter 20

Provisional Government

IF THERE BE A PRINCIPLE THAT OUGHT NOT TO BE QUESTIONED WITHIN THE UNITED STATES, IT IS THAT EVERY MAN HAS A RIGHT TO ABOLISH AN OLD GOVERNMENT AND ESTABLISH A NEW ONE. THIS PRINCIPLE IS NOT ONLY RECORDED IN EVERY PUBLIC ARCHIVE, WRITTEN IN EVERY AMERICAN HEART, AND SEALED WITH THE BLOOD OF AMERICAN MARTYRS, BUT IS THE ONLY LAWFUL TENURE BY WHICH THE UNITED STATES HOLD THEIR EXISTENCE AS A NATION. – JAMES MADISON

As a result of the decision of the people of Texas to leave the United States of America, the State of Texas set about to create the Republic of Texas. There was never any doubt about what the independent nation of Texas was going to be called. The time had come to start the transition from a state of the United States, to the Republic of Texas as an independent nation.

The first thing to happen was to restructure the state government to add those additional tasks that would relate to creating a nation. The goal was to provide for a functioning mechanism for the conduct of all aspects of a national government pending the ratification of a new Constitution for The Republic of Texas. The

Governor would become the Provisional President of the Republic of Texas, and the Lt. Governor to become the Provisional Vice President. The House and Senate would remain as is, but additional committees formed to take on the additional functions of a national government such as foreign affairs.

Additional people would be needed to staff the new functions. There would be an increase in the number of people employed in the Military Department, and as the National Guard was still a federal asset, the additional staff would have to be found elsewhere. That elsewhere was mainly from retired officers, and that included the General, who now would be part of the Provisional President's military staff.

The Department of State had been renamed the Department of the Interior, and a new Department of State was being established for the purpose of conducting international diplomacy. As with the Military Department, this area was the exclusive domain of the federal government as long as Texas remained a state within the United States. The first task assigned to the new Department of State of the Republic of Texas was to conduct the negotiations for the exit of Texas from the United States. As a practical matter it meant communicating that to the federal government, determining who would comprise the Texas delegation to that negotiation, and then the more esoteric items such as creating passports to be issued by the Republic of Texas.

One of the more sensitive subjects was the creation of an intelligence organization. Texas foreign policy had been one of the questions that was the subject of debate in the Texas independence movement. Some adherents of Texas independence were more disposed toward a non intervention to isolationist foreign policy for the Republic of Texas. There were others who held the view that a Republic as large as Texas would have to play a role in the affairs of the world, and should be actively involved in world events. One point on which all agreed was that the Republic of Texas would not be a member of the United Nations, that organization being viewed as a Third World dictators club at best and the major source of evil in the world at worst.

The Lone Star Party and the conservative Republicans were using the legislation creating the governmental departments of the Republic of Texas as an opportunity to reform the state government as they went. The first target was the Military Department. The assumption was that it would become the Department of Defense for the Republic of Texas. That was not what the Lone Star Party had in mind. The Republic of Texas was going to have a War Department consisting of the regulars and militia. That militia would be universal so that over 2.5 million Texans would be in organized units arranged to provide a credible military deterrent.

The first task assigned to the War Department was to be border security on the Mexican border. That was going to be expensive, and the Lone Star Party insisted on increasing the budget for that activity from the current .5% of the state budget to 15% of the RoT national budget for the War Department. The House session got raucous when the Democrats asked where the legislature was going to get the money to do that and were told from welfare programs. This put the moderate Republicans in a jam. They had to either vote for more security and less welfare programs, or against more security.

The Lone Star Party Representatives had part of the answer. Removing many of the non citizens would relieve pressure on many of the social service agencies of the state. The schools were a perfect example. Every student cost the state about $10,000 US per year in aid to the school district in which the child was enrolled. With an estimated 10% of the school population the children of illegal and non citizens, reducing this population would save almost 10% of the budget spent on education. Add in the cost of other programs funded by the state, and the increased border security might even result in a savings to the RoT.

Lone Star Representatives had other ideas in mind, such as eliminating bi-lingual education and any money from the federal government for school programs, too. That fight would come at a later date, but not having the population that caused a disproportionate portion of state expense was a first step in changing the way the government was funded, and how much money might be needed.

Longer term, the LSP intended to eliminate property taxes, and fund the operations of the Republic of Texas solely via sales tax and tariffs. That dream was also off in the future, but the conditions for it to happen were being put in place now.

The next reform was the Treasury Department, which now became the entity for holding and spending the money allocated by the legislature. The Treasury Department was authorized to contract for the minting of coinage, purchase of silver and gold bullion for Texas currency, print or contract for the printing of Republic of Texas currency, and the issue of Republic of Texas bonds if authorized by the legislature to do so. The Treasury Department promptly contracted with the Freedonia Transaction Company to provide coinage and currency. Thus, Republic of Texas currency and coins would be identical to or interchangeable with the coinage and currency issued by the Freedonia Transaction Company.

The Comptroller became the tax collection arm of the Republic of Texas. For now, the Lone Star Party avoided the issue of property tax, and the whole realm of how Texas collected money for the government to operate. That issue would get sorted out later. The Lone Star Party was willing to trade elimination of the property tax for a higher sales tax. Unfortunately, the sales tax was increased to 7% and exemptions eliminated, without the promised decrease in property tax. This was not a surprise to the Lone Star Party. That result would help pay for the War Department while providing a campaign issue for the election of the permanent government of the Republic of Texas.

The Department of Public Safety had its tasks modified. It would no longer be involved in border security, as that was now a military mission. Those personnel would now be used to detain and deport persons in Texas without authorization in addition to the investigative functions that cross county boundaries, and the intelligence agency of the Republic of Texas would be placed in this department.

The Department of Transportation would be responsible for building highways using funds provided by the gasoline tax. The gasoline tax would be used for no other purpose than road construction, and as soon as there was no more gasoline tax being sent to the federal government, there would be ample funds for road construction and maintenance. The Lone Star Party was determined to end toll roads in Texas.

For the present, other departments and agencies would be left as is, pending review to determine if the Republic of Texas really needed a plumbers' examining board, cosmetology board, florist license, and other such offices.

Finally, the legislature approved the calling of a Constitutional Convention to write the Constitution of the Republic of Texas, which would be submitted to the people of Texas for approval. The convention was to take place in Austin starting in September. Once ratified, the required elections would be held, and the Provisional Republic of Texas would then become permanent as a nation equal to other nations.

The only problem with the plan was that the United States of America considered Texas to be a state within the United States, and not an independent nation. That issue had yet to be sorted out.

It was in the interest of Texas for the United States to think that a military solution to the problem was unappealing. There were two ways to make that happen. Either a strong enough military deterrent as to make the cost of that option too high, or incentives for a negotiated settlement could work. Or, both options could be pursued simultaneously.

Chapter 21

To Raise and Support Armies

THE AMERICANS ARE A VERY LUCKY PEOPLE. THEY'RE BORDERED TO THE NORTH AND SOUTH BY WEAK NEIGHBORS, AND TO THE EAST AND WEST BY FISH. – OTTO VON BISMARCK

Jim Roberts got a call from the General. Among those who had formed the Texas militias and incorporated them into the Texas Military Forces, there was only one General that mattered. The former commander of Texas' 36th Infantry Division in the TXARNG and former commander of the TXARNG was the General. The General was now the TMF Army Deputy Chief of Staff for Operations. He had been the advisor in forming the militias into a functioning military organization as a branch of the Texas State Guard and their commander as they were mobilized. The General was now going to perform the same task on a larger scale. "Jim, are you a good news first or bad news first kind of guy? I have both kinds of news for you. Which will it be?"

Most people listening in on the conversation would have found it odd for a General to ask such a question to a Major. The General and Roberts had taken a liking to each other personally at their first meeting and had a great deal of respect for each other as military professionals. Roberts responded with "Sir, I'm a bad news first kind of guy. At least it is not bad news followed by more bad news is it?"

"You are now assigned to TMF Army DCSOPS (Texas Military Forces Army Deputy Chief of Staff – Operations)." said the General.

"Ouch – now I need the good news." was Roberts' reaction. He liked the General and working for the General would normally be a pleasure for Roberts. He didn't like the idea of a staff job where he would help to create an Army, and then he would sit by and watch while that Army he helped to create took the field.

Now the General could deliver news that Roberts would like. "You have been promoted to Lieutenant Colonel and placed on active duty with the Texas Military Forces."

Roberts decided to have some fun with the news. "Sir, I gather the promotion is the good news? It certainly can't be the part about moving to Austin."

The General decided to have a little fun with Roberts. "It won't be that bad, we are adding on post housing and have made arrangements so you won't be bothered by liberal neighbors, or federal agents for that matter. You are going to build us an Army."

Arriving at camp Mabry in Austin, the first thing Roberts noticed was the construction boom of an additional headquarters building for the Texas Military Forces that was even larger than the 36th Division HQ used by the Texas National Guard. One of the oddities of the situation was that the Guard leadership was left out of some of the planning and discussions of the future of the Texas Military Forces, being considered part of the federal forces (which the Guard is), while the individual members of the Guard were in favor of the separation as a rule. They didn't like being diverted from critical Texas defense tasks to missions given to them by the federal government.

The rest of the construction was for housing of senior officers on post and the provision for increased security of a military installation located inside of Austin itself. Conservatives in Texas always referred to Austin as the city in Texas that wished it was San Francisco. The seat of government always attracts those seeking government largess whether personally in way of employment or for more sinister purposes. It was the intention of Jim Roberts to have as little interaction as possible with the population infesting Austin, returning to Freedonia every weekend.

Jim and Lise went first to the Adjutant general's section to pick up the official sets of his orders. Roberts had one set assigning him to the DCSOPS and another set of orders placing him on active duty, with a third set of orders promoting him to Lieutenant Colonel. He had been assigned on post housing at Camp Mabry, so the next stop was to the Post Quartermaster to see where they would live and get the key. Later that day, the movers would show up with some of their furniture, and Lise would start to put the house in order.

Jim left Lise at their quarters and drove over to the main HQ building to report in to the General. He found the General's office, with his secretary and the Major that served as the General's aide in the outer office. With the General getting his third star, Roberts had considered it possible that he might have been selected as the General's aide, but was glad it didn't turn out that way. Most officers hated the aide job, although officially the job is supposed to give promising officers insight into the higher levels of command.

Roberts walked over to the major's desk and handed him a copy of his orders assigning him to DCSOPS. "Hi my name is Roberts and could you tell me when would be a convenient time to report to the General for duty?" He had sympathy for the officer performing aide's duty and wanted to make things as easy on him as he could.

"Sir, the General has been expecting you and wishes to see you right away." The major walked to the General's office door, knocked and then announced, "Colonel Roberts, sir."

The General returned Roberts' salute and remarked "I see you were able to find your new rank insignia. I would have liked to have pinned that on myself. But, exigencies of the service as it were. Have a seat, and I'll get to the critical tasks I have for you.

Initially, DCSOPS is myself and six officers not including my aide. Your job is to create force structure, design it in terms of TO&E, get the right mix of regulars and militia units, with a primary mission focus of border security and possible mission of defense against invasion. We already have a plans guy as one of the six. You will have to slice the budget and between us DCSPERS and DCSLOG figure out how we allocate the people, training, build units, and supply them. There is no TRADOC, FORSCOM, or anything else in the way of schools other than the State Guard Academy. You have to figure out everything. Got it?"

Roberts responded "Yes sir, I think I do. I'd say the first thing we need to know is what is the Army budget. Is that known?"

"We should have the working numbers Friday. At least what is authorized. When we get the money may be a different story." was the General's reply.

"Sir the first thing I can get to you for your approval is the militia infantry battalion TO&E. That will get us started putting militia units into a structure, tell DCSLOG and DCSPERS what to look for first in terms of unit equipment, and potentially get something going as a force that can be fielded. I can see three battalions being put together rapidly. It gets problematic after that, but at least we have something for every other part of the Army to focus on for the next 30 days.

My main concern is the process we are using. It looks like we are starting to replicate how the Defense Department in Washington operates. We have two separate spheres operating. One is the budget sphere where the challenge is to see how much money the Department gets and then we play a zero sum game among the services to see who gets how much of the pie. The other sphere is the assigned missions. We get tasked to do something without considering if missions conflict or if the resources required for that mission are available.

We need to be able to fuse the two and say this mission requires X amount of money and the following units from each service. If the budget isn't there, then we need to push back in order to modify the mission based on budget, or the legislature knows how much more cash is required to do what they want. We tend to say that its OK and we'll cut corners to try and get the mission done. At this level there will be the tendency to keep cutting corners off the polygon until it becomes a circle and there are no more corners left to cut.

In summary sir, I'm campaigning for a real General Staff to do that. Not what the US Army calls a General Staff, which Congress never wanted in any case, but the real deal. Otherwise, we are going to replicate the current Washington budget and procurement mess. We have a chance now to break that cycle as this War Department is built. " offered Roberts.

"That's a good start. Now let me show you to your office." The General took Roberts a couple of doors down the hall. "And bring Lise over for dinner at 7."

Roberts attended the budget meeting for the War Department of the Republic of Texas. At least in his mind saying that he attended the meeting was a misnomer. He considered himself to be one of the flunkies sitting against the wall. The real reason why he and the officers from the other services in the service staffs were there was because the meeting would provide additional perspective. This was where the "big picture" was being painted.

The legislature had authorized 1 Billion TXD for the War Department for the year. This amount was now going to be sliced among the services. The split became 350 million each for the Army and Air Force, while the Navy got 300 million. The Navy was starting from nothing, The Air Force from next to nothing as the F-16s were in the Air Guard and not directly available, just as the National Guard equipment in the 36th Division was still in the hands of the federal government. The Army at least had some militia units and the State Guard.

Next meeting was Army only, chaired by the Vice Chief of the Army. Like the US model, the service chiefs were the Provisional President's advisors and met jointly for defense policy and priority of effort. The Vice Chief would actually run the Army. At the meeting was the DCSPERS (Deputy Chief of Staff for Personnel), the DCSIntel (Deputy Chief of Staff for Intelligence), DCSOPS (Deputy Chief of Staff for Operations), DCSLOG (Deputy Chief of Staff for Logistics), the Finance chief, and their key staff officers. The decisions on how the Army was structured and how it would train to fight were the remit of the DCSOPS, which as far as the staff went made it first among equals. Supplying the people and equipment the DCSOPS said the Army needed were the responsibilities of the other staff areas.

The Army was now going to start the first iteration of staff work to create a land force to defend Texas and support the foreign policy of the Republic of Texas. The DCSOPS motioned for Roberts to start the presentation.

Roberts started in with the planning assumptions. "At this funding level, we are going to attempt to seal the border with Mexico. Currently, we have neither the manpower, nor the equipment to do so, thus the budget this year will be directed at building the structure necessary for long term success. Cost of the border operation breaks down as follows – manpower 100,000 troops, and operations cost 40 million. At that rate, a full scale border operation costs 200 million TXD per year. This will leave 150 million for procurement and training along with operational costs for the rest of the force.

The reality is that we can't build up to that 100,000 troop level anytime soon, so funds will be reallocated at the end of every month to meet the needs of other activities or additional procurement. We also have the problem of not knowing if and how many of the US Army regulars will find their way to the Texas Army, what will be the final status of the TXNG, and we have differing pay scales among the components of regulars, State

Guard and militia. A private in the regulars is paid about 100 TXD per month, a State Guard member on state active duty about 300 TXD per month, and a militia soldier either the State Guard rate or nothing. Recommendation is to pay all active duty at the regulars rate.

Given that we will want to find a home for the regulars from the US Army that become Texas Army, the number of regulars we want to immediately access into the Army from the 100,000 figure is small – we want to keep it at 1000 or less, and until we have regular units ourselves, use militia units to fill the rest of the manpower need. Ultimately, between regulars and militia, we could have 2.5 million on the rolls, so personnel systems need to be scaled accordingly. Our regulars will be the staff here, and the trainers for the militia units, and other specialized personnel needed to build the force.

Immediate procurement needs are to equip 100,000 troops which means 500,000 uniform sets, 250,000 pair of boots, underwear, and so on. Not to mention weapons, ammunition procurement, and HMMWVs, trucks, field kitchens. To start procurement we need to approve patterns and source it. Obviously we want to give preference to any supplier that manufactures in Texas, but time and quantity constraints means using a pattern currently or previously in use by US forces. Sourcing from the Sierra Army Depot depends on if the Department of the Army will sell to us.

Short term operational need will be for 10,000 sets of individual night vision, field gear, and body armor, with more needed 90 days from now. That is probably 30 million TXD right there. So procurement is likely to run through the budgeted amount quickly." Roberts had only scratched the surface. Building units that would be needed was not covered as that was the problem of DCSOPS alone. And that meant it was Jim Roberts' problem.

DCSPERS briefed on decisions required on retirement policies, promotion policies, Texas already had its own medals and awards, and what additional awards might be necessary, and whether to use the same occupational specialties in use with US forces. DCSOPS needed to provide additional unit structure in addition to the infantry battalion, so personnel could be staffed for those units.

DCSIntel briefed on the priority intelligence requirements that were currently being targeted. First priority went to the border operation to identify likely smuggling routes, cartel operational bases and contacts in Texas. Second priority was the probability of the US forces conducting an invasion or operations against the Republic of Texas if ordered to do so.

DCSLOG briefed on procurement policy. Initial procurement was anywhere an item could be obtained, but within 180 days wanted to contract for items produced or assembled in Texas. If the scale of procurement on certain items rivaled that of the US, there would be incentive for suppliers to move operations to Texas.

There were a few more discussion points and then the meeting ended. The next meeting was then the internal DCSOPS meeting. This meeting was to coordinate Roberts' activities with the Plans section and the Training section. Training was working on the methods to train the soldiers needed and units being designed by Roberts. As Roberts had modeled the Texas Army closely on US forces, there was a quantity of material already available to modify. They did not have the staff, or other resources to create an Army from no pre existing template whatsoever. Coordination with the Plans section consisted of what type and number of units would theoretically be available for various contingencies. That gave Roberts his priority of work on establishing the next types of units to be needed.

Although he was working from a template, every line had to be reviewed, confirmed, or modified. Going through the organizational documents for every type of unit was tedious and time consuming. It was easy to lose track of time while pushing through all of the decisions that had to be made, and then submitted to the General for approval. Adding one more radio to an infantry company, meant 4 more radios in the battalion, or 12 more for the brigade, or 36 more for the division, and with the number of divisions in the projected for structure, that was easily a one million TXD decision. Based on Roberts experience as a company commander determined whether or not that million dollars was worth it or not. The same decision making process was required for every piece of equipment in a unit and the number of personnel, and the jobs those personnel performed.

There was the issue of the US "up or out" promotion system. Roberts didn't like it because it tended to put people with little experience into critical positions. Roberts wanted the Texas Army to have more of a regimental system and the regulars being promoted more similarly to the militia officers. He recommended that officers who were competent remain for up to 20 years for First Lieutenants, 30 years for captains, and 40 years for other officers. Too much investment was made in the training of a competent officer to force him out after less than 20 years of service.

Then there was force structure. Almost by definition, militia units would be light infantry. But there was a whole infrastructure that needed to be in place to make those light infantry units capable of fighting. For the first large formation to be formed, Roberts wanted the battalion commander, staff, and headquarters company to be regulars, and let light infantry militia companies rotate through the battalion every 30 days. This would provide continuity for the operation while the bulk of the manpower for the operation came out of the militia. It also provided for the largest possible number of militia units to get real experience and training. This was how Roberts intended to have the border security mission performed.

As the security mission was unlikely to need some functions such as artillery support, not all types of units would be needed to build the brigades and the eight to ten divisions that would eventually seal off the border. This would let every militia member in the 2.5 million member Texas Militia have 30 days on the border over the course of three years. That would at least give the whole Army a baseline of minimal experience. The next phase would be to expand the number of battalion, brigade, and division headquarters units to allow the entire Army to be mobilized if needed. Competent militia company commanders would be identified by the regular army trainers, and later promoted to the battalion positions as the militia battalions were built, then the process repeated for the larger units.

While that at least gave some foundation for an Army, any serious military threat would require regulars. Ideally there would be a corps of regulars consisting of two divisions with a cavalry regiment and armored units included. If Texas ever fought a real military, something more than a bunch of guys with rifles would be needed. There was one other reason for such a force. If Texas was going to be a player on the world stage, credible military power would need to be an option for the Republic of Texas. And that requires the ability to project military power.

Roberts was working on one such issue when the General came into Robert's office. "Lise called and said that you are late for dinner."

"She did not." Roberts replied.

"No, but she should have. Get out of here. Texas will still be here in the morning." The General knew the scale of the task, and there was no point in killing the staff. There were limits as to how much could be done.

Chapter 22

The Art of the Deal

GENTLEMEN, WHEN THE ENEMY IS COMMITTED TO A MISTAKE WE MUST NOT INTERRUPT HIM TOO SOON. – ADM HORATIO NELSON

On the part of the Republic of Texas, a negotiated and amicable separation from the United States of America was desirable. The challenge was to get the United States Government to feel the same way. This was one of the objectives of a Free Texas information operation which had been underway for almost one year. With the election of the new President, the negotiation was certain to be more complex, and the information operation was now conducted with this in mind.

The operation was conducted to work on the United States Congress as a target. If Congress passed a resolution agreeing to the withdrawal of Texas from the United States, it would be helpful to the cause. This served two purposes. First, it would meet the terms for secession laid down by the US Supreme Court in the White v Texas case. Second, it would provide cover for the President to negotiate the terms by which Texas left the union. The Democrats would be targeted for this effort, to give them a means of weakening a President they loathed.

The first indicator on how the negotiation was likely to go would be the reception given to the Provisional Secretary of State communication requesting the naming of a delegation to negotiate the terms and conditions of the withdrawal of Texas from the United States.

Jim Roberts was deep into the problem of how to give some 2.5 million militiamen a basic training in military skill without spending anything in the way of money when his cell phone rang. Roberts was irritated that he had forgotten to turn the phone off while in the office, then he noticed the call came from the Washington, DC 202 area code. He decided to answer the call.

"Is this Colonel Jim Roberts of the Texas Military Forces?" the caller asked.

"Yes it is." was Roberts reply.

"This is the White House switchboard. Would you please stand by for the President."

To Roberts surprise the next voice on the line was the President of the United States. "Mr. President to what do I owe the honor of your call?" Roberts said to the President.

The President got straight to his point. "This Texas situation needs to get resolved, and everywhere I look into it, your name comes up. You have influence in what is going on in Texas and I want to talk to you about it. Can you come to Washington next Thursday?"

The question presented a hard choice for Roberts. "Mr. President, I'd be happy to meet with you, however I doubt I will be able to make it to your office, as I suspect the FBI has other plans for me."

The President knew that was going to be a sticking point. He had a solution in mind before making the call. "OK, I can solve that. We go with both sides having sovereign immunity. I issue pardons for all that has happened to date to your and your people, and the Governor does the same for all 248 agents arrested in Texas. That will show we are both dealing in good faith. Agreed?"

"Mr. President, I can't speak for the Governor, but I will convey your offer to him and I hope that he accepts it." replied Roberts.

"One hundred percent. I'll call him later today. Bye." And the President was off the phone line.

Roberts contacted the General's aide. "The oddest thing just happened. I got a phone call from the President of the United States about the situation here in Texas. I need to see the General and then the Chief and the Provisional President to discuss the substance of the call."

It took about 30 minutes to set up everything. Roberts was called to the General's office, where in addition to the General's aide, the Army and Joint Chiefs and their aides were present. The office of Provisional Secretary of War had yet to be filled. Roberts repeated the conversation he had with the President of the United States. Then he added, as it was his opinion, that he thought that he had been selected as the back channel so that ideas could be brought up for future negotiations without there having to be a response or if there was a need to deny making an offer.

Then the call was made to the Provisional President with the Joint Chief setting up Roberts to repeat the conversation he had with the US President. "What do you make of it Roberts?" the Provisional President asked.

"Sir, I think he wants to diffuse the situation and bring Texas back into the fold. For him, this is a low key way to get that ball rolling." Roberts replied.

"How badly are your friends going to beat up on me for pardoning the feds? Are you going to smooth the way for me on that one?" the Provisional President asked.

"They'll take the deal. We know they are never going to be tried in a Texas court, so we get something in exchange and get to start the negotiation. You won't get slammed for it." was Roberts answer.

"At least it turns out OK for you doesn't it?" said the Provisional President.

"Sir, if you have some other way of getting me into the White House ...." Roberts needled the Provisional President.

"All right, I'm going to issue the pardons. They will be delivered to you so that you have some leverage on your end. Make sure I don't catch any grief over this and let me know how it turns out." was how the Provisional President ended the conversation.

Monday afternoon the guard at the main gate of Camp Mabry rang up Roberts. "Sir there is an FBI agent here to see you. He says he has a message from the President."

"Let him in." Roberts directed the guard.

"But sir, the FBI, they ....." the guard was searching for the right phrase to use to describe his opinion of what might happen next.

"I'm armed, and I have a number of friends also wearing the same uniform I am. Hopefully, we will have him outnumbered if it comes down to that." rejoined Roberts.

A few minutes later, the FBI agent was at the door to Roberts' office. "Come in." Roberts told him.

The agent said without emotion "I have a letter for you from the President and will return your reply."

Roberts opened the packet. It contained the pardons and a sealed envelope addressed to him personally. As he examined the contents, he remarked to the agent. "Do you know what is in the packet? You sound disappointed it isn't the warrant for my arrest."

The agent responded "I wish I was arresting you, and yes I know about the contents."

Roberts looked at the agent coolly "And you too are unlikely to get shot today. I also have a packet for you to take back. It contains 248 pardons for government agents. Have you ever heard the saying that the medium is the message? The President made sure the FBI delivered this in order to send me a message. I suspect he is also sending a message to the FBI as well. You can tell the President that I will be there. Good day."

Five minutes after the FBI agent left the post, Roberts called the General's aide and told him of the visit, and that the meeting with the President was on. That news was relayed up the chain of command to the Provisional President.

Thursday morning, Roberts went to Bergstrom airport. He was dressed in a civilian suit. For a moment, he thought about going unarmed, but decided against it. The US Air Force C-38A from the

257

201st Airlift Squadron was waiting for him as he arrived on time. Roberts headed for the stairway and the Airman at the bottom of the stairs saluted. Roberts returned the salute. As he got to the top of the stairs he asked one of the crew members "Where do you want me to sit?"

That comment got smiles from the crew. "Your choice of seat sir, there will be no other passengers. When we are airborne, drinks and snacks will be available."

Roberts took a portside seat and said "This is much nicer that the last time the Air Force delivered me somewhere. When we are wheels up, a Coke will be fine. Hopefully this puts me on the 'not an ass' list."

Although universally denied, crews of the 201st Airlift Squadron kept tabs on the VIPs, tracking those that respected and treated the crews well, and those that were the mission from Hell. His remark elicited more smiles from the crew. The flight to Andrews Air Force Base was uneventful.

The C-38A taxied into position, where there was a car and driver waiting for Roberts. The driver took Roberts to the White House, and being on the agenda for meeting the President went through the gate and was met by the Secret Service detail. Roberts turned to one of the Secret Service agents and said "Mind holding my 1911 for me while I'm meeting with the President?"

The agent looked shocked "You're carrying a firearm? How did that get in here?"

Roberts told the agent "It fits in a holster." and showed the agent where he had the gun. "I'll pick it up on the way out. We Texans have a reputation to maintain. I hear that Washington, DC is a very dangerous place."

When Roberts entered the Oval Office, the President was there along with three other people he did not recognize. Introductions were made and Roberts recognized a couple of the names as policy advisors. The President asked Roberts "Mind if we make this a working lunch?"

"By all means Mr. President." replied Roberts.

One of the aides pressed a button and a waiter appeared. Roberts ordered last – a bacon cheeseburger with potato chips and a chocolate shake. Another of the aides seemed bemused. "The White House chef is famous for making almost any of the world's finest dishes, but I'm curious to see how this comes out."

"We'll see how it compares to the 21 Club. Think of it as sending a message, just like having a packet hand delivered by the FBI." was Roberts' comment.

The President broke in "I thought you would understand, and by the way, the Secret Service is already plenty excited about your visit. Trust me, I'm here to negotiate."

Roberts responded, "On our end we are assuming this is the back channel. Nothing about this will be made public so we can have an open discussion."

"One hundred percent Let's get to it. I wasn't elected President to supervise the break up of the United States. What does it take to keep Texas in the US?" stated the President.

"After the referendum and recent actions by the Texas Legislature, that may be hard to walk back. I'll suggest to you that a key to how this goes for you will be actions of the US Government vis a vis the Constitution. A major trigger for events in Texas is a federal government doing what it is not authorized by the Constitution to do. No matter what law Congress may pass, or regulation invented, it had better be one pursuant of the eighteen enumerated powers of the US Government, or it isn't happening in Texas. It is the only way you may keep Texas as a state." Roberts had just articulated the core position of the Texans.

"I understand, I'm a businessman. You want to be able to do business. It is how the economy grows. Believe me, that is what I want, too. You people make it sound like you want to be your own country next week." the President was looking for a common interest.

"We do have a number of us that would rather that Texas became an independent nation last week. I'm a realist. Even if we agreed on the end state, it would take time to achieve it. That time works to your advantage to convince Texans that they don't need to leave the US, and that time allows us to make a rational transition with the minimum amount of disruption. I'm suggesting that we have a mutual interest in a careful deliberate negotiation." suggested Roberts.

"It is going to be hard to negotiate when we have a different desired end state as a result of the negotiation." reasoned the President.

"My guess is that the desired end state of one of the parties is going to change over time. Either you convince us this was all a bad idea, or you will realize that the US will not be able to keep a state in the Union that wants something different from other states. Whatever success you may have in saving the country may easily be undone by the next President. Thus we are taking advantage of the opportunity we now have." Roberts observed.

Lunch had arrived and the discussion slowed. One of the President's aids remarked to Roberts "This has gone differently than I expected so far. You seem like a reasonable guy."

"If your source for information was the FBI, I'll suggest to you that is not the best source of useful information." said Roberts.

The President broke in "I've already discovered that myself. What would you propose as a way forward from here?"

"The Provisional Republic of Texas has created a Department of State that is tasked with negotiating with the US Government. Figure out who you want on your end to talk to them. That will be the public mechanism for discussing our differences and negotiating a solution. Once you get the Texas proposal, counter with your proposal to keep Texas in the US and how the issues of concern to Texas will be addressed.

Essentially work two negotiating tracks (A) redress of Texas grievances with the US Government and (B) what agreements would be necessary to allow for a split. For example, could Texans born in the US have dual citizenship and as dual citizens they would still be required to file US tax returns and pay income tax. That alone could take some time to negotiate, as I suspect some of my cohorts have not thought through the implications there. Kind of makes a January 1 split seem reasonable due to the complexity of that issue alone. Now as to January 1st of which year ......

If it starts to go sideways, we open the back channel to get discussions back on track. Seem reasonable?" Roberts proposed.

"Sounds like you think we have the better position." Said one of the President's aides.

Roberts addressed him "On the contrary, I think the course of history is with the breakup of the United States. That was for me a very painful conclusion to reach. We have large political factions which are unable to be reconciled. The US Government is $20 Trillion in debt, and as any businessman knows, there is a point at which the business has too much debt and it can't be serviced. I think we are dangerously close to that point. With the FED raising interest rates, that point has come even closer, if it has not already been reached. The US Government doing a Chapter 11 bankruptcy is probably not an option because of the impact on the US Dollar and the individual citizen's stored wealth.

Despite all of your heroic efforts to save the country, your chances of success are slim in my view. I sincerely wish you every success in saving the United States. It will be made more difficult by the number of people in this town who will gladly slip the knife into you for any number of reasons. It won't be us. I'm guessing that at least one of them will succeed in thwarting some of your plans. When that happens, no matter what you may desire, the independence of Texas and potential breakup of the other states into various alliances becomes almost certain.

We have the option of letting events take their course, negotiating a mutually acceptable compromise, or actively working against you. I was just stating that the last of those three options isn't worth the bother to me."

The President broke in "I realize there are some very serious challenges we face in fixing the country, and I'm determined to do the utmost to make America great again. It seems that if we look like we are negotiating a solution to this issue, that contributes to public confidence in our good intentions. Much more productive than active conflict being waged. I think we can give negotiations a try."

Roberts replied "Then I will take back the message that negotiations regarding the relationship of Texas to the United States can occur. We should expect there to be a number of issues on the tangent to arise, and the process will take some time to complete. Therefore, none of us should have any unrealistic expectations as to the timeline the process may require. Is this acceptable to you?"

"Agreed one hundred percent." said the President. He then buzzed in one of the Secret Service agents to escort Roberts out of the White House. "Don't forget to pick up your gun on the way out."

The men shook hands and Roberts was on his way to Andrews Air Force Base, where the same plane and crew returned him to Austin. After leaving the airport, Roberts phoned the General's aide and told him that he had returned. He asked the aide if the General wanted the debrief now or in the morning. Roberts was informed the debrief had been scheduled for tomorrow morning.

The Friday morning debrief featured a number of interested parties. The Provisional President was there, accompanied by the Provisional Vice President, and the Provisional Secretary of State (that office having been filled), the Chairman of the Joint Chiefs acting as the Secretary of War, and the General as Robert's direct superior. Including aides and flunkies, Roberts made the total number of attendees at almost two dozen. With that many people in attendance, if there was bureaucratic conflict between the agencies represented in the room, somebody would be trying to score points off of him during the debrief.

Roberts began with his summary of his meeting with the President. "I was invited to the White House to discuss the current situation between Texas and the Federal Government. The meeting took place in the Oval Office with the President and three of his political aides. The meeting lasted just over 30 minutes and lunch followed with more informal discussion.

The President is seeking a method to resolve the conflict between Texas and the US Government. From his perspective, if the US Government conducts the type of reforms he has included in his political agenda, many of the points of conflict will be resolved. Thus, there is the perception that events to date and the referendum are a means of expressing displeasure to the President that has refused to listen to concerns of the state. The current President wanted to make it clear that he was listening.

I made the points that the events have a much greater seriousness. There is a percentage of the Texas electorate determined to have a nation independent of the United States. That effort is centered on a peaceful negotiation as the means of that separation. The effort has now manifest itself in a transition phase of government intent on conducting those negotiations.

Rather than allow the existing impasse to continue, there is a willingness on the part of the President to receive the Texas delegation after US Government negotiators are selected, and conduct meetings. We can expect Federal negotiators to concentrate on identifying measures that will tend to defuse the

Texas independence movement and try to obtain agreement that such measures when implemented, have resolved the issues between Texas and the US Government. Clearly we can use this strategy on their part to identify measures that the US Government will be unable to accomplish to resolve differences between the parties, thus steering negotiations in the direction of our choosing.

I will now take your questions."

One of the people Roberts had identified as a State Department flunky was the first questioner. "Why did the President decide to meet with you?" The question told Roberts that the State Department was trying to establish its turf and resented somebody from the War Department representing Texas.

"The President indicated that he thought I was influential in the current affairs of Texas, and could give him an accurate view of the various constituencies and if necessary, would be able to fairly represent his views to someone in Texas who might be misinformed as to the President's intentions." Roberts shot back.

The Provisional President interjected "And maybe the President wants to deal with someone who he thinks is capable of shooting someone who gets out of line and fails to adhere to the terms of a deal."

That was always the elephant in the room. Over the past few years, thousands of Texans had come to believe that Jim Roberts and other militia leaders had their best interests in mind. One call and the largest armed in force in Texas would assemble, and then tend to do exactly what Jim Roberts suggested. Any office holder in Texas ignored that fact at his peril.

The Provisional President's comment also told Roberts about the relationship between the Provisional President and the State Department and himself. The Provisional President had respect for Roberts' ability, even if their personalities clashed. The Provisional President also did not like how things were going in the State Department.

The Provisional President continued "Where do you see things going from here Roberts?"

That elicited the following analysis from Roberts "Sir, I think getting a commitment for negotiation removes further use of force as an option for them. The President is probably not inclined to go that way as it has been ineffective for them in the past. They will use the negotiations to ensnare us in tangle foot to delay agreement until circumstances change or even until the President leaves office. Barring extraordinary events, de jure independence is years away. On the other hand, the speed with which we can build economic insulation from the rest of the country and have a credible military deterrent provides de facto independence when we stop paying income taxes and secure our border."

"What happens next?" asked the Provisional President.

"I think our State Department hears something within two weeks." replied Roberts.

The briefing then broke up, a couple of the attendees having private questions for Roberts. The General asked if he and Lise were going to Freedonia for the weekend. After the question being answered in the affirmative, the General told Roberts that he would be visiting Freedonia and several members of the legislature from the Lone Star Party were also heading for Freedonia that weekend. "The impending Constitutional Convention is a mess."

"I keep telling everybody that politics stinks." said Roberts.

"But you are constantly in the middle of it." noted the General

Roberts explained "An ancient Athenian once said 'You may not be interested in politics, but politics is interested in you.' I am merely engaged in a self defense mechanism."

Chapter 23

Constitutional Convention

LET OUR GOVERNMENT BE LIKE THAT OF THE SOLAR SYSTEM. LET THE GENERAL GOVERNMENT BE LIKE THE SUN AND THE STATES THE PLANETS, REPELLED YET ATTRACTED, AND THE WHOLE MOVING REGULARLY AND HARMONIOUSLY IN SEVERAL ORBITS. – JOHN DICKINSON

To complete the process of transforming the State of Texas into the Republic of Texas, it was necessary that the people of Texas approve of the Constitution that would govern such a republic. Almost everything relating to a Constitution for the Republic of Texas was likely to be contentious. At best, it would be an attempt to apply the lessons learned from over 200 years of self government to further improve the safety and happiness of the people of Texas. At worst, the seeds leading to a future tyranny would be planted to grow over time, until that tyranny matured and caused untold grief.

The first fight to occur was the determination of who would be appointed to the convention to write the proposed Constitution of the Republic of Texas. Every possible constituency wanted to get at least one representative into that convention. Finally, the question came down to determining how many delegates the convention would have. Then, the fight over who those delegates should be could take place.

To try to break the logjam, Free Texas invited the other Texas independence organizations, Lone Star Party, Republican Party Texas legislators, and a few of the other like minded groups to Freedonia for a workshop to try to devise a plan that might make it through the legislature. Too many lobbyists and reporters were around Austin to make it possible to have a private meeting where issues could get sorted out. Freedonia served as a location where the liberty movement could gather in peace and have a demonstration model of what might be possible if only the proper laws passed and improper laws repealed.

A large number of the Free Texas members, and some legislators from the Lone Star Party, plus a few Republicans had gathered at the Green Dragon to hear from Jim Roberts about his sojourn to the White House. Ed McMasters started the conversation. "What was the President like?"

This was the prompt for Roberts to elucidate about his experience. "He was much more personable than I expected. I left with a much higher regard than I had for him before. That is always the challenge when meeting someone with a well defined public persona. You tend to get either a pleasant surprise or a disappointment. It may seem strange to some of you here, but I really hope he can turn the country around. But, like most of us, I have concluded things are too far gone to be reversed.

Anyway, the meeting gave me an insight as to how they intend to handle us. They seem to have reached the conclusion that the real issues between us are government policies like regulation and tax rates. If they can fix those issues, they seem to think that the desire for independence will fade, all will be well, and we'll be one big happy American family again. Currently, they can't conceive of not being able to pull this off. There is a commitment for negotiations between Texas and the US, and that is going to take a long time."

McMasters broke in "How long do you think?"

Roberts continued "If the President and the Republican National Committee are successful, as long as it takes for the people of Texas to decide that this was all a mistake and we really are happier as a state in the United States. The idea that we are looking long term beyond the current President is lost on them. In any case there are legitimate issues that will take some time to resolve. How will our people react if they are told they have to give up US citizenship and can't be dual citizens. What if there is dual citizenship and dual citizens of Texas, like dual citizens of the US and other countries have to still pay US income tax.

My point being that is just one example of something that has to be agreed to between Texas and the US. Once we agree on how that is going to work, to be put into place cleanly it has to occur at the end of the tax year for individuals and businesses. Just that one issue alone is going to take months to resolve and implement. And this assumes the US isn't actively trying to screw us, which they will.

We are going to have to negotiate all of this stuff point by point for a clean and legal break. This brings me to the other possibility. Events could easily overtake the negotiations. In that case, we have to hope we have an economy that has become independent enough to withstand the shock of US collapse, and that we have enough military power to defend ourselves.

At least as long as there are negotiations, we are unlikely to be visited by the FBI, IRS, ATF, EPA, and the rest. If we can get the US Government to realize that their unconstitutional crap is the real problem, and they are not going to solve it without annoying too many Republican contributors, that will help change the dynamic in our favor. At some point Texans will get frustrated with the lack of progress toward real independence or federal government restraint and demand something happen. It is going to be frustrating for someone to have voted for independence and a year later still be paying federal income tax.

That leads us to the Constitutional Convention mess doesn't it?"

McMasters said "Yeah, but you've already made my brain hurt enough for one night. We'll tackle that with the other attendees in the morning."

The workshop got started shortly after 9 AM Saturday. The Lone Star Party legislators and some of their more trusted Republican allies were attending. Care had been taken to make certain that no more than 40% of the legislature was present. If too many members had been present, provisions of the Open Meetings Act would apply, and this workshop was organized with a view of making progress on the subject, and not being a public spectacle. Also attending were some allies in government, a few members of the War Department, several of the directors from Free Texas, and some representatives from other Texas sovereignty movements.

The Lone Star Party caucus leaders started discussion with a report on what the legislature had done to date, which was very little because the first roadblock had been reached, Other than agreement there should be a committee appointed to write a Constitution for the Republic of Texas, the size and composition of the committee was where action had stalled. The group assembled here today needed to work out a plan of action to move events forward and provide the framework for the support from the public needed to let that action plan work.

Each of the legislators gave his perspective on the problem and they tended to make the pitch for what items they thought were important enough to be included in the new Constitution. So far a few themes emerged. Size and composition of the legislature was an issue. How many Representatives and Senators should there be and what would constitute the constituency for each. Would it be the current method of allocation based on population, or should there be a geographic component at the county level, like the Lone Star Party operated in selecting convention delegates.

Another of the themes was what would be the requirements for being a citizen of the Republic of Texas and who should have the right to vote and hold office. There was a strong sense that just being born inside the borders of Texas should not be qualification for citizenship. That opened the question of what should be the criteria used to define a citizen. There were a number of competing proposals to determine who would be a citizen. It could be based on having a parent who is a citizen. It could be based on property ownership. One proposal was for third generation residency to establish citizenship. There were a number of ideas. What there wasn't at this point was consensus and a mechanism to document who is a citizen and who isn't.

What should be in the proposed Bill of Rights also became a laundry list of items. All manner of prohibitions were wanted from any restriction on firearm ownership to no toll roads, and other items. People were attempting to find new ways to prevent government usurpation of powers not granted to it. While the

272

discussions were intense, at least they were polite. If nothing else, that was something unusual in Texas politics. Like what was happening in Austin, there was loads of talk about what it should be, but little in the way of how to actually create the document.

There had been one mid morning break, and the participants broke for lunch as the time neared noon. The Lone Star and Free Texas attendees headed for the Green Dragon. The Republicans and many of the Native Texan Movement people headed for one of the other restaurants in Freedonia. That was in keeping with the alignment between the political parties and affiliated Texas independence organizations.

As they were walking toward the Green Dragon, one of the Lone Star Party legislators said to Roberts "You haven't said a thing all day."

"I'm listening to what everyone has to say." replied Roberts.

"What do you make of it so far?" the Representative asked.

"I doubt a solution can be crafted that solves every problem anybody thinks we have. We need a plan to staff a committee that can produce a Constitution the voters will approve. And we have to hope that Constitution does not do us any damage, but puts a framework in place that allows for the detailed issues to be addressed later. I think the scope of what you are trying to accomplish needs to be more limited." opined Roberts.

"Are you going to mention that this afternoon?" continued the Representative.

"When the opportunity presents itself, I'll try to make a suggestion." concluded Roberts.

After lunch, the assembly picked up with what should be in the Bill of Rights. Eventually, the subject came up as to what the independence organizations represented in the workshop had to say. Their members had their own list of issues they wanted addressed such as prohibitions on income tax and a prohibition on taxing property.

The Representative that had spoken with Roberts before lunch asked to be recognized in reply. He said to the group "I want to hear what Jim Roberts thinks about the problem we have." A few other attendees voiced assent to the idea.

This was Roberts' opportunity to plant some ideas among the legislators. "I think you have several difficult challenges to meet.

First is composition of the committee to write the Constitution. I'd suggest that what we learn from the past is that is needs to be a small group. The larger the committee, the more will be the desire for every group in Texas to get a member on it. That will bog down the process to a standstill. One possible solution is to have each of the three parties in Texas representing their supporters and voters. That could be six House members, two from each party, and one Senator from each party, for a total of nine.

That number of people is barely manageable. It gives enough strength to vote down the off the wall suggestions, while demonstrating minority representation. If the Republicans need to split votes on an issue, they can while the issue gets resolved in our favor.

The next challenge is the scale of the Constitution. The options are to go very general like the US Constitution or to take on the State Constitution and modify it. If you go general, you might get something out of the committee in a reasonable amount of time. The more detail you cover at this time, the more likely we are to end up with something like Martians have a right to free health care. If you concentrate on putting in the structure that can be used to pass at a subsequent time, the restrictions and amendments we have been discussing today that would generate less controversy than some provision that barely made it into the document.

I'll also suggest that the composition of the House and Senate is potentially the most critical item. Something that could really tilt the field in our favor would be to have one Representative from each county, and the Senate represent population, say no more than 1 million population per senator and no less than 800,000, and a Senate district must contain entire counties, unless the county has a population of over 1 million.

Let the fight be over the composition of the Texas Congress as the proxy issue for all of the things we have been discussing today. That increases the number of Representatives and Senators to almost 300, or not quite doubling the current number. Let the opponents argue why they want less representation rather than more.

Clearly our issues resonate more with the rural and suburban population. That puts in place the structure that makes the other reforms possible." Roberts then resumed his seat.

There was now discussion of "the Roberts plan" by the legislators as to if it could work its way through the legislature. The Lone Star Party legislators liked the idea, as it was similar to how the Lone Star Party was organized internally. The Republicans wanted to study the idea a bit more before committing to support the plan as the means of moving a Constitution through the legislature and to the voters for approval.

After the workshop ended, Ed McMasters asked Roberts "What do you think is the hold up with the Republicans?"

"They have to sell it to as many of the rest of the Republicans as they can. They also have to navigate around a national Republican Party that wants Texas to stay in the United States, and deal with constituents. We could use some help from the Native Texas Movement on them." said Roberts.

"Even if it makes it through, there is still left a lot to do to get our program put into the Constitution." remarked Ed.

"Whether it is in the Constitution or law, the real issue is enforcement. If there is no enforcement, both Constitutions and laws are without meaning." Roberts observed.

Chapter 24

Silent Missions

THE ART OF STATESMANSHIP IS TO FORESEE THE INEVITABLE AND TO EXPEDITE ITS OCCURRENCE. – CHARLES MAURICE DE TALLEYRAND

The General entered Roberts' office at Camp Mabry. "I have just left a meeting with the Provisional President and the Provisional Secretary of State. Through discussions via Switzerland with NATO and EU countries, we are going to send a representative to establish preliminary diplomatic and military contacts with potential allies. You will be that representative as you have lived in Europe for several years, speak German, you can get by in French, and your reputation will precede you when we notify the Swiss. Of course we can't send a Lt. Col. on such a mission."

"Of course not" Roberts wasn't sure where this was going.

"A Colonel is the lowest possible rank of officer that could be sent on such a task. Thus, you have been promoted to Colonel. Start packing, Colonel Roberts." The General liked delivering good news, and he had recently gotten his third star himself.

"I haven't been a LTC for even a year." Roberts had been a very old Captain, almost like the days of the Indian Wars when it was common to retire as a Captain. He had been fairly old to be a Major, too.

"Think of it as you are catching up with your contemporaries." The General told Roberts.

"I've never commanded anything larger than an armed mob. They at least had the opportunity to command real battalions." It still annoyed Roberts to not have had much time to command at the battalion level.

The General understood. "Your armed mob was larger than a battalion, and a much more challenging task than commanding a conventional battalion. I and others are well aware of the skill you exhibited under trying circumstances.

The mission has been arranged via the Swiss, and you will be going on an European tour to establish diplomatic and military contacts with potential allies in Europe. Tomorrow morning, you will meet with your contemporaries selected for other regions of the world, the Provisional President, Provisional Vice President, Provisional Secretary of State, Provisional Secretary of War, Chief of Texas Military Forces, Army, Air, Navy Chiefs and their operations Vice Chiefs such as myself. And tell Lise that she is going with you."

The next morning, Roberts was one of the first to arrive. He found the seat he had been assigned. There was a briefing packet prepared for him. The first thing that caught his attention was that the packet contained two passports. A black Diplomatic Passport issued by the Republic of Texas for him, and a red Official Passport issued by the Republic of Texas for Lise. Also in the packet was a projected itinerary. Jim and Lise Roberts were going on an European tour. It was also clear they were not going to get frequent flyer miles as this travel would be using a Gulfstream jet.

By this time, the other participants were arriving. Roberts was the only person in the room other than military aides wearing a uniform who was not a General or an Admiral. It looked like the War Department had infiltrated a State Department operation. This tended to confirm his suspicions about the turf battle between the War Department and State Department. The men with the other regional packets for East Asia, Middle East and Africa, South America, and Central and North America were what Roberts made to be suits. To Roberts a suit was someone who had spent a career alternating between government positions and various public policy related organizations with an occasional real job just to have credibility with people who only had real jobs.

The Provisional President started the meeting. "Welcome everyone. Before we get started there is an important ceremony that requires our attention. General, would you please read the order."

The Chair of the Joint Staff announced "Lieutenant Colonel Roberts, attention to orders."

Roberts stood up and the order promoting him to Colonel in the Regular Army of the Republic of Texas was read. The Provisional President then changed Roberts' insignia to reflect his new rank.

Roberts concluded the Provisional President had just sent a message, and the War Department had just scored one on the State Department. It was clear that the State Department had not selected Roberts for this task. He didn't fit the profile of the other four packet holders. Someone in the War Department wanted him on this mission to Europe in place of who the State Department was going to send. The case had been made to the Provisional President, and carried the day.

The meeting was now turned over to the State Department, and the Secretary of State took the floor. "The State Department has been given the charge to open preliminary contacts with other nations around the world as the first steps in an independent Texas assuming a role in world affairs. As we have not yet negotiated our separation from the United States, this is a particularly sensitive mission requiring the utmost in discretion and skill. With one exception, the diplomats selected for these missions have an impeccable list of credentials starting with their education, and experience at almost all levels of the consular service."

Roberts briefly considered asking who the one exception was, but decided to hold his tongue. He could now guess why there was conflict between the War and State Departments. The Department of State was being populated with the "right sort of People" meaning Texans with Ivy League backgrounds and US Department of State experience, probably for previous Republican Presidents. If there was going to be a Republic of Texas, mainline Republicans intended to control the foreign policy of the Republic. The War Department was concerned about Europe, and wanted to have somebody there who was not going to Europe with the intention to sit in the hallways of the Foreign Ministry between dinner parties.

The Secretary of State continued "The Swiss Government viewed the results of the referendum as a measure of self determination as the will of a sovereign people. As a result, they have agreed to serve as intermediaries for the Provisional Republic of Texas, pending future developments. Now we will have a look at the specific regions."

The Secretary gave a bit of the background of the selected diplomat that explained why he was chosen for the region, which countries he would visit and what were to be likely discussion topics. While the Secretary was speaking, an Army officer quietly entered the room and sat down. Roberts noticed the officer held a letter sized envelope marked "CONFIDENTIAL".

When the Secretary of State said "And finally, we come to Europe and Colonel Roberts" the officer arose and interrupted the Secretary to tell him that a message had arrived for him from the Swiss consulate marked urgent. The Secretary opened the envelope and as he read the message, his face tightened. As he regained his composure, he looked at Roberts and said "Mr. Martel of the Free Democratic Party asks me to pass along his warmest regards and says he looks forward to seeing you again while you are in Bern."

The Generals in the room looked at each other and grinned. Score another one for the War Department. The Secretary had been rattled.

The Secretary tried his best to recover "It seems our information on Colonel Roberts is incomplete. Do you know this gentleman, Colonel?"

"Yes sir, personal friend. I know some other FDP office holders through business relationships while I was working in Switzerland. As junior partners of the governing coalition, they will be the most approachable about a free trade agreement between Switzerland and Texas." answered Roberts.

The Secretary was now completely off track. The brass hats in the War Department were dropping sandbags on him left and right. All he could say to Roberts was "Well, while you are over there, at least try not to get us into any wars, won't you?"

The Provisional President had enough "He managed to make it into the Oval Office to meet with the President and back without anyone getting killed in the process, didn't he? That was something none of your guys was able to do." The meeting was over.

There was a follow on to the meeting at the War Department. Attendees were the Secretary of War, the Joint Chief, Army Chief, Army DCSIntel, Army DCSOPS, their military aides, and Roberts. The Secretary of War spoke first. "Colonel, I was told you were quite a character and your reputation is fully justified, but I've got to admit I was impressed with that ambush. Do you really know that guy in Switzerland?"

"Yes sir, I sent an email to him last night asking to help me out and send me a note via the Secretary of State. After the trip to Washington, I figured I owed the State Department one. I never expected the timing to be that perfect." Roberts answered.

The DCSIntel jumped in "I'm taking credit for the timing. When that message came in over night, I knew it was gold. I gave the delivery instructions to one of my staff. I gather you found his performance of duty satisfactory?"

Roberts responded "I owe that guy a steak dinner."

The Secretary of War continued "He was trying to goad you to lose you temper and justify his opposition to you, but he never had a chance."

"I wouldn't give him the satisfaction." Roberts confirmed.

Roberts' boss the DCSOPS broke in "Now let's get serious. Jim, you have obviously figured out that we rigged having you go as our diplomat to Europe. I'm sure you can guess why we did it. What do you think we need from your mission?"

Roberts gathered his thoughts for a moment. "First let me take military considerations. The split of Texas off from the United States is going to worry NATO members as to if the US will maintain its NATO commitments or the possibility of Texas joining NATO and picking up the slack from a diminished United States. There are also escalating tensions with Russia on the Eastern boundary of NATO.

As we are currently the only western entity working on a large buildup of military power, our intentions are going to be an object of curiosity. If we are still part of the US as we build, the Texas Military Forces could potentially end up being committed in Europe. We need to know the lay of the land. Which NATO countries have a capable military force and how committed are European countries to the preservation of western civilization and possible cooperation with us.

Next we have the Muslim invasion of Europe and need to know which nations will push back, as opposed to those who are going to roll over and go paws up. As we have dealt with the problem, those who want to defend themselves will be interested in learning from our experience and thus one of the factors as to why I was selected for this mission, along for the ability to assess military capability.

In the realm of the purely political, we share a common culture with Europe. The change in political circumstances manifesting itself in the rejection of the European Union, repelling invasion from a civilization determined on conquest, and a shift in public opinion toward less government interference in personal lives are of as strategic interest to Texas in terms of alliances, markets for our goods and services, and potential sources of capital for our economy. Many of the political parties that are a part of this movement would be natural friends of a Republic of Texas. We could potentially tip the balance by the skillful use of diplomacy that is active and engaged in Europe."

The DCSOPS said "See, I told you he was relatively bright, even for a Colonel."

The DCSIntel joked "I am so disappointed that it seems I will not be getting the benefit of the Colonel's thinking on the strategic importance of the War Department fighting climate change. I'm sure the State Department would be much more proficient in this area."

"Seriously sir, while I'm over there, I'd like to take a week of leave. We could visit Lise's family and I have a couple of things I'd like to do." Roberts asked.

"You have the plane and the crew. Go look up some of the people you served with in the NATO armies too, and as for how much time you take, it will just be permissive TDY. Do a little snooping around. We'll see you back here in four weeks. Take the rest of the day for you and Lise to get ready for your departure." said the DCSOPS.

Roberts contacted his assigned aircrew and told them he would prefer an evening takeoff so as to arrive on the European continent mid day making essentially an over night flight, so the pilot could schedule the necessary crew rest. Commercial traffic preferred planes to arrive in Europe early morning, so they could fly back to North America for an early afternoon arrival and repeat the cycle. The plane and crew were tasked with supporting Roberts' mission, so time of departure that was not a consideration. Roberts didn't sleep on planes, so he considered the arrival day in Europe to be a total loss.

The first stop on the journey was Bern, Switzerland. The plane landed just after noon, and already Roberts noticed something different about travel in a private jet with a diplomatic passport. There were no lines to get your bags, and no customs line to delay getting on with the trip. But the best part of all was that there was no interaction with the Transportation Security Administration whatsoever. It reminded him of his first trip on a plane in the days before metal detectors. You simply arrived at the airport, checked your bags, and got in the plane.

After checking into the hotel, Jim took Lise on the one must see tourist activity in Bern. They went to the bear pit. There is a legend that Bern will prosper as long as there are bears in the hills around Bern. Not willing to leave prosperity to fate, there is always a bear kept in the bear pit in order to assure the prosperity of Bern. Next on the Roberts agenda was food and sleep. The real mission would start in the morning.

The first meeting of the trip was with the Swiss Foreign Minister. This was not unexpected because of the tradition of Swiss neutrality which allows Switzerland to facilitate meetings and negotiations between parties in an international context when those parties might not otherwise be able to find a suitable venue for diplomatic exchanges. Switzerland considers this to be its contribution to the international community. Thus, the idea of Switzerland facilitating the Republic of Texas assuming an international role was not unusual after it was clear that creating an independent republic was the will of the people of Texas.

For this reason, and the fact that the first meeting of an official representative of the Republic of Texas would take place with a cabinet level official of a foreign country, Switzerland was the first stop. Contributing factors to the decision were that Roberts spoke the language and would not need an interpreter, and Roberts had lived in Switzerland for several years. The last and perhaps most important factor is that Texas would likely pursue a policy toward Switzerland that the Swiss would find much more favorable than the attitude taken by the United States toward Switzerland.

Meeting the Foreign Minister, Roberts expressed his appreciation and the appreciation of the Republic of Texas for the assistance of the Swiss Confederation in making the first meetings with foreign government officials possible. Texas has every interest in having the best possible relationship with Switzerland, and the Republic of Texas was prepared to take active measures to assure this positive relationship.

Among the things the Republic of Texas could offer Switzerland were (1) continued use of Sheppard Air Force Base for pilot training and Ft. Bliss for air defense training (2) unlike the United States, a cash and carry policy on arms sales with no approval by the Republic of Texas required, unlike the United States (3) the Republic of Texas respect for the sovereignty of Switzerland by having no reporting requirements by Swiss businesses on the activities and financial status of its citizens, unlike the United States (4) a desire for a free trade agreement based on the fact of there being an equivalent standard of living between the two countries, Swiss citizens and businesses being subject to the same taxes as their Texas counterparts.

Roberts also stated that it was a long term goal of the Lone Star Party, one of the parties now part of the coalition running Texas to

286

eliminate all income, capital gains, and property taxes. Therefore a free trade agreement with Texas would provide Swiss investors with an attractive economy that would not steal their profits. Texas would also have an interest in a bilateral agreement to ease residency and work permit grants for the citizens of the two countries in order to improve economic cooperation and friendship between the two countries.

The Swiss Foreign Minister said that this was a welcome and positive development and that as Roberts knew, his friends in the FDP would be very friendly to the idea of a free trade agreement with Texas. And the willingness of Texas to respect Swiss laws and especially the banking secrecy laws of Switzerland is especially welcome. He also stated that the Swiss foreign ministry would continue to assist the Republic of Texas in facilitating diplomatic exchanges. As Texas was not yet a recognized country, any other contact with Swiss officials would be unofficial. The question of if and when the Republic of Texas would be recognized by Switzerland was of course, a matter left entirely with Switzerland.

Roberts hoped all of the meetings would go as well, but the next one in London was likely to be one of the more difficult because of the traditionally close relationship between the US and Great Britain. The Swiss had made the arrangements, and what he had to work with was based on the Swiss relationship with the British, which was generally good. Roberts had toyed with the idea of arriving at Stansted airport instead of Heathrow because of the low profile nature of his mission and the outrageous landing fees Heathrow charges, but the British hold appearance in high regard, and that consideration took precedence. Heathrow would be the landing location of the representative of the Republic of Texas, like every other nation.

Roberts was surprised to be met by a car and driver from the Rifle Regiment. His first trip to Great Britain had been as a young Lieutenant as part of a program commemorating 200 years of diplomatic relations between the United States of America and the United Kingdom of Great Britain, Scotland, and Ireland. The British Army unit supporting the event had been the Royal Green Jackets, which had now been amalgamated with other units to form the Rifle Regiment. It would seem that Texas had friends in the British Army. The driver introduced himself and inquired if the Colonel had accommodation in London sorted. Roberts replied that he did at the Victory Services Club on Seymour Street. The driver was familiar with the location.

If travel on a diplomatic passport offered no other benefit, they had bypassed the one hour wait to see an immigration officer who would inquire as to their purpose in visiting the UK, and anticipated length of stay. Jim and Lise checked in at the club, and thankfully after the most recent refurbishment, both of them and their luggage could fit in the lift. Roberts told the driver that he would not be required until their departure in two days time.

One of the benefits to being a member of the club is nice hotel rooms in London at about half the price that the hotel chains charge, and all of the members are military. Given the diversity displayed so far in London, the club was a welcome relief for those kindly disposed toward western civilization. Roberts had previously purchased a Life Membership.

One of the reasons for the extra day in London was for some shopping and sightseeing for Lise. The first order of business for Jim Roberts London shopping trip was to head for Jermyn Street. He decided he needed more shirts and Turnbull & Asser was where they were to be had. Roberts went around the corner off of

Jermyn Street where the main entrance for the store was located to the Prince of Wales Room entrance. He was greeted promptly and said that he was here to order some more shirts, and would like to look at the fabric samples. He selected six patterns of fabric and said he wanted them cut just like his last order, giving the order number, and when completed would like them sent to Freedonia. Roberts paid and left.

Jim and Lise had a short walk from Jermyn Street across Piccadilly to Saville Row, where Jim had an appointment at his tailor. Gieves & Hawkes at the southern end of the street was his destination. As is the custom in high end shopping in London, he was promptly greeted and said he was heading for the back where he had an appointment. The first thing a customer sees on entering the Bespoke section is a painting of Admiral Nelson. Tailors never say who is or is not a client, but the portrait tells what needs to be told. The Bespoke Cutter greeted him warmly. "A pleasure to see you again, sir. It has been a very long time."

"Much too long, I'm afraid." Roberts replied. "Might I look at the fabric samples for the next suit?" and the book of lighter weight woolen fabrics was produced. "Yes, remember this one from last time. I'll go with the expert opinion and would like it cut the same as this one."

"Excellent choice, sir." affirmed the cutter.

The Next destination was Fortnum & Mason back on Piccadilly, where Jim wanted to find something for Lise. As Tea Time was approaching, they had Tea there at F&M, so that item could be checked off the bucket list. Lise did not want a bespoke outfit made at Gieves & Hawkes, one of the little known facts being that most of the Saville Row tailors also do women's clothing. In fact

Roberts' tailor was a woman because Roberts was an American, and therefore could be touched by a woman who was not a family member, unlike a British gentleman. Finally, the issue of shopping for Lise was resolved, and they headed back to the Victory Services Club, being a leisurely walk through the Mayfair district.

The rational observer would have considered the shopping expedition extravagant, and it was. However, it had an objective behind it. The UK is still a very class conscious society and the circumstances of birth play a large role in the possibilities a person has for his future. The people who hold key positions in the UK both government and business have in common attending certain schools, bespoke clothing, the same forms of recreation, club memberships, and so on. It is possible for an outsider such as an American to play in that league if he is astute and it is done well. One of the ways to bond and be able to influence the players in Britain is for them to be able to see that you fit into their lifestyle. Wearing the right clothing and being able to small talk about one's tailor or shirt maker is a means of showing that one is a player in Britain.

Roberts wasn't sure who he was going to see the next day, but he was going to send the message that Texas had sent someone who could play the game in the UK. Jim and Lise were in the club library spending time before the evening meal. Thanks to Tea Time, and European custom, they would be eating around 8 PM in the club dining room. It seemed that going out to eat for the most part in London had become a choice of Indian, Halal, or American fast food. One of the club members had decided to "chat up" Jim Roberts, and the accent betrayed him. "American eh? I suppose that's all right, after all, the Americans did help out a bit at the end."

Whitehall, where many of the government offices of the UK are located was not far from the St. James district where Jim had been the previous day. He would be meeting with a nobody in the Foreign Office. Roberts made this as a we are just going through the motions, but on the off chance that the Texas independence thing does happen, we can say we in the Foreign Ministry were not taken by surprise meeting.

It was suggested to Roberts that leaving the United States would be a particularly difficult task. Did he think the people managing the Texas effort were capable of managing independence from a United States that would be hesitant to let them go. Roberts responded that he was hardly an unbiased observer, but imagined there were similarities with the Scottish Nationalist Movement. A small region of the world without a sophisticated economy has a lesser chance at breaking off from a larger country and going its own way than does a region that is entirely self sufficient. After all it wasn't as if Texas had never done this before, and played some role in the world, including an almost alliance with Great Britain in the 1840s.

Roberts left with the reminder that the Republic of Texas would be kindly disposed toward the UK, would welcome British troops continuing to train at Ft. Hood, and would be interested in negotiating trade agreements with the UK. Also, Texas would be keen to expand the "Five Eyes" agreement to "Six Eyes" and share intelligence with the UK, Australia, New Zealand, Canada, and the US. Roberts then decided to play a card that might get the attention of the British Government. Texas had not yet decided on NATO membership and that was an open question.

Discussion with key figures in the UKIP went much better. They shared common goals and values, which rapidly becomes the foundation of cooperation. It might strike most observers as odd for a couple of guys wearing tailor made London Saville Row suits to be chatting about how to obtain more freedom and economic success for the average person in Texas or the East Midlands, but both could appreciate the irony of it all.

From London, Roberts was going to do the Eastern Europe swing. Poland, the Baltic Republics, Czech Republic, Hungary, and Romania were on the agenda. This was the eastern border of NATO to Russia. Military considerations would be a major factor for this part of the tour. The reception was likely to be much warmer than that in London. These were countries that valued liberty and appreciated the way the Cold War was conducted in the 1980s that resulted in that liberty.

The reception in Warsaw, Poland was cordial. Roberts was greeted at the airport by an official of the Foreign Ministry, but not the foreign Minister himself in deference to Poland's desire to keep good relations with the United States. That relationship had been strained by the decision of the US to cancel missile defense of Poland without first informing Poland, and the statements made by the new President about NATO countries not contributing enough to their own defense. For the past few years, Poland had been improving its military, buying tanks and artillery form Germany and some US made military equipment.

Out of sight of the public, the Foreign Minister did meet with Roberts. The first question was where did Texas stand on the issue of Russia. Roberts expected this as the Native Texan Movement had gotten press from floating the idea that Russia would support Texas independence. The Republic of Texas War Department had a very different view. Roberts told the Foreign Minister the only common interest Texas had with Russia was the same interest

292

Poland had – we don't want to see Christian nations in Europe over run by Muslims. Roberts told the Minister the only other commonalty was a desire to sell gas and oil to Poland, and we would rather that you buy from us. That broke the impasse, and the conversation improved from there.

The questions then poured forth. Would Texas join NATO? Roberts replied that had not been decided. There was hesitation to get entangled in a massive bureaucracy that could interfere with Texas military policy. A Texas in NATO would have its forces stationed in Europe if any, counted under the limits of the CFE Treaty, and Texas was opposed in principle to having the disposition of its military monitored by any supra national entity. As a practical military matter, Texas would operate any forces stationed in Europe in cooperation with NATO.

Would Texas be willing to station forces in Poland in order to assist the defense of Europe? Roberts was careful in his answer. We have not gotten that far in deciding our policy. We have our own security challenges that demand our attention. It can not be ruled out that there could be circumstances that would cause Texas to agree to a military presence. We would also have to have the air and sea power to support that force, and it will take some time to be in the position to make that decision. In Texas we have people who want no foreign alliances, and we have people who want Texas to be active and engaged in world affairs.

Roberts was now asked if he would go "Off the table" or in diplomatic terms the next part of the conversation was no reflection of policy by either government at all. Roberts replied of course he would. The Foreign Minister asked if Roberts thought Texas could really leave the United States. Roberts believed it was very possible due to political factions becoming more strident, this causing an irreconcilable split in the country, or the excessive debt of the US Government leading to massive economic collapse. In either case, Texas had no intention of letting the rest of the country lead it to ruin.

Roberts was than asked if he would be available to give some advice to the military based on his experience in dealing with "unpleasant domestic situations". How does one keep border security while facing a major world power as an enemy is a challenge Poland faces and was not strong enough to defend itself without the assistance of powerful friends. Would Roberts take a look at the situation? Roberts agreed to do so. It would give him a look at the state of Poland's military while, identifying key officers who would be important to the future of Poland's military. Building good will never hurts either.

Poland and the Baltic republics had a real defense problem and the name of the problem was Kaliningrad. This was the former German city of Königsberg which the Soviet Union took and shifted Poland's borders after the Second World War. Russia now had a large military base behind the NATO front line in case of any conflict. A high priority concern for those NATO countries would be how that threat was to be neutralized.

The next scheduled stop was Estonia. A tiny country annexed by the Soviet Union in 1940 after becoming independent after the First World War, Estonia regained independence after the collapse of the Soviet Union. To say that Estonia hated Russia would be an understatement of the intensity of emotion felt by Estonians. In addition to a small army, there was the Estonian Defense League, a near universal militia equipped with whatever weaponry the citizenry could afford. The Estonian government had an unusual request for Roberts. He was asked to arrive in uniform as the official representative of the Texas Army and inspect the honor guard. There was going to be nothing low key about the visit of the diplomatic representative of the Republic of Texas to Estonia.

Roberts considered the request. It was obvious Estonia intended to send a message to the Russians. Roberts thought there was intent to send a message to the United States as well. Because of tensions with Russia, Estonia had requested the basing of US Forces in Estonia. At most, the US would deploy a few hundred troops for a few weeks as part of a NATO exercise. The US appeared unwilling to increase tensions in Europe by basing troops outside of areas where US troops were stationed prior to the collapse of the Soviet Union.

Appearing in uniform would imply that the Republic of Texas was potentially going to ally with Estonia. This would irritate the Russians into thinking Texas intended to sell energy to Europe, potentially station troops in Europe, and having an economy about the size of Russia's, show itself to be a global competitor. This would annoy the United States because Texas was not a country, and indicate Texas was serious about independence. Once the Republic of Texas Secretary of State heard about it and saw the images, he would possibly have a heart attack. The idea of making the visit official became more appealing the more Roberts thought about it.

Roberts carefully crafted the messages he would send. One of the issues in using unsecure communications is that other people are going to read your mail. The message sent to the Estonians via the Swiss, was that Roberts would comply with the request. He expected a copy of that message to be read in Moscow before his arrival. The message going to the Secretary of State, via the Swiss was that Estonia had requested that his visit be of an official nature rather than an unofficial visit, as had originally been scheduled. Roberts had decided to accede to the request, and was informing the Secretary accordingly. Roberts expected the National Security Agency had a fair chance of having broken the Swiss diplomatic codes, and his message would be read in Washington before it was read in Austin.

Before Roberts had left Austin, the Secretary of State was adamant about not using the War Department's messaging system and using the Swiss for communications. Roberts suspected it was more a case of the State Department did not want the War Department reading its mail. The War Department used Lotus Notes as an off the shelf product with at least some security potential because connections were encrypted. Roberts sent a message to the DCSIntel outlining his analysis of the situation and intentions. As a reminder of the commitment of Estonians to freedom, he gave a brief outline of the Forest Brothers, the last of which were captured in 1974 after starting operations against Soviet forces in 1945. If the NSA could read that, there wasn't much they could not read.

As the Gulfstream carrying Roberts arrived at the airport in Tallinn, it was directed to the tarmac where a red carpet had been laid out, and the honor guard stood ready. Roberts guessed most of them were vets of Estonian deployments to Iraq and Afghanistan where they had fought along side the British Army. The air crew, who were now dressed in uniforms of the putative Texas Air Force, following the ground guide, taxied to place the plane's stairway in front of the red carpet.

As the stairway lowered, the honor guard came to attention, and a man in a suit and two men in uniforms approached the stairway. One of the air crew finished with lowering the stairway, descended and saluted the men in uniform, who returned the salute. Roberts then descended the stairway, followed by Lise and another air crew member. The man in the suit introduced himself as the Foreign Minister, and was accompanied by the head of the Estonian Defense Forces. Roberts then saluted the General who returned the salute. The General's aide then said to Roberts "Welcome to Estonia Colonel, the General apologizes for not being able to speak to you in English, as for most of his service Russian was the language of our military, but we have switched to English for the last years and the junior officers will be able to speak to you."

"Please tell the General that I thank God every day that I was not forced to learn Russian." Replied Roberts.

Roberts remarks were translated for the General and the response was translated into English "The General requests that you exercise your rank as ambassador and walk to his right for the inspection."

The regulars were well turned out as Roberts expected from a small professional military. In his honor, based on his background, the Estonian Defense League also made an appearance. As a citizens militia, there was some discrepancy in dress and a hodgepodge of weapons. There was the occasional M16 and M60 machinegun, but most of the weaponry was European, and all of it capable of automatic fire. The weapons and equipment were well cared for and gave a good impression. The Estonian government entrusted weapons to its citizenry that the United States did not Roberts observed with irony.

At his office, the Foreign Minister had yet another surprise for Roberts. Estonia was prepared to recognize the Republic of Texas and exchange ambassadors. Estonia was also prepared to negotiate reciprocal trade deals and military cooperation. From the perspective of Estonia, there was nothing standing in the way of warm relations between the people of Estonia and the people of Texas.

Roberts thought that Estonia was about to get more attention from the US Department of State in the next 48 hours than it has gotten in the last 48 months. Roberts response was an expression of gratitude that Estonia would make such a show of support and that further actions on the part of the Republic of Texas would require action from the Secretary of State himself. As Roberts wrote the memos for the Secretary and to the DCSIntel, he thought if the coverage of his visit in the press did not induce a stroke, when this memo hit, that this memo would do it to the Secretary.

The rest of the travels through various countries of Europe was uneventful. Reception in Latvia and Lithuania was almost as warm as Estonia. Most of the other countries gave cool if polite reception to his visit. However there was one incident in Austria when Roberts was approached by the Russian ambassador, who got within two feet of Roberts, put his tight index finger on Roberts' chest and said "Roberts, you may be good soldier, but Diplomat you are not."

From Vienna, Jim and Lise drove to see Lise's family and check on how the immigration to Texas was progressing. At the rate the US Government was moving on this, Roberts figured that they could just order the Texas passports now.

Jim and Lise then returned to Switzerland where Roberts had kept a condo since the time he had lived and worked in Switzerland. Walking up the steep mountain trails caused some discomfort in his left knee, and he had to admit his skiing days were probably over.

"Maybe we will be able to come back in the winter, and you will be able to ski." Jim said to Lise.

"No, we are staying in Texas this winter. I am not going to ski." Lise responded.

"Why not?" Jim asked.

"Because we are going to have a baby." Lise announced.

Chapter 25

Home to Texas

FORCE IS NEVER MORE OPERATIVE THAN WHEN IT IS KNOWN TO EXIST BUT IS NOT BRANDISHED. – ALFRED THAYER MAHAN

In keeping with what was supposed to be the low profile nature of the mission, the Gulfstream jet carrying the Diplomatic Representative of the Republic of Texas and his wife taxied to the active runway at the airport in Samedan, Switzerland for the flight to Texas. Jim Roberts was working on typing the notes from his meetings for presentation to the DCSOPS and the officials of the Provisional Government of the Republic of Texas who had authorized his mission. He wanted to structure the document so that the first section was a summary of meetings and discussions, then a section on analysis, followed by conclusions and recommendations.

The flight time back to Texas would give him a good ten hours mostly uninterrupted, to work on the document. Once the jet was wheels up, Roberts began writing the document.

TOP SECRET

Report of Discussions Held With Certain European Governments With Respect to Relations With The Republic of Texas

(S) TO: The Provisional President of the Republic of Texas

(S) THRU: Army DCSOPS
                Army Vice CoS
                Army CoS
                Joint Chief
                RoT Secretary of War
(S) CC: RoT Provisional Vice President
                RoT Secretary of State
                Army DCSIntel
                AF DCSIntel
                Navy NavalIntel

(TS) Summary of Discussions Held With Various European Governments Relating to the Republic of Texas

(TS) The primary concern of European Governments relating to the Republic of Texas is the impact on the ability of the United States to maintain its commitments to NATO and European defense. This is especially an area of concern with a president in office not convinced of the seriousness of the efforts of other NATO nations to contribute to the NATO alliance. A secondary concern is the method by which the RoT is created and the impact that would have on their relations with the United States. Therefore the concern to be addressed by our diplomacy is the extent to which the RoT will compliment or conflict with US commitments to NATO and European security.

(S) NATO members are keenly interested in the question of RoT membership in NATO. The most obvious reason for this interest is the perception that the existence of the RoT weakens the US and its ability to lead or influence NATO. While members complain of US dominance, they are also aware that the US provides a role that can not be performed by any other NATO member. NATO members are fearful that North American events could serve as a pretext for the US ending its involvement in European security organizations. Should such an event occur, NATO members consider it unlikely that the RoT could successfully perform the role of the US, even should the RoT be willing to do so.

(TS)   Communicated to those governments is the policy that the RoT is not considering NATO membership. The RoT would not commit to defend nations that do not recognize the RoT. NATO membership would place any RoT Forces stationed in Europe under the constraints of the Conventional Forces in Europe Treaty between NATO and the Russian led Confederation (formerly Warsaw Pact). The RoT is not a signatory to the CFE Treaty and does not recognize its limitations as applicable to the RoT. This policy position provides the RoT with additional leverage in diplomatic negotiations.

(S)   Many European nations use US produced or designed military equipment, and US forces and the RoT use or will use European military equipment produced under license. Of interest to the RoT are small arms licenses that allow production of small arms from Fabrique National of Belgium and M1 tank components from Rheinmetall and Dynamit Nobel of Germany. On the part of the RoT, our policy of cash and carry for military sales would provide a competitive advantage in the sale of military equipment. Purchasers would be relieved from complying with obtaining approval of the US Department of State, and in many cases the US Congress for the purchase of US produced military equipment. It should be noted that France refused to risk having its military supplies be at the mercy of a foreign government and this led to the withdrawal of France from the military structure of NATO.

(C)   Trade and Trade Agreements

(C)   Considerations on trade relate to the relationship a particular country has with the European Union. Most countries have governments who view EU membership as beneficial, which often puts the government at odds with a substantial percentage of its population. As a government policy, most countries will view trade agreements with the RoT to be an item regulated by the EU. Notable exceptions are Switzerland which is not an EU member, and possibly Great Britain after it withdraws from the EU.

(C) Switzerland will be the most likely trade partner with which the RoT could negotiate a trade agreement. One of the ruling coalition political parties (FDP) has a long standing platform of negotiating a free trade agreement with the US, so that Switzerland can serve as a counter weight to undue EU influence on trade. By not trying to impose US operating restrictions on Swiss banks that conflict with Swiss banking secrecy laws, the RoT could use this opportunity as a means of gaining influence in Europe. Such an agreement could give the economy of the RoT easy access to capital based in Switzerland to finance anticipated economic growth in the RoT.

(C) Estonia is another target for economic cooperation, not due to anticipated economic benefits to the RoT, but for political considerations. Should mutual diplomatic recognition occur, a trade agreement with the RoT would demonstrate our commitment to friendly nations, and give the RoT a secondary channel into the European markets, particularly the European financial system and recognition of the TXD in the international financial system.

(TS)   Analysis of the Political and Military Situation

(C)   Europe faces a major security threat from Muslim invasion and a long standing geopolitical risk from the relationship of Russia to the Eastern and Central European states. To date the Muslim invasion and settlement of Europe has been little hindered by European governments closely aligned in the EU, and moderately resisted by the governments of Eastern Europe. Russian expansion has been a long standing policy for some 300 years and is driven by the considerations of warm water ports to allow for year around access to the Atlantic and trade, and a land buffer zone as protection against invasion.

(C)   Muslim invasion has been a security consideration for Europe for most of the past 1000 years. The most recent cycle stems from the breaking of the greatest intrusion into Central Europe, resulting in Vienna being placed under siege, which was broken and reversed by a Polish Cavalry Regiment on September 11th, 1683. This resulted in Muslim influence being pushed back to the border of now Turkey by the second half of the 1700s. Since the Balkan Wars of the early 20th Century, Muslim influence has gained in Europe via official or unofficial policy of European Governments, either as an appeasement measure, or for access to cheap labor.

(S)   Many European governments now find themselves unable to control areas of their own countries. Muslim communities displace native populations and impose their standards of conduct within areas they control. The native populations are subject to harassment, theft, mass rape, and murder unless they either convert to Islam or accept becoming de facto chattels of Muslim rulers. European governments are now in a dilemma they are unwilling to resolve. Either the tide of invasion continues until the governments are overthrown, or some form of mass deportation takes place and the resulting conflict is pursued with vigor. Currently, the most

304

affected governments possess neither the resources or will to defend themselves. Notable exceptions are the belt of countries stretching from Estonia to Hungary, who are in conflict with the EU on immigration policy and maintain border controls.

(TS)   Local populations who are exposed to the Muslim invasion threat are beginning to offer resistance to the invaders and in some cases their own governments for allowing the invasion to happen. Arson is the current most favored tactic to hinder invasion by the destruction of facilities governments use to process "refugees". A series of elections are under way in Europe that will determine if European governments will elect political parties with the will to resist the invasion. Such parties will seek to implement policies such have taken place in Texas to provide security for their citizens. These political parties are naturally sympathetic to the RoT, and would probably influence accordingly the diplomatic policies of their countries.

(S)   The same countries most resistant to Muslim invasion also see Russia as a security threat to them. Estonia, Latvia, and Lithuania have a minority ethnic Russian population in their countries as a result of Soviet policy to gradually transform populations into a more Russian identity. Protecting these minority populations is a tactic used to justify Russian activities in targeted countries and change boundaries in favor of Russia, such as has recently happened with Russian reannexation of Crimea. The eastern boundary of Poland is the demarcation line of the Nazi – Soviet agreement of 1939 on the partition of Poland. The former Soviet occupation zone of Polish territory is now in Belarus. Most of Poland today was formerly German territory in East Prussia.

(TS)   The relationship of the RoT with Russia will determine the diplomatic relationship the RoT has with these eastern European countries. To the extent Russian policy destabilizes Europe, that policy is not in the interest of the RoT for European countries with which we share a common heritage and basis of civilization, to be subsumed in an entity that does not share the same interests as the RoT. Our common interest with Russia, is in containing Muslim invasion and influence in Europe. In other regards, the RoT is a competitor to Russia for trade and therefore influence in Europe.

(S)   Russian military power aligned along the border from Estonia to Ukraine consists of some 30 divisions. Most of the equipment and organization is a result of Post Cold War efforts to modernize the military of Russia. With few exceptions, most NATO military equipment dates from the late 1980s and early 1990s. NATO military power now consists of approximately 13 divisions, of which the US has the equivalent of one division, of which one brigade is in Italy, and thus not on the Central Front of NATO. This situation drives the issue of how RoT participation in NATO will affect the US commitment to NATO, and the balance of power in Europe. Any signal that the RoT will align with Russia, will cause European diplomacy to oppose the RoT.

(TS)   Conclusions and Recommendations

(S)   Since the end of the Second World War, European security and prosperity has depended on security guarantees supplied by the United States. NATO serves as the manifestation of this security assurance. An accepted maxim was that the purpose of NATO was to keep the Americans in, the Germans down, and the Russians out. The current reality that this maxim no longer applies drives the actions of the major powers of Europe. The United States is reducing its involvement in Europe due to economic costs and political policy. Germany now exerts its influence via the EU, which allows German policies to have a multi national appearance.

306

Russia influences Europe not only via military intimidation, but by the sale of natural gas and control via proxies of oil pipelines to Europe.

(TS)   The RoT has the capability to influence events in Europe to the advantage of the RoT. As an energy supplier, the RoT could export energy to Europe, lessening dependency of Europe on Russia and the Middle East. This would allow European Governments the flexibility to respond to the desires of its populations not to make accommodations to Muslim invasion or Russian intimidation. Tariffs on European exports would provide additional revenue to the RoT and assist in paying for the defense needs of the RoT or contributing to the economic prosperity of the RoT.

(TS)   Economic and tax policies can give the RoT a competitive advantage that will appeal to business interests. The anticipated tax policy of the RoT (at a minimum having no income taxes) provide a competitive advantage of lower taxes than other entities and being friendly to business enterprises is well established in Europe and influences where companies locate activities. This policy has contributed substantially to the prosperity of Switzerland, Monaco, Luxembourg, and Liechtenstein.

(TS)   The relationship between the RoT and the US will influence how well European countries will be receptive to RoT diplomacy. US policy toward Europe will also influence how receptive European countries will be to RoT diplomacy. To the extent the RoT is seen as complimentary to or a more capable replacement for US efforts, the RoT will achieve greater influence in Europe.

(TS) Influence in Europe is also a function of military power. Providing continued access to military training facilities located in Texas will maintain good will. The ability to be better able to supply military equipment to NATO countries could be an incentive for US military suppliers to move production to Texas in order to supply Texas and NATO requirements without government regulation. This is another argument for the structure and equipment of Texas Military Forces to adhere to NATO and US standards.

(TS) Possible deployment of Texas Forces to Europe is a diplomatic tool available for use. Poland and the Baltic republics would be receptive to the stationing of Texas Forces in Europe. Those countries would consider such a move a further guarantee of RoT commitment and interest in Europe. The concept could also be used as a counterweight to US policy, should US policy attempt to work against the interests of the RoT.

(TS) A deployment of Texas Forces to Europe would primarily be a political act. Actual deployment would require the Forces to work within the framework of NATO defense policy and coordinate with host nation and NATO Forces. Garrison locations should be consistent with RoT political objectives, and a realistic military strategy.

(TS) Deploying ground and/or air forces have several implications within the RoT. Such a mission represents additional investment in military forces, where the RoT has its own border security considerations. Should the host nation agree to materially support the deployment, the RoT would still bear costs relating to sustainability and supportability.

(TS)   Any possible deployment should take into account the proximity of ports and potential hostile forces. Specifically, Russian naval and air units at Kaliningrad make initial deployment of forces to the east of this Russian territory undesirable. A RoT naval effort to protect a sea lane to Europe will be a difficult undertaking, and of the countries wanting to deploy RoT Forces, Gdansk is the post logical port of landing and supply.

(TS)   The loss of western countries who share our culture would adversely impact the RoT economy by limiting commercial opportunities. Should Europe fall under Muslim domination, additional resources would then be exploited to subvert and conquer the North American continent, including the RoT. The justification of US participation in NATO applies to the RoT being engaged in Europe. It is in the interest of the RoT to conduct the defense of western civilization as far from the borders of the RoT as possible.

James L. Roberts
COL, AR
TX Army DCSOPS

Roberts then prepared a similar document for the Secretary of State, but adding more detail of the summary of discussions in each country and meeting participants. This would allow the State Department to start to build profiles of officials in various countries of Europe. He expected at some future date, this information would be used in conducting negotiations or establishing relationships with those governments. Building up its files on who is who around the world was something the RoT intelligence service would need to do.

Secretly, a copy of that State Department report would be given to the Secretary of War and the Army DCSIntel. There would be yet another report for the DCSIntel containing more detail on each of the NATO military establishments that he observed.

Landing at Austin took place early in the afternoon. This allowed Roberts the opportunity to turn in his reports the same day and undergo an initial debrief. He would have a friendly debriefing at the War Department. His debrief at the State Department would occur the next morning.

The DCSOPS greeted Roberts with the comment "Lo, the Prodigal Son returns!"

"It is good to be back, sir." Roberts replied.

"We noted that while you were in Europe, you did manage to get the Russians and the United States to agree on something." said the DCSOPS.

"What was that, sir?" Roberts asked.

"Diplomat you are not." joked the DCSOPS.

"I suppose it depends on your perspective, doesn't it?" observed Roberts.

As expected, the meeting with the Secretary of State was less friendly. No time was wasted in getting to Roberts failure to adhere to department standards as an envoy of the Republic of Texas. "You had one job, which was to represent the policies of this department to those entities we authorized you meet. When circumstances went beyond those parameters, you were to contact

310

this Department for further instructions. As I suspected, it took you almost no time at all to create an international incident."

Roberts kept his cool. "Well sir, there is only so much information I feel comfortable in messaging via a system where at least one foreign government can read it, even as helpful as the Swiss have been."

The Secretary continued his rebuke. "Has your education included reference to Secretary of State Stimson?"

Roberts replied "I believe 'Gentlemen do not read each other's mail' would be the operative quote here."

The Secretary glared at Roberts "Well?"

"I have not met very many gentlemen." stated Roberts "It is also my information that two months ago your office had no communications with the US Department of State, and now there are in fact regular communications."

A "Colonel you are dismissed." from the Secretary ended the meeting.

A few days after reading the reports, the Secretary of War had occasion to chat with the DCSOPS. "You were right about your man Roberts. He is quite a character. What is he doing wearing a uniform? The guy that wrote those reports should be at the War Department. But for some reason, he goes around getting into firefights with the FBI, blowing up mosques, intimidating government officials, and when I asked him about working for me as a civilian, he said he would rather command a regiment."

The best way the DCSOPS could explain it to the Secretary of War was "Sir, that is what warriors do."

Epilogue

You have now reached the point in the tale, where Texans determine to bring back the Republic of Texas. The stage was set for an independent Texas in *We Defy!* This book, *Independence!* is the path to the realization of that republic. The next book, *Republic!* will take the tale through establishing the Republic of Texas and what role that republic may play in the lives of its citizens and the impact of that Republic of Texas on the world stage.

One of my objectives in writing this series is to provide what I consider to be a realistic view on the issues pertaining to a Texas independent of the United States. It is my opinion that much of the existing literature on the subject only examines one particular aspect of the problem, or takes a very simplistic view of the public policy that must be addressed by those who would wish an independent Texas. A reader may agree or disagree with the views and conclusions presented herein, but I contend that the issues discussed here are vital and will require attention and care of an active and involved citizen.

In Hoc Signo Vinces

www.ingramcontent.com/pod-product-compliance
Lightning Source LLC
Chambersburg PA
CBHW060235290526
45789CB00001B/59